10-23-62

D0365339

$ 4.90

Vogt Memorial

1962-1963

Social Relations
in the Urban Parish

It is the special property of human institutions and laws that there is nothing in them so holy and salutary but that custom may alter it, or time overthrow it, or social habits bring it to naught. So in the Church of God, in which changeableness of discipline is joined with absolute immutability of doctrine, it happens not rarely that things which were once apposite and suitable become in the course of time out of date, or useless, or even harmful.

LEO XIII

Social Relations
in the Urban Parish

By
JOSEPH H. FICHTER, S.J.

THE UNIVERSITY OF CHICAGO PRESS

IMPRIMI POTEST: A. W. CRANDELL, S.J., *Praepositus Provinciae Neo Aurelianensis*

NIHIL OBSTAT: PATRICK GILLESPIE, *Censor Librorum*

IMPRIMATUR: ✠ JOSEPH FRANCIS RUMMEL, *Archiepiscopus Novae Aureliae*

Die xiv Julii, Anno Domini, MCMLIII

Library of Congress Catalog Number: 54–11207

THE UNIVERSITY OF CHICAGO PRESS, CHICAGO 37
Cambridge University Press, London, N.W. 1, England
The University of Toronto Press, Toronto 5, Canada

Acknowledgments

RESEARCH and analysis in social science pass through the hands of a kind of middleman who brings together the thinking of theoretical scholars and the behavior of people in society. Both kinds of people have contributed to this book, but many of them remain unnamed, some by their own choice, some by the decision or the forgetfulness of the writer. Footnotes help to acknowledge indebtedness to professors, scientists, and scholars, but it has become almost a sacred rite to place an anonymous shroud around the human subjects of sociological research. They are represented in this book by a statistic, an example, or a quotation. If anyone recognizes himself in these pages as a dormant or marginal parishioner, let him see to his own conscience, for the similarity is probably not accidental.

Detailed research in the sociology of relugous groups requires especially the co-operation of the participants and functionaries of religion. It is as though the social theorists provided the framework of research, the participants supplied the content, and the priests guaranteed the validity of the combination. The encouragement and assistance of certain priests at different administrative levels have been particularly valuable. For various reasons they too wish to remain anonymous, but their eager interest in this research, their presentation of problems, and their discussion of analyses cannot be sufficiently appreciated.

Students of society will recognize in this book the influence of social scientists like J. O. Hertzler, E. T. Hiller, Everett Hughes, Robert Merton, Talcott Parsons, and others, whose writings have gradually evolved and blended into an identifiable species of sociological approach. There is no reason to conceal one's indebtedness to these scientific thinkers.

I appreciate also the fact that funds were forthcoming for such research in religious groups. The series of projects underlying this book were made possible in part by a research committee at Loyola University, New Orleans, Louisiana, from funds made available jointly by the Carnegie Foundation and Loyola University. Checking data and references, compiling statistics, and typing numerous revisions of the manuscript were largely done by Joy Landry and Charles S. Palazzolo. The content and formulation of the book are, however, my responsibility and not that of the University, the Foundation, or the various advisers and assistants.

J. H. F., S.J.

Table of Contents

Chapter One

Introduction: Religion and Social Science

SOCIOLOGY is a secular science which studies religious groups and institutions with the same methodological tools with which it studies familial, recreational, economic, and other groups and institutions. Therefore, as Wach says, "there is no such thing as Christian or Jewish or Moslem sociology,"[1] even though the sociologist who studies religious behavior may be a convinced believer in Christianity, or Judaism, or Moslemism. This does not mean, of course, that the social scientist is prohibited from stating his social and moral values in an explicit way when he analyzes the results of his research.[2]

The confusion that exists in the so-called conflict between religion and social science seems to lie in the peculiar attempt to interpret religion as exclusively sacred, and science as exclusively secular. There can be little question that the basic and essential purpose of religion is to deal with the divine, to promote the sacred relationship between God and man, to achieve the sanctification and salvation of human beings. Thus, at first glance, if social science is essentially *secular*, it appears to be in conflict with religion, which is essentially supernatural. But religious behavior in groups and institutions is social behavior carried on in observable and measurable ways. Even when the sociologist studies this religious behavior, his methodology and conceptual frame of reference remain secular (not in the anti-religious sense but in what might be called the "nondenominational" sense).

On the other hand, sociology is sometimes interpreted as a *normative* science. This too creates a confusion because of the tendency

1. See Joachim Wach, *Sociology of Religion* (Chicago: University of Chicago Press, 1944), pp. 7–8. For a contrasting view see the works of theologians and social philosophers like Luigi Sturzo, Charles A. Ellwood, T. S. Eliot, Bernard Iddings Bell, and Vigo Demant. See also the sympathetic treatment of "Catholic Sociology" by Melvin Williams, *Catholic Social Thought* (New York: Ronald Press Co., 1950), pp. 83–109.

2. See below, chap. 15, for a discussion of the "major issues" of the sociology of the parish.

I

to include sociology in the same category with moral theology and social philosophy. The proper province of philosophy and theology is undoubtedly the important realm of norms and standards and values, but this does not mean that the sociologist is excluded from the study of the social expressions of these high values. Sociology is mainly a descriptive and analytical science, and, while the sociologist may be reluctant to advocate certain religious and philosophical values, he must certainly recognize and interpret their appearance in group life.

That values and science, secularism and religion, have not always been clearly distinguished by sociologists is indicated by Hobbs's sharp criticisms of sociological textbooks. He says that the "authors generally claim that they [scientists] support rather than oppose religion, but their support of religion is similar to their defense of democracy and education in that it involves a redefinition in sociological terms. Religion is redefined in terms which make it practically synonymous with social work. In the sociological religion a social problems textbook would be a more important reference than the Bible. Supernaturalism, veneration of traditional codes of behavior, ritual and mysticism are criticized, and strong emphasis is placed on the necessity of religion becoming secularized."[3]

This trend toward a secular interpretation of man and society is not exclusively sociological. Tawney has pointed out that, when the naturalistic and secular view of society develops, there is likely to be a changed view of the nature and function of religion.[4] MacIver says that "revelation stands in the way of revaluation," indicating that the institutionalized Church is reluctant to submit to secular, scientific analysis.[5] Davis, who is anything but a "religionist," thinks that scientific analysis would destroy religion, and he takes this attitude because he is convinced that the bases of religion are mythical, fictitious, and subjective. "Dependent as it is on subjective faith, religion withers like a leaf before a flame when the scientific attitude is brought to bear on it. . . . Systematic analysis is the opposite of crowd enthusiasm. If the public in general undertook an analysis

3. A. H. Hobbs, *The Claims of Sociology: A Critique of Textbooks* (Harrisburg, Pa.: Stackpole, 1951), pp. 129–30.
4. R. H. Tawney, *Religion and the Rise of Capitalism* (New York: Harcourt, Brace & Co., 1926), chap. i.
5. R. M. MacIver, *Society: A Textbook of Sociology* (New York: Rinehart & Co., 1937), p. 319.

of religious behavior, using systematic research tools, it would be the death of religion."[6]

Assertions of this kind help to give the "secular" aspect of social science a bad name among people who know that religion is not merely an illusion. But there are also other questions involved. If the terms "religionists" and "secularists" may be used here without opprobrious connotation, they tend to represent different points of view in the discussion of religion and social science. For example, the religionists accuse the secularists of departmentalizing the lives of people in our society and particularly of interpreting religion as a part-time, peripheral, and indifferently useful activity. If the social scientist analyzes religion as he finds it—and if he finds it this way—he can hardly be "blamed" for this interpretation.

The secular scientists now maintain that the religious role is simply one in an integrated series of social roles which the human being plays in society and that it can be studied and analyzed like the other roles. Social scientists have veered away from the abstract conceptualization of the economic man, the political man, or the religious man as though he lived within a closed system of economic or political or religious activity. The contemporary theoretical trend seems to come closer to the facts of social life: that culture is manifested through multiple institutions in which each human being plays multiple social roles.

Thus, the secularization and compartmentalization of religion may also be discussed in terms of either the single-role or the mutiple-role schema of human behavior in society. Many of the religionists seem to favor the single-role paradigm (which tends to compartmentalize society) even while they are complaining that secularism is guilty of compartmentalizing religion in society. This may be a confusing and paradoxical statement, and the explanation probably lies in the following statements.

a) Religion, as a way of life, provides ideals and values which should govern the moral behavior of men. Since all behavior is

6. Kingsley Davis, *Human Society* (New York: Macmillan Co., 1949), p. 536. The sharpest criticism of this positivistic and secular metaphysics is found in William L. Kolb, "Values, Positivism, and the Functional Theory of Religion: The Growth of a Moral Dilemma," *Social Forces*, XXXI, No. 4 (May, 1953), 305–11. Kolb puts the moral dilemma bluntly when he says that "a sociologist who believes that people must believe in the validity of values but that such values actually have no validity must either deceive his public or help in dissolving the forces which hold society together."

3

moral in the sense that a man must be held responsible for his actions (whether they are economic, familial, political, recreational, or any other type of action), one may say that the religious role should be consistent with—some say even dominant over—all other social roles of man. The theoretical conceptualization of religion as a penetrative institution which can be separately analyzed is accepted by the Protestant theologian Paul Tillich, who writes that "religion is the expression of the meaning of our life as a whole. It is related to every realm of human existence. Religion is not a province beside other provinces of the human mind. It is never 'beside' even in the sense of 'above.' It is the ultimate concern in all preliminary concerns, the center of all theoretical and practical activities, the inexhaustible meaning in everything that has meaning. Religious thought can influence social outlook, because religious thought deals with the ultimate meaning of man's scientific, moral, political, aesthetic existence."[7]

b) At the same time the religionists, especially some of the full-time functionaries of religion, tend to fence off the religious role as a sort of sacred property. It must not be submitted to the scrutiny of the social psychologist, the sociologist, or the cultural anthropologist. In this sense they, too, compartmentalize religion. The paradox lies in the concept of the religious role which can be at one and the same time a comprehensive role penetrating and embracing all other roles in society and a single social role held apart and inviolable from other social roles.

7. Paul J. Tillich, "Trends in Religious Thought That Affect Social Outlook," in *Religion and World Order*, ed. F. Ernest Johnson (New York: Institute for Religious Studies, 1944), p. 17. The comprehensive and socially integrative force of religious values for both the in-group and the out-group is discussed several times in the present book (see the relevant sections of chaps. 4, 14, and 15. Robert Merton (*Social Theory and Social Structure* [Glencoe, Ill.: Free Press, 1949], pp. 30–31) questions the "large, spaceless and timeless generalizations about the integrative functions of religion" and points out three obvious nonintegrative examples of contemporary society: (1) How do many different conflicting religions help toward integration of a total society or community? (2) Nonreligious people in a society may be integrated by subscription to common values and ends which are not religious. (3) The religious doctrines and values held by one Church are at odds with the nonreligious content and values held by a large segment of the population not belonging to that Church. Wach (*op. cit.*, pp. 34 ff.) alludes to both the integrating and the disintegrating influences of religion on society. "The sociologically relevant facts are just those concepts, rites and forms, reflecting a very definite experience which integrates a religious group and at the same time separating it as a sociological unit from the outside world."

This paradoxical concept is a modern and particularized version of the old fight between religion and science,[8] but in this case the shoe is on the other foot. The religionists once complained that the scientists would not co-operate with religion; the scientists now complain that the religionists will not co-operate with science. It is difficult to estimate how widespread this latter refusal is, but it is found in the words of some critics who look upon the study of religious institutions as a "statistical fad," who object that church-goers "are simply being used as sociological guinea pigs," and who assert that "religious behavior cannot be analyzed by sociological methods."

Criticism against social scientists in their study of religious behavior and institutions seems to stem from an estimable desire to keep holy places holy. The cold and mundane eye of the sociologist picks up objective facts without the aid of "value-colored" spectacles. This appears to be a profane intrusion in sacred places. As one minister of religion remarked: "Neither the church nor the rectory should be turned into a common public place for statistical observation. Nor should a church parish be turned into a kind of guinea pig for the sake of almost unlimited dissection." Similar annoyances have been expressed in less holy places (communities, factory systems, hospitals, labor unions), but social scientists continue to study and analyze them successfully.[9]

The intelligent Christian who recognizes the limitations of scientific methodology and who knows the objective validity of religious truths will not fear the intrusion of science into the sanctuary. He will disagree with both the positivistic claim that science will destroy religion and the piously sentimental claim that science will cheapen religion. Parsons makes neither of these mistakes. He says that there is a conflict only when a religious claim is advanced which would attempt to make the empirical investigation of the scientist superfluous. Thus, the scientist "cannot admit *a priori* and without scientific investigation that within the specific field of his competence, *in principle* any other source of specific knowledge must

8. See Oliver Reiser and Blodwen Cavies, "Religion and Science in Conflict," and G. Bromley Oxnam, "Religion and Science in Accord," *Annals of the American Academy of Political and Social Science*, CCLVI (March, 1948), 132–47.

9. That some of these complaints are justified is seen in the discussion below, chap. 16, of the ethical limitations on the research scientist.

be held to supersede his own. To do so would be tantamount to the abjuring of his profession."[10]

There is another sense in which the religionist tends to "compartmentalize" his religious life, and this seems to be a function of the philosophical individualism of Western civilization. Speaking of this "nineteenth-century error," Guardini says that religious life was "individualistic, disintegrated and unsocial. The individual lived for himself. 'Myself and my Creator' was for many the exclusive formula. The community was not primary; it took the second place."[11] And Plus makes a similar observation: "Many Catholics, even frequent communicants, have a selfish Catholicism; they go through life with blinkers on and have no fellow-feelings for mankind. The enemies of the Church delight in pointing this out, and use it as an argument against her."[12]

Thus the extremists among both the secularists and the religionists seem to come full circle and to arrive at a similar, scientifically untenable spot. In divorcing religion from the whole of life, and especially from the social community, both have reduced it to merely a personal matter—a relationship between one's conscience and one's God. While they differ considerably concerning the moral obligation and the significance which attaches to this relationship, they would both agree that there is no common meeting ground of empirical investigation for religion and social science.

This book provides sufficient evidence to show that this is an erroneous agreement and that there is a limited but *de facto* level on which the social scientist can competently analyze religious groups.

10. Talcott Parsons, *Religious Perspectives in Sociology and Social Psychology* (New Haven: Edward Hazen Foundation, 1951), p. 22.
11. Romano Guardini, *The Church and the Catholic* (New York: Sheed & Ward, 1940), p. 15.
12. Raoul Plus, *Christ in Our Brethren* (St. Meinrad, Ind.: Grail Publications, 1947), p. 70.

PART I

A Typology of Parishioners

Chapter Two

What Is a Parishioner?[1]

O NE of the knottiest problems of both theory and research in the sociology of religion is contained in the definition of the local congregation as a distinctive social organization. Hiller's definition of a social group has been applied to the local Catholic parish: "a distinctive and organized plan of relations by designated persons participating in the pursuit of some one or several implicit or explicit values."[2] This interpretation means that the parish is not simply a "branch office" of the Church, or a periodic audience of people, or an occasional public.

Whether one accepts the definition of the parish as a formally organized social group or prefers to think of it as a mere "statistical category,"[3] he still faces the problem of discovering the designated persons. Who belong to the group or category, and by what process are they designated as parishioners? In other words, what criteria may best be used in order to discover the actual members of the Catholic parish? Hiller helps to clarify this point in explaining his formula for a social group. "The participants are designated and identifiable. The membership does not include just anybody but only those who are admitted by some *test of acceptability*, whether by birth or by initiation."[4]

This question is faced by all denominations which seek to employ an intelligent approach for discovering or describing their membership. The Jewish congregation usually counts as its members the heads of households who have identified themselves to the rabbi. The total "attending" congregation of the temple or synagogue

1. See the article of the same title, *Theological Studies*, XIII, No. 2 (June, 1952), 220–27.

2. E. T. Hiller, *Social Relations and Structures* (New York: Harper & Bros., 1947), p. 286; quoted in *The Sociology of the Parish*, ed. C. J. Nuesse and Thomas Harte (Milwaukee: Bruce Publishing Co., 1951), p. 6.

3. Or employs any of the other conceptualizations of the parish discussed below in chap. 14.

4. *Op. cit.*, p. 286. (Italics mine.)

9

would also include women, children, and other individuals who are not heads of households, but their number would be known only if the rabbi conducts a census. Some rabbis refine this whole category of people into "regular" and "irregular" worshipers.

The method of finding the "designated and identifiable" persons among the Protestant congregations is multiple, but in all cases it seems to imply a voluntary action on the part of the individual member. A letter of membership, or the public pronouncement of "the vows,"[5] is frequently the test of acceptability, especially when the person transfers from one place to another. Even where infant baptism is practiced, most Protestant churches do not usually count their membership until the individual signifies willingness to belong to the Church. This may be through confirmation, or through the act of "coming forward" at a church service, or by the simple declaration of membership.

It is sometimes said that a person "joins" a Protestant church but that he "becomes" a Catholic. If there is a difference between these two methods of attaining membership, it seems to lie in the deliberation of the individual himself. The Catholic attitude seems to be that the person is "acted upon" by the sacrament of baptism; for example, God Himself through baptism makes the infant a member of the Church, even though the deliberate, vocal consent is given through the godparents. Of course, an adult convert to Catholicism joins the Church by a deliberate action.

The problem of defining membership in the parochial unit may be approached in various ways. In a sense, every validly baptized person is a subject of the Church of Christ,[6] but a papal encyclical declares that "only those are really to be included as members of the Church who have been baptized and profess the true faith and who have not unhappily withdrawn from Body-unity or for grave faults been excluded by legitimate authority."[7] By positive ecclesiastical law every lay Catholic (apart from the exceptions of national and personal parishes) is automatically constituted a parishioner, with a view to certain canonical effects, by the fact of resi-

5. See Murray Leiffer, *The Effective City Church* (New York: Abingdon-Cokesbury Press, 1949), pp. 155–56.

6. Canon 87: "By baptism a person becomes a subject of the Church of Christ, with all the rights and duties of a Christian, unless so far as rights are concerned there is some obstacle impeding the bond of communion with the Church." In this discussion, however, we are excluding those validly baptized persons who belong to a non-Catholic religious denomination.

7. Encyclical *Mystici Corporis*, English trans. (New York: America Press, 1943), p. 12.

dence within a parochial territory.[8] At a minimum, therefore, it may be said that baptism is the test of acceptability through which the person becomes a member of the Catholic Church and that place of residence is the test of membership in the particular parish.

The sociological definition of the parishioner starts at this point. The sociologist's problem here arises because he is interested in real social relations and must find some concrete evidence of actual participation by lay persons, or of their willingness to participate, in the social unit called the parish. There is a need for criteria of membership which can give significance to the comparative data from various parishes.

The following six criteria are suggested on the basis of empirical research in southern urban areas. The first three may be called "institutional" in the sense that they stem from a regulatory pattern established by the Church itself. They are: baptism, place of residence, and racial origin. The last-named criterion is interchangeable with national origin in places where national parishes have been canonically established.[9] The other three criteria may be called "personal" in the sense that they depend mainly upon the belief and the behavior of the individual Catholic. They are: intention, religious observance, and social participation.[10]

Since the general purpose of even the smallest unit of the ecclesiastical system is the sanctification and salvation of human beings, we may say that *every person* living within the territorial boundaries of a parish is either potentially or actually a member of the parish. In this broadest sense (after making the required racial and national exceptions), the "care of souls," for which the parish priests are

8. Canon 94, n. 1: "Through domicile or quasi-domicile each of the faithful gets his proper pastor and ordinary." A domicile is acquired by actual residence of ten years or by intention of staying in a place permanently. A quasi-domicile is acquired by residence in a place for the greater part of the year. See Canon 92, nn. 1 and 2.

9. But foreigners who speak English do not have to belong to national parishes. *Acta Sanctae Sedis*, XXX (1897), 256, also says that "the children born in America of foreign-language, non-American parents, upon reaching their majority, are not obliged to join the parish to which their parents belong, but have the right to join a parish in which English, the language of the country, is used." See the comments of Harte's chapter on "Racial and National Parishes in the United States," in *The Sociology of the Parish*, pp. 159–60. As far as the present writer can discover, this "right" to leave his racial parish does not extend to the Negro at the age of twenty-one.

10. The division into institutional and personal criteria is not meant in any sense to be theological or canonical. It is obvious from the nature of the matter that the Church has also set up regulations for what we call the "personal criteria."

responsible, extends to every soul in the parish. The "missionary" aspect of the parochial function is directed toward the potential parishioners, and in an ideal sense it may be said that both clerics and laics should be concerned about the incorporation of non-Catholics into the parish. But, for practical purposes of social research and parochial administration, these non-Catholics cannot be considered participants of the parish as a social aggregate.

There is another category of potential parishioners which must be excluded from the sociological definition of the parish. These are the lapsed Catholics, or "dormant parishioners," who through lack of Catholic belief or failure in Catholic behavior (or both) can no longer be called members of the parish.[11] A conservative estimate, based on several detailed research projects, is that at least 30 per cent of the infants baptized in a normal urban parish cease later to function as Catholics and parishioners.[12] There is undoubtedly some meaning to the popular axiom that "once a Catholic always a Catholic," but it is not a sociological meaning (nor is it a theological meaning if the person has "lost the faith").

The relegation of lapsed Catholics to the category of potential parishioners does not resolve our problem. It simply states the problem in another way. If we can specify and count the non-Catholics and the dormant Catholics in any parochial territory, we know that the remaining persons are actual parishioners. But precisely herein lies the difficulty. Both the ecclesiastics and the sociologists make it sound easy by declaring that there is a dividing line between potential and actual parishioners. The study of real social life, however, shows that the imaginary line between two categories of people is in actual fact never sharp and clear cut.[13]

It is obvious that an element of arbitrariness must enter into the analysis of this problem of "designating" the members of the parish. This is why we feel compelled to add the second set of "personal" criteria. After the conditions of baptism, residence, and race or national origin have been met, the decision concerning the difference between the member and nonmember of the parish must be made by some official in the group, by the people themselves, or by some

11. This does not mean that dormants have been expelled or excommunicated from the Church (see below, chap. 6, for this question).

12. See *Dynamics of a City Church*, Vol. I of *Southern Parish* (Chicago: University of Chicago Press, 1951), pp. 38–39.

13. Sex categories are clearly defined; classification according to marital status is multiple but can be logically refined. But even a simple arrangement of age categories is ultimately reducible to a continuum if the precise moment of birth is taken into consideration.

external observer. An "ideal decision" would arise out of the consensus of all three parties.

If the Catholic parish were like a social fraternity or a labor union, the priest could easily decide who is a member and who is not a member, because he could quickly discern whether or not the individual had fulfilled the requirements for membership. If the parish were like a school, where periodic tests of achievement are administered, the priest could easily decide who is to remain and who is to be expelled on the basis of these tests. But every large urban parochial territory has within its boundaries certain persons who seem to be "fringe" Catholics, because their status of membership or nonmembership cannot be clearly decided by the priest alone.

It would be most helpful to both the ecclesiastic and the sociologist if this "fuzziness" could be removed. Neither of them can talk intelligently about the structure and function of the Catholic parish unless there is relative agreement about the "universe" of persons under discussion. If the pastor says that 40 per cent of the marriages performed in his church during the last twenty years have been mixed marriages, we know that the universe (or 100 per cent) consists of those marriages kept on record in the rectory. It includes revalidations, but it does not include civil marriages or the marriages of his parishioners (usually males) in other Catholic churches. But if the priest says that "40 per cent of the married couples now in my parish are in mixed marriages," we do not know what he means, because we do not know how he defines a parishioner. What must the married person think or do, as a Catholic, in order to be considered a member of the parish and thus be included in the universe of married parishioners?

One of the first problems which faced us in our own parochial research was this question of designating the parishioners.[14] From the *City Directory* we transferred onto 4×6 cards the names and addresses for every dwelling unit in the parochial territory. We checked these names against the address directory of the telephone company and against the records of the power and light company and those of the retail credit association. Dividing the parish territory into sections of approximately ten square blocks each, we sent canvassers from door to door in each section. On the prepared card for each dwelling unit they entered the informa-

14. The practical working solution which we employed, and which can undoubtedly be improved, is indicated in *Dynamics of a City Church*, pp. 13–14.

tion concerning the number, sex, age, marital status, occupation, telephone subscription, homeownership, race, and religion.

Within the territorial limits of the parish we were thus able to discover all those persons who, by the institutional criteria of baptism, place of residence, and racial origin, should be called members of the Catholic parish. Meanwhile we had prepared detailed census schedules similar to those used by Coogan and Kelly in their Florida study.[15] Fortified with credentials from the pastor, we revisited every dwelling unit which had reported the presence of white Catholics. It was through this process and at this point that we recognized the need for further criteria of parochial membership.

A relatively small percentage of these people refused to answer the census schedule because they "couldn't be bothered," or they were "too busy," or they "didn't want the priests to know all their business." Through the help of neighbors, friends, and relatives, and through telephone calls to the individuals themselves, we were able to fill their census schedules. But a much larger number, involving about 40 per cent of those who reported their religion as Catholic, refused the schedules because they "didn't go to church any more" or because they were "supposed to be Catholics but didn't bother with it." Most of the adults among them did not even know the name of the parish church. But the notable fact here is that these people had in mind a fairly clear distinction between a Catholic and a parishioner. They identified themselves as Catholics but not as participants of the religious and social unit known as the parish.

This obviously indicates that there exist criteria of parish membership in the minds of lay persons other than baptism, place of residence, and racial origin. Are these criteria the same as those which exist in the minds of the parish priest or of the sociological researcher? For practical purposes it seems that we must know the *intention* of the lay person. The lapsed Catholic not only does not "go to church any more" but he does not even intend to be considered a parishioner. On the other hand, there are numerous lay persons whose intention it is to be considered parishioners even though some of them have not made their Easter duties and some had not attended Sunday Mass once during the previous year.

15. See Father Kelly's contribution to *The Sociology of the Parish*, pp. 244–45; also his doctoral dissertation, *Catholics and the Practice of the Faith* (Washington, D.C.: Catholic University Press, 1945), pp. 208–9.

By adding the criterion of "personal intention" to the three accepted criteria of baptism, residence, and race, we can obtain a more accurate count of the actual membership of a parish. This number includes all children below the age of seven years whose intentions are interpreted through their parents (even though some of these children may not yet have been baptized). It includes also those persons, most of them living on the periphery of the parish territory, who prefer to attend services in any of the neighboring parishes. It includes also an unknown number of adult individuals whose intentional attitude may have been dubiously interpreted by the member of the family who answered the census schedule.

It has become an accepted procedure among social analysts of religion to make a general division of a given population into three classes: (*a*) church members; (*b*) nonchurch members with a preference for some denomination; and (*c*) nonchurch members without a preference. The first two classes are then redivided according to the numerous denominations in the community, so that each denomination recognizes both actual members and "preferential nonmembers." In writing about his research in Madison, Wisconsin, Bultena says that "each church group may be thought of therefore as having a loose 'outer fringe' of potential members and interested persons which for the average church constitute about one-fifth of the total."[16]

This is saying in another way that the intention of the respondent toward his religious status has to be known. Does he consider himself (*a*) Catholic and a parishioner; (*b*) Catholic but a nonparishioner (i.e., a baptized person who is not a member but still has not joined another denomination); (*c*) or simply a non-Catholic? No one can answer this question better than the lay person himself. We have used the term "dormant parishioner" for the second classification, made up of people who could be called "nonchurch members with a preference for the Catholic Church." We excluded them, on their own testimony, from the social unit called the parish.[17]

The problem of interpreting the intention or meaning of the

16. Louis Bultena, "Church Membership and Church Attendance in Madison, Wisconsin," *American Sociological Review*, XIV, No. 3 (June, 1949), 384–89.

17. Bultena's 20 per cent "outer fringe" cannot be generalized for all churches everywhere, nor can our 40 per cent dormant Catholics be generalized for all Catholic parishes. Until agreement can be had on criteria and other similar studies are made, these conclusions can apply only in the specific instances where they were made.

respondent to a questionnaire is one that constantly plagues the social researcher. The great majority of Americans, if asked what social class they belong to, will say that they are of the middle class. This seems to be a reflection of our democratic value system. The person in the upper class does not want to be guilty of unseemly boasting; the person in the lower class knows that he is supposed to aspire, as an American, to the "average" middle class. To avoid confusion, and to arrive at a relatively objective rating in social stratification, the Warner school has devised a series of measurable norms for stratifying people within a community.

Just because a person says that he is in the middle class, we must not necessarily conclude that this is so. Is the same doubt present when a person makes a declaration of his religious status? The analogy seems to fall down because of this difference: everyone is necessarily at some point in the social stratification of his community, but not everyone is necessarily included within a religious category. In the case of the parish, the four criteria already mentioned bring the persons within the social unit of the parish. They may then be classified within the religious structure by the use of the two final "personal" criteria: religious observance and social participation.[18]

But these are not merely a technique for refining the categories of people who are already members of the parish, as we use them in subsequent chapters. They are also a further means for identifying and designating those who belong to the social unit itself. A person who neglects his spiritual obligations and fails to participate in any way in the parish can hardly be called a parishioner in the sociological sense of the term. These criteria imply two important questions which must be involved in any definition of a *social group* and which cannot be answered merely by census-taking. If one accepts Hiller's definition quoted at the beginning of this chapter, he must ask: (*a*) Are these designated parishioners in pursuit of some one or several implicit or explicit values? (*b*) Are they actually participating with each other in the parish?

The implicit or explicit values of the parish, as a constituent segment of the Catholic Church, must be primarily religious. It is not difficult to learn from the teaching and preaching of the Church what these values are. In so far as they are translated into be-

18. In chap. viii of *The Sociology of the Parish*, C. J. Nuesse suggests that studies of religious observance and studies of participation are among the important "empirical problems of research" in the Catholic parish.

havior patterns they can be measured by the various religious observances which are expected of "practicing" Catholics. Thus the fifth criterion of membership in the parish can be reduced to the question: Does the individual fulfil the *minimum* requirements of formal religious practices?

The Catholic Church has clear-cut rules concerning excommunication of its members, but these rules are not helpful in making the sociological distinction between parishioners and nonparishioners. Some nonparishioners neither have been formally expelled by the Church nor have formally renounced the Church. We have seen that by the criterion of personal intention there are people who claim to be Catholics but who do not consider themselves parishioners. These we have called dormant parishioners, and they do not practice any of the religious observances expected of Catholics. They never attend church services, and, in the colloquialism of the Catholic, these are the people who "never go to the sacraments," which means that they have given up the practice of confession and the reception of Holy Communion.

In attempting to draw the outside boundaries of the parish according to this one criterion of religious practices, we may say that the minimum patterns are as follows. A lay Catholic may still be included in the parish if he attends Mass once in a while, perhaps not as often as once a year, and this Mass attendance may be only for special occasions like the weddings or funerals of family members. If he has children, he will have them baptized and in most instances have them receive their First Communion but will probably neglect their confirmation. His own marriage was witnessed by the priest, and he will probably want the ministrations of a priest again for the "last sacraments" before he dies.

It may appear to the faithful and regular religious participant that these outside limits of religious observance are too far outside. Some may insist that these people are really "dormants" and can no longer be called parishioners. The answer to this objection seems to lie in the combination of this criterion with the four which we have previously discussed, particularly that of the intention of the individual. The person who thinks of himself as a parishioner and who *also* makes these minimum gestures of formal religious practices can hardly be excluded from the total category of parishioners. The dormant Catholic, in contrast to the nominal Catholic, is the person who has completely divorced himself from the practices of the Church.

If the parish priest maintains a fairly accurate and up-to-date census of his people, he is most likely to have the names of these minimal Catholics in his files. Since the dormant Catholics have no contact whatsoever with the Church, their names are most likely to be excluded. Since, however, the method and the accuracy of keeping census files vary widely from one parish to another, this would not be a completely dependable source of information. The priest who has been in a parish for several years is usually able to point out those parishioners who are on the "border line," and he probably recognizes the practical limits of the parish as a social unit.

The final personal criterion of membership in the parish, that of *social participation*, presents the greatest analytical difficulty from an empirical point of view. We are confronted here with the problem of deciding upon the minimum acceptable degree of social interaction among the members of the urban parochial unit. The fact is that the great majority of people who fulfil all the five previous criteria of membership do not have continuous, integrated social relations on the parish level. A relatively small number can be said to form a parochial group, in the technical definition of the term.[19]

The problem amounts to a dilemma. If we insist that functional participation and social relations are prerequisites in the definition of a social group, and if at the same time we insist that the urban Catholic parish is a social group, we must drastically reduce the number of parishioners already designated by the five previous criteria of baptism, residence, race, intention, and religious observance. In other words, it seems that we must make one of two conclusions: (*a*) either the large urban parish is not a social group in the strict sense or (*b*) the numbers of persons who fail to meet some minimum requirement of social participation must be considered nonparishioners.

On the basis of genuine research data so far obtained from American urban parishes, the present writer tentatively accepts the first conclusion. The social facts of parochial life indicate that the urban parishioners do not constitute an "organized formal group"[20] but rather a social unit which might be called a statistical popula-

19. See the discussion of nuclear parishioners, chap. 3, below.
20. In *The Sociology of the Parish* the editors think otherwise and remark (p. 6) that a parish is not simply a "branch office" of the Church, or a periodic audience of people, or an occasional public but is a formally organized group.

tion, a social aggregate or category. It is not the purpose of this chapter to argue this point, which requires more evidence than can be allowed here.[21]

There can be no doubt that the parish represents, in Hiller's words, "a distinctive and organized plan of relations." This says nothing about the degree of social integration among the parishioners or about the amount and kind of primary or secondary relationships and contacts which are to be expected. The widest possible interpretation must be given to the term "social participation" if it is to be a genuine and usable criterion of parochial membership. It seems possible to do this if the emphasis is placed, not upon the person-to-person relations among the parishioners, but upon the relation of the individual parishioner to the organized parochial patterns of belief and behavior.

To clarify this point, a profane analogy may be made with the local urban segment of a political party. In order to participate in the primary elections in a southern city, a citizen has to register not only as a voter but as a member of the Democratic party. Even though he does not vote in every election, he is considered a Democrat. Some persons (like nuclear parishioners) may be very active at the center of the party and have close association with one another. Others may participate only to the point of voting and may have hardly a nodding acquaintance with fellow-Democrats living in the same territory. Perhaps this local Democratic party could not fulfil the strict definition of a social group either; but even the least active members could be said to have some participation with, or relation to, the political patterns of belief and behavior of the party.

It may well be pointed out here that the participation of the parishioner need not be limited to purely religious functions. The best example of this religious participation on a large scale is probably found in the Dialogue Mass and in other services where the congregation prays together with the priest. But other forms of genuine social participation are found in educational activities, such as in the Parent-Teachers' Association; in economic pursuits, such as fund-raising organizations; and in recreational, ameliorative, and other co-operative efforts of parishioners. No individual will participate in all these forms of social relations, but it is probable that every person will at least occasionally be identified as a parishioner in one of these activities.

21. See, however, the discussion of this point in chaps. 4 and 14 below.

The theologian or ecclesiastic is probably not interested in the refinements which are required by the sociologists for the study of social functions and structures. The ordinary layman may well be satisfied to set down the definition of a Catholic as one who "has been baptized and has not been excommunicated" without counting the number of parishioners or studying the manner in which Catholics fall under the sociological definition of a parishioner. In the relation of Catholicism to life, however, it seems necessary for both the parish priest and the social scientist to understand and apply the practical criteria of parish membership. Without these our analysis of the whole sociocultural system of American Catholicism becomes confusing and relatively inconclusive.

Chapter Three

Nuclear Parishioners and Leaders

THE analytical discussion in the previous chapter has been preliminary to a more detailed analysis of the various categories of
parishioners. By employing certain logical criteria, we have been
able to establish an operational definition of the Catholic parishioner. Neither the criteria used nor the definition arrived at is final or
exclusive. There are other ways in which the social relations of lay
Catholics can be studied, and there are numerous ways in which the
urban Catholic parish can be conceptualized.[1]

There is no single sovereign description of the urban lay Catholic
in the social structure of the parish. The test of any interpretive
description is its utility to the student of social relations and its
conformity to the factual data of research. In this and the following
chapters we shall discuss each of the types of parishioner in connection with a relevant problem of the parish. Lay leadership is
discussed in relation to the nuclear parishioner (chap. 3); social
solidarity of Catholics, in relation to the modal parishioner (chap.
4). Institutional inconsistency is related to the marginal Catholic
(chap. 5); defection from Catholicism, to the dormant Catholic
(chap. 6).

Any attempt to arrange a typology of religious groupings, even
on the broadest bases, involves a number of theoretical difficulties.[2]
A similar series of complicated abstractions is involved in the
attempt to arrange a typology of the persons participating in a
specific religious structure like the city parish. The four categories,
or types, which we have established have admittedly only a rough
resemblance to the social realities in and around the parochial system. The dividing line between any two of these categories is
necessarily "fuzzy" in that some people do not fall unambiguously
into either of them. The criteria which we employed in order to

1. See, e.g., the discussions below in chaps. 11 and 14.
2. See below, chap. 11, pp. 138–42.

place people are relatively arbitrary, and the psychosocial analysis of the persons within each category is not satisfactorily conclusive.

In spite of these and other difficulties, we have been able to construct various general categories from our research in urban Catholic parishes. We have tentatively classified the urban white Catholics of this study into four general groupings: (*a*) *nuclear*, who are the most active participants and the most faithful believers; (*b*) *modal*, who are the normal "practicing" Catholics constituting the great mass of identifiable Catholic laymen; (*c*) *marginal*, who are conforming to a bare, arbitrary minimum of the patterns expected in the religious institution; and (*d*) *dormant*, who have in practice "given up" Catholicism but have not joined another religious denomination.[3]

At the core of the urban Catholic parish there are always a number of people who best exemplify in practice the high ideals of the Church. They may be termed the "most Catholic" persons in the parish. We have called them nuclear parishioners. Not only have they satisfied the institutional criteria[4] of parishioners but they also fulfil to a high degree the personal criteria: they intentionally belong to the parish, they are most faithful to the religious observances, and they participate most actively in the social relations of the parish.

It would seem at first blush that the terms "nuclear parishioner" and "leading parishioner" are synonymous. This appears to be true, however, only if one interprets leadership in the widest possible sense, so that it would include the meaning of "influence by example." If, however, we define a leader as a person who "initiates, directs, and controls group thought and action" in the formal or informal groupings of the parish, we find that the nuclear parishioners are more numerous than the lay leaders of the parish.

Generally speaking, it may be said that it is out of the core of faithful and active parishioners that lay leadership develops but that the correlation between the nuclear status and the leadership status is not always exact. If we say that the nuclear parishioner is one who is highly faithful both in religious observances *and* in active parochial participation, we find that there are several categories of parishioners who do not exemplify this combination of characteristics.

3. See also the various classifications below, chap. 14.
4. See above, chap. 2. See also chap. 14, p. 192, for the definition of major categories: dormant, marginal, modal, and nuclear.

These exceptions are as follows: (*a*) There are always a few persons who are nuclear from the point of view of active participation in social relations but who are modal parishioners in the sense that they do not demonstrate high fidelity to religious observances. (*b*) There are some highly religious nuclear parishioners who are either merely good followers in the parochial groups or who do not even belong to these groups. (*c*) Some nuclear parishioners exert their leadership qualities in religious organizations which are city-wide or diocesan rather than parochial. (*d*) Finally, there are also some "leading Catholics" who are prominent in their business or profession, in political or civic life, but who do not participate actively in parish groupings. A few of these are nuclear from the point of view of religious behavior, but most of them are not.

For purposes of a clearer understanding of the factors involved in each category, we here discuss the nuclear parishioners and the leaders separately.

NUCLEAR PARISHIONERS

If a parishioner lives up to the complete ideology[5] of the Catholic Church, he is a saint. The social scientist cannot pretend to classify or even to define the saints whom he studies in the parochial structure. The intangible and immeasurable inner perfection of the Christian can be judged only by God. The best that the scientific observer can do is to provide a rough description of a class of persons who tend to approach the ideal type of nuclear parishioner as defined by certain arbitrary criteria.

The most faithful religious practitioners and the most active participants co-operate with other parishioners and with the priests in the functions of the parish church. They portray Christian behavior in their personal and social life; they hold high religious values; they conform to the sacramental expectations of the Catholic Church.

It may be said that the nuclear parishioner is an integrated Christian, in the sense that he is guided by the same set of values in all the institutions in which he participates. His moral code, which is based on his religious beliefs, extends to and controls the roles he plays in economic, familial, recreational, political, and other institutions. He does not succumb to a kind of cultural

5. See the discussion on complete ideology in *Dynamics of a City Church*, Vol. I of *Southern Parish* (Chicago: University of Chicago Press, 1951), pp. 259–60.

schizophrenia by which he would compartmentalize his patterns of thought and behavior according to the exigencies of social situations.

It is obvious that the social philosophy of the nuclear parishioner cannot be either individualist or collectivist. He can be neither a complete liberal nor a complete traditionalist. The dichotomy of personal morality and social morality has no meaning for him, because the same basic moral and religious principles underlie all aspects of his behavior. While he realizes that eternal salvation with God is the ultimate objective of his life on earth, he realizes also that this objective entails a recognition of his duty as his brother's keeper.

In order to set up a rough category showing the proportion of nuclear persons in any given parish, two elements must be taken into consideration: (1) the size of the parochial universe and (2) the strictness of the criteria selected. By reason of the first element, we exclude all dormant Catholics, that is, all those who fit the institutional criteria but not the personal criteria of parish membership. By baptism, race, and residence, they belong to the parish, but they lack intention as well as religious and social participation. For obvious reasons, we exclude also all children below ten years of age.

The criteria selected to mark off the nuclear parishioner must be among those which measure religious observance and social participation. Here it seems necessary to employ a combination of standards of measurement for the *same* person. For example, he must not only make his annual Easter duties and attend Sunday Mass regularly; he should also be a person who receives Holy Communion weekly or oftener *and* belongs to a parish organization.[6] No matter how carefully the criteria are selected, there seems always to be an overlapping of social categories; for example, some daily communicants may not be able to join parish societies, and a few very active people in the organizations may not even have made their Easter duties.

In a study which we made of three urban parishes, application of our strict criteria indicated that, of the 8,363 white Catholic parishioners ten years of age and over, there were only 476 (5.7 per cent) who could be called nuclear parishioners. Table 1 indicates

6. Those who do all these things and are also *active* in the parish programs and societies constitute a still smaller category and should probably be called the "nuclear leadership group."

percentages of religious observants and social participants according to age categories.[7] The last column does not represent all the members in parish societies but only those who receive Communion weekly or oftener. These people, of course, made the Easter duties and regularly attend Sunday Mass, and many of them also attend evening services and other religious devotions. They are the most "dependable" people in the parish, the ones on whom the priest can call to carry the brunt of the lay functions of the local congregation.

TABLE 1

RELIGIOUS PRACTICE AND PAROCHIAL PARTICIPATION
BY TEN-YEAR AGE GROUP

Age Group (in Years)	No. (100 Per Cent)	Percentage Receiving Monthly Communion	Percentage Receiving Weekly Communion	Percentage Belonging to Parish Societies
10–19	1,668	71.3	29.3	15.0
20–29	1,994	40.9	5.7	1.8
30–39	1,987	31.6	6.2	2.4
40–49	1,462	39.3	9.2	5.4
50–59	737	38.4	16.0	4.6
60 and over	515	25.6	8.4	5.6
Total	8,363	43.3	12.2	5.7

These comparative statistics show that the youngest age category exhibits the highest fidelity to both religious practices and group participation. None of this youngest age group, either male or female, is married, and this may account for the fact that they have more leisure time than other groups to devote to parish societies. They are in the youth organizations of their parish, athletic and social programs, sodalities, and Junior Holy Name societies. It is notable too that the percentage rises in the forty-to-forty-nine-year category, when the married parishioner presumably again finds more time for parochial activities.

We have suggested above that the nuclear parishioner tends to be an integrated Christian in the sense that he carries over into other institutional activities the high behavioral ideals implicit in his religious convictions. As far as we have been able to discover, all the parshioners who are here included in the nuclear category are also exemplary in their private and social behavior. This does

7. See below, chap. 7, "The Religious Life-Profile," for a more detailed discussion of age and sex categories.

not mean merely that the youths have escaped delinquency and that the married persons have never considered divorce. It means that all these people have a "good reputation" in their neighborhoods, in their social contacts, and in their business and civic affairs.

It cannot be repeated too often that there is no necessary correlation between formal religious observances and community dependability. The fact is that there are in any urban community a number of people who exhibit a high degree of social awareness but at the same time are not active participants in the religious group. The opposite is also a common phenomenon: some people who are very religious either resist or neglect the extension of their religious beliefs and obligations into the wider social life. This failure to *combine* the individual and social aspects of religion is undoubtedly one of the principal factors accounting for the small percentage of persons who may be called "core Christians" or nuclear parishioners.

Aside from the selection of criteria for distinguishing the nuclear parishioner and the approximate percentage of the parish unit which can be identified as nuclear, there are two further considerations which may help in understanding this religious category. These are the study of (*a*) the social background and the study of (*b*) the motivational system of the nuclear parishioner.

a) In the *social background* of every person there are, of course, a great variety and a large number of factors which are relevant in some way to his social and religious behavior. The following items appear to have an influence on the functions of the nuclear parishioner: (1) familial status, (2) educational status, (3) the fact of being a "born Catholic" or a convert, (4) economic and class status, and (5) the ethnic and migrant factor. Neither the list nor its discussion can be exhaustive in a study of this kind.

1. The nuclear parishioner usually belongs to a nuclear family in that he is a member of a "good" Catholic family closely attached to the parish center. This statement is relative and must be interpreted cautiously. For example, if the nuclear person under consideration is a parent, there is a good likelihood that the children are also faithful to religious duties and to parochial participation. The reverse is not always true. Our statistical comparisons are unbalanced in the youthful age category, and we have found numerous instances of children who are nuclear and whose parents are modal, sometimes marginal, Catholics. The size of the family does not seem to have any connection with the presence or absence of nuclear Catholicism. In our

study the largest number (110) come from families in which there are four children, and the next largest (76) from five-child families, but in proportion to the number of families of varying size the nuclear parishioners seem to be fairly well distributed among the different-sized families (Table 2).

TABLE 2

THE DISTRIBUTION OF 476 WHITE NUCLEAR PA-
RISHIONERS ACCORDING TO THE NUMBER OF CHIL-
DREN IN THEIR FAMILY OF ORIENTATION

NO. OF CHILDREN IN FAMILY	NUCLEAR PARISHIONERS No.	Per Cent
One or two...............	111	23.3
Three or four.............	137	28.8
Five or six...............	98	20.6
Seven or eight............	62	13.0
Nine or ten...............	46	9.7
Over ten.................	22	4.6
Total	476	100.0

TABLE 3

THE DISTRIBUTION OF 236 NUCLEAR PARISHIONERS WHO HAVE
COMPLETED THEIR SCHOOLING ACCORDING TO THE AMOUNT
AND TYPE OF FORMAL EDUCATION

AMOUNT OF FORMAL EDUCATION	TOTAL FORMAL EDUCATION		TOTAL CATHOLIC EDUCATION	
	Per Cent	Average Years in School	Per Cent	Average Years in School
Grade school or less...	24.6	6.9	46.3	6.2
Some high school......	33.0	11.5	39.7	10.4
Some college..........	35.6	14.8	14.0	15.2
Postgraduate	6.8	19.0	0.0	0.0
Total	100.0		100.0	

2. The educational record of the nuclear parishioners tends to be slightly better than that of the modal parishioners in the sense that the nuclear parishioners have had more years of formal schooling and more years in Catholic schools. One of the most notable phenomena in this regard is the number of persons who have had some higher education. Since we are using the two general criteria of religious observance *and* group participation to identify nuclear parishioners, it may be said that, generally speaking, the less-educated nuclears are more active in the parish organizations while the better-educated ones are more notable for their religious observances.

Table 3 shows both the amount of formal schooling and the

amount of Catholic schooling. The statistics are drawn only from the 236 nuclear parishioners who are no longer in school. Concerning the type of education, this study shows that the nuclear parishioner has had most of his formal education in the Catholic schools, where, through frequent contact with priests, brothers, and nuns, he has developed an ease of social relationship with the professional functionaries of the Church.

3. The nuclear parishioner tends to be a "born Catholic" rather than a convert. In this limited study of three white urban parishes we did not find one individual (of the 278 converts above the age of ten years) who qualified by our arbitrary criteria to be included among the nuclear parishioners. This fact raises an interesting problem concerning the integration of converts into the city parish after their reception into the Catholic Church. Among the subjects of our study, those who are active in parish societies are at best modal parishioners in their religious observances, while those who exhibit high fidelity to the sacramental and liturgical functions do not participate actively in the parish organizations.

This problem certainly requires further study and careful analysis before any generalizations are to be drawn. The axiom that "the convert frequently makes the best *Catholic*" is not negated by our findings, which simply indicate that he does not always "make the best *parishioner*." Some of the converts whom we interviewed are extremely active in what they called "the broader apostolate." They devote much time and energy to groups like the Catholic Evidence Guild and the Retreat Movement, which are supraparochial organizations. They appear to find more persons of similar background and zeal in these groupings than in the strictly parochial societies.

4. The economic and class status of nuclear parishioners is for the most part that of the lower middle class. They tend to be salaried and wage workers rather than self-employed or professional persons. They do not usually belong to exclusive "social clubs" or to congeniality groups with pretensions of upward mobility. The social relations which they have on a supraparochial basis also tend to be in religious and welfare activities with other Catholics.

5. The ethnic and migrant factors also seem to have some relationship to the nuclear status of the parishioner. Families that have migrated from the country parishes seem to integrate better into the urban parish, and to become nuclear parishioners more often, than those who are city people and have moved in from other urban parishes. This is not true of foreign-born immigrants, who appear

to have such great difficulty in adjusting themselves to the urban parochial system that they must be classified sometimes in the modal category but most often among the marginal parishioners.

The ethnic background of the nuclear must somehow be correlated with his immigrant or native status, and this appears to be the reverse of the rural-urban comparison. Roughly speaking, the longer a family has been in the city, the less likely are its members to be nuclear parishioners. Again, roughly speaking, the longer a family has been American, the more likely are its members to be nuclear. For example, in our study, people of Irish, French, and. German background, who are third- and fourth-generation Americans, are proportionately more numerous in the nuclear category than are the first- and second-generation Mexicans and Italians.

b) The study of the *motivational system* of nuclear parishioners involves all the difficulties which are usually attendant on the analysis of motives.[8] The following series of statements are therefore merely inferential and suggestive. They were evolved from observation, interviews, and discussions, and they elude the relative precision of conclusions based on statistical evidence.

1. Orthodoxy of religious beliefs appears to be a characteristic of the nuclear parishioner. He does not question the dogmatic and moral teachings of the Catholic Church, and he exhibits the state of mind which is said to "think with the Church." It is empirically demonstrable that this unwavering adherence to a satisfying system of religious principles helps the individual to pursue his high behavioral objectives. He does not attempt to "adapt" these principles either to his own whims or to the so-called cultural expectations of the society in which he lives. For example, the nuclear person is not likely to assert: "I am old enough to choose my own movies and can ignore the Legion of Decency ratings"; he does not complain that "the Church's teaching on hell does not fit our culture."

2. The religious institution is pivotal for him, and in this regard he tends to "go against" the culture in which he lives. If a clear-cut division could be made between the secular and the sacred institutions of our culture, it may be said that this Catholic is marginal to the former and nuclear to the latter. It is generally conceded that in our urban, industrial culture the economic institution is the pivotal and most influential of all the institutions. The nuclear

8. The problem of religious motivation presents one of the greatest difficulties in the strictly scientific approach to religious behavior. It is discussed below, chap. 15, pp. 209–11, as one of the "major issues" in the sociology of religion.

parishioner, contrariwise, does not allow this central position to the economic but replaces it with the religious institution.

3. The institutionalized religious role is also pivotal for the nuclear parishioner. In the complex of social roles which he plays he places more importance on the religious role as a sort of core into which all other patterned activities must be integrated. This does not mean that the nuclear neglects his "lesser roles" but rather that he subordinates them and permeates them with the values of the religious role.

4. It is logical also that the nuclear parishioner operates under an integrated value system. This tends to constitute for him an inner psychological unity which is externalized by cutting across all his institutional roles and activities. For example, he does not think of the commandments and precepts as exclusively religious principles which operate only within the formalized ecclesiastical structures. They are principles for a "philosophy of life" according to which he acts in every institutional situation he enters. This is another way of saying that he does not employ one set of values for his family relations, another in his business contacts, a third in his recreational and leisure activities, etc.

5. Relations between this person and the clergy tend to be cordial and spontaneous. The nuclear parishioner understands his status as a lay person within the stratified social system of the Catholic Church. He knows that the priest is the "head man" of the parish and that decisions can be made by the laity only in so far as the priest permits or encourages them. He considers himself an "assistant" to the parish priests, and this attitude is demonstrated in his sympathetic approach to the problems of the priest, his penchant for defending and supporting the actions of the priest, and his willingness to co-operate in some of the more tedious and "thankless" functions of the parish.

PARISH LEADERS

Because we could not obtain a sufficient number of interviews from proved leaders in the three white urban parishes which form the basis of our study of nuclear parishioners, we extended our inquiries to include lay leaders from other parishes in the same general urban area. We obtained completed interview schedules from 245 white lay persons (147 men and 98 women) above the age of twenty-five who are or were officeholders in the parish societies. These persons were selected for interviews not only because of their experience in parish groups but also because they were recognized and recommended for their "leadership qualities" by other parishioners.

In order to work out a description of the Catholic lay leader, we asked these experienced persons to give us a listing of the qualities which they considered most important in a parochial leader. To avoid an interminable list, we asked them to mention no more than five qualities in the order of importance. Actually, the responses averaged only about three suggestions per person. In some cases the terms supplied were synonymous, so that in the analysis of the answers were were able to work out ten main characteristics or qualities and an additional category of miscellaneous suggestions. Table 4 shows the percentage distribution of the 745 answers given by these leaders.

TABLE 4

PERCENTAGE DISTRIBUTION OF QUALITIES AND ABILITIES
REQUIRED OF LAY PARISH LEADERS

	No. of Times Mentioned	Per Cent
Must be a practicing Catholic with a good knowledge and appreciation of the Catholic religion	134	18.0
Must have a good approach to people, treating them with tact, diplomacy, and courtesy	112	15.0
Must be willing to treat others in an unselfish, charitable, and unprejudiced way	97	13.0
Must be open, honest, and sincere; a person who you know can be trusted	74	10.0
Must be recognized as a good moral character who sets the example for other parishioners in all things	71	9.5
Must have a willingness and ability to work hard even when the job is not considered an important one	66	8.9
Must be enthusiastic, militant, courageous, and aggressive	56	7.5
Must have ability to express thoughts clearly to co-workers and to speak well in public	49	6.6
Must have executive ability and be a good organizer and manager	41	5.5
Must be active and successful in community, neighborhood, and occupation	32	4.3
Miscellaneous qualities and abilities (broad-mindedness, possessing vision, willing to contribute and collect money, etc.)	13	1.7
Total	745*	100.0

* Wherever a synonym was mentioned in the same interview, it was omitted from this count. Without these subtractions the actual number was 763.

There was no appreciable difference of opinion between males and females in the listing of qualities of leadership. Similarly, in the ranking of the various qualities, those which are most often mentioned were also considered most important by the individuals who ranked them.

By asking these lay persons an oblique question, we felt that we could make a better judgment about their opinions concerning the qualities most needed in a leader. We told them that we were interested in the training of young leaders, that is, the persons eighteen to twenty-five years of age who would later take their places

TABLE 5

	No. of Times Mentioned	Per Cent
Give them opportunities, definite jobs, and responsibilities	119	30.0
Provide for them social, recreational, and athletic programs	96	24.1
Have the young people form their own clubs and organizations which they run independently	67	16.8
Integrate the young people with the older persons, increasing association between the two age groups	61	15.3
Develop better relations between the priests and the young people	34	8.5
Improve the content of the meetings of existing organizations so that young people will be interested in attending	21	5.3
Total	398	100.0

as parish leaders. The question was: "What do you think should be done in order to prepare and train younger persons for future leadership in the parish?" Table 5 gives the percentage distribution of their answers.

It is interesting to note that, while these respondents put in first place the importance of the knowledge and practice of Catholicism as a leadership quality, they made no suggestion for the training of young leaders which would include the development of spirituality. Perhaps they felt that this spiritual training would be provided otherwise and that the Catholic youth need more than anything a training in responsibility. The third suggestion (that the young people run their own clubs) also indicates the conviction that future leaders must develop a sense of responsibility. The second and sixth suggestions center on the importance of youthful interests, apparently on the hypothesis that young people will develop leadership if they are really interested in the proposed functions.

In an attempt to discover more information concerning the organizational activity of parish leaders we asked them to name the organizations to which they belonged. We placed these organizations in five categories and found that these 245 lay leaders had 713 memberships in religious groupings, 237 in business or professional groupings, 186 in civic or community organizations, 111 in congeniality groups,[9] and 17 in political associations. Table 6 shows the distribution of these persons according to their frequency of membership in the different categories of organizations.

TABLE 6

DISTRIBUTION OF 245 LAY LEADERS ACCORDING TO THE NUMBER AND
TYPE OF SOCIAL ORGANIZATIONS TO WHICH THEY BELONG

| | | | No. of Memberships in: | | | | |
No. of Persons	No. of Organizations	Religious Organization	Business or Professional Organization	Civic or Community Organization	Congeniality Organization	Political Organization	Total No. of Memberships in All Organizations
19	2	31	2	2	1	2	38
41	3	57	35	27	3	1	123
43	4	123	21	18	5	5	172
43	5	132	19	45	16	3	215
47	6	169	41	35	37	0	282
16	7	54	22	11	24	1	112
15	8	23	38	42	15	2	120
8	9	47	16	4	5	2	72
7	10	40	22	6	2	1	70
6	11	37	21	5	3	0	66
Total	65	713	237	186	111	17	1,264
Average membership in each type of social organization		2.95	0.96	0.76	0.45	0.07	5.15

These statistics show that the parochial leader is a person with wide and diversified experience in organizational activities, having an average of about five memberships in different kinds of groups. He is most absorbed in religious groupings and least in political. No leader belongs to less than two groups, and doubling-up tends to take place more in the religious societies than in others. Memberships average less than one per person in each of the remaining group categories. There are 237 memberships in occupational groupings and only 17 in the political groups.

9. "Social" in the broad sense of recreational and fraternal groups.

Before proceeding to an analysis of the leader-in-action within the parochial unit of the Church, it seems important to point out that the parish priest is the primary leader in all the parochial groups.[10] In the strict sense, he is the only full-time leader in the only consecutively functioning organization, the parish itself. The lay persons can be only part-time leaders in part-time organizations which function sporadically.[11] Thus the inherent nature of the parochial substructures excludes the probability of "bureaucratic leadership" as defined by Max Weber and of "executive leadership" as defined by Chester Bernard. These two types of leadership may be found among the clergy of the Catholic Church but not among the volunteer lay leaders in the parish.

Besides this subsidiary, part-time position of the lay leader, there are other distinguishing characteristics of the leadership function in the Catholic parish. The layman is not able to receive or dispense rewards that may act as a significant incentive to group action.[12] The person who is elevated to the Knighthood of St. Gregory or receives the "Pro Ecclesia et Pontifice" medal may be a leader in his own parish, but the award usually comes to him for praiseworthy activity in a wider field—the city or diocese. How can the parish priest compensate his parochial leaders except by praises and recognition? This in itself, unless adroitly performed, may alienate some of the followers in the organizations. The lack of effective symbols for incentive seems to be a problem of all voluntary religious leadership as compared with professional secular leadership.

On the other hand, the inability to dispense rewards is also a dysfunctional factor in the development and maintenance of lay parochial leadership. From the point of view of the active membership, a parish society appears to be one of the most democratic groupings in existence. This, too, is a problem of incentives, first, for original inception to the group and, second, for active adherence to the organization's program and leaders. In our present urban society it is no longer culturally compulsive for the lay person to be actively identified as a member of a church society (it may be temporarily expedient for the young business and professional man who at the beginning of his career needs a reputation for

10. See below, chap. 10, the discussion of priestly roles in the parish.
11. This excludes the relatively few instances in urban American parishes where full-time functionaries are employed as directors of athletic programs, social work activities, etc.
12. This does not mean that these individuals are lacking in spiritual and supernatural motivation. The ideal situation would probably be one in which these "higher" incentives sufficed without the need of lesser motives.

stability and sobriety among his prospective Catholic clientele).[13] Furthermore, a member may quit a lay organization at any time without "losing face" and without the necessity of explaining his defection. Finally, there are numerous secular organizations whose functions and goals may interest the Catholic more than do those of the parochial lay groups.

All that has been said above indicates that leadership, as a general and abstract concept, has very little practical meaning in the parochial situation. The abilities and qualities of the ideal lay leader must be related to the kind of organizations in which they are employed and to the actual social situation in the urban parish. Before we began this study, we thought that some existing conceptual scheme of leadership could be easily employed and that comparisons could be made with it. But the evidence has forced us to think otherwise. Leadership in the lay societies of a Catholic urban parish presents peculiar elements which cannot be generalized for all types of social structures.

The following facts highlight that peculiarity: (*a*) The lay person can never be a "total" leader; the priest is above him; the layman can give only part of his time to the work; the incentives which motivate the leader and with which he motivates his followers are intangible. (*b*) The parochial organizations in which he works are not "total" organizations; they function intermittently, and, above all, they are "volunteer" groups. Because of these reasons the lay religious leader with voluntary followers seems to require even greater knowledge and ability than is demanded of the professional leader with paid followers.[14]

These generalizations about the peculiarities of both leaders and organizations in the urban parish must be kept in mind when considering the more specific remarks here made concerning lay leadership. The leader does not operate in a vacuum, and at least four elements must be combined for successful functioning. His role implies at least two sets of patterned relationships: (1) the one toward the priest-director and (2) the other toward the membership of the group. The success of leadership seems to depend, at least in part, upon the proper balance and integration of these rela-

13. On the other hand, he may feel the necessity for being very "broadminded" about religious beliefs and practices in dealing with persons of different religious denominations, being asked also to contribute to their charities.

14. A similar analogy may be drawn in the comparison between a labor leader's relation to his union members and an executive's to his workers, or between a political leader's relation to his followers and a civil service administrator's to his employees.

tions. The lay person cannot be an effective leader if either of these
relations breaks down. A certain amount of social skill is required
in order that this line of communication and of subsidiary authority
from priest to leader to members be kept open and operative.
Leadership also implies (3) an intimate knowledge of the function
and goal of the groups and (4) a developed and sustained interest
by all participants.

1. In the relationship between the priest and the leader it may be
said that the degree of independence and initiative allowed to the
leaders is a most important factor in successful leading. Voluntary,
effective lay leadership cannot be had by appointment or dictation.

TABLE 7

Opinions of 245 White Catholic Lay Leaders (147 Males and 98
Females) on the Question: "When It Is Not a Matter of Faith
and Morals, What Is the Best Position for the Priest To Take
in the Parochial Organizations?"

	MALE		FEMALE		BOTH	
	No.	Per Cent	No.	Per Cent	No.	Per Cent
Complete control.............	11	7.5	2	2.0	13	5.3
Power of final decision only...	35	23.8	7	7.2	42	17.1
Advice and direction only.....	91	61.9	84	85.7	175	71.5
Equal vote with parishioners...	10	6.8	5	5.1	15	6.1
Total	147	100.0	98	100.0	245	100.0

The priest who can find and maintain the delicate balance between
the minimum of necessary authority on his part and the maximum
of constructive initiative on the part of the lay leader is probably
himself the exemplar of parochial leadership.

The 245 lay leaders whom we interviewed were asked their
opinion concerning this question: "When it is not a matter of faith
and morals, what is the best position for the parish priest to take
in the parochial organizations?" Four choices were given, and
none of the respondents was hesitant about his or her choice. The
overwhelming majority (71.5 per cent) said that the priest should
"give advice and direction only." A much smaller percentage (17.1
per cent) thought that the priest should have the "power of final
decision only." The remaining minority was divided between the
two extreme views: 6.1 per cent said that the priest should have
no more than "an equal voice with the membership," and 5.3 per
cent thought that the priest should have "complete control" over
the organization (Table 7).[15]

15. It is interesting to note that, of the thirteen who are in favor of complete
control by the priest, eleven are men and two are women.

These answers show that experienced lay parochial leaders are neither authoritarian nor anarchic; they want neither complete control by the priest nor complete emancipation from him. They would like a certain amount of freedom to determine their organizational activities, and at the same time they recognize that they are functioning within an ordered social structure in which the priest must play an important part.

2. In the relationship between the lay leader and the lay members of the organizations it would seem that the ability to obtain cooperation is a most important factor. We asked these 245 lay leaders what the position of the leader should be if he is to obtain maximum co-operation, and again we gave them a choice of four answers. Table 8 shows the results.

TABLE 8

OPINIONS OF 245 WHITE CATHOLIC LAY LEADERS (147 MALES AND 98 FEMALES) ON THE QUESTION: "IN ORDER TO OBTAIN CO-OPERATION FROM THE MEMBERS OF THE ORGANIZATION, WHICH OF THE POSITIONS SHOULD THE LEADER TAKE?"

	MALE		FEMALE		BOTH	
	No.	Per Cent	No.	Per Cent	No.	Per Cent
Act on his own at all times..	7	4.8	5	5.1	12	4.9
Act on his own only in emergencies	4	2.7	3	3.1	7	2.9
Submit all important issues to the membership..........	108	73.5	80	81.6	188	76.7
Submit all issues to the membership	28	19.0	10	10.2	38	15.5
Total	147	100.0	98	100.0	245	100.0

These opinions indicate that the lay leaders neither wanted nor expected to have complete control of their organizations. Only nineteen (7.8 per cent) of them felt that the leader should "act on his own" in the sense of being independent of the will of the membership. The great majority, however (76.7 per cent), seemed to feel that a certain amount of leeway could be allowed in the less important issues which confronted the leaders but that all important problems required consultation and consent of the members.

3. The function and the goal of each particular parochial organization constitute another important element in successful lay leadership. Almost all these leaders pointed out that there are great differences in the kind of group activities pursued within the parish. The occasional religious function of a sodality or a Holy Name Society

differs vastly from the frequent visiting of the poor by members of a St. Vincent de Paul Conference and from the direction of athletic teams for the young people. Thus, quite aside from the abilities of leaders, some types of organizations inherently function more easily and successfully than others.

Judged by external criteria, it may be said that the success of a lay leader is measured by the success of his organization. The latter may be measured by the degree to which it has attained its goal. Hence it is extremely important to know the function and the goal of each group, not only as these are stated in written constitutions and public expressions, but also as they are understood informally by the priest, the leader, and the members. If there is disagreement or vagueness on this point within the group, lay leadership cannot function effectively.

4. Since no goal is achieved spontaneously and no group functions automatically, successful lay leadership depends also upon the interest which the priest, leader, and members have in the particular operations of the group. This fact is demonstrated in remarks like the following: "You can get lots of women out to a bingo party but very few to a meeting of the Altar Society"; or "The men will work hard to put on a boxing program, but they won't come out for a parents-teachers' meeting."

This is another way of saying that people will co-operate more actively in the attainment of goals which are consonant with their practical ideology or value system. If they are secular-minded, their primary interests will not be centered in the more spiritual activities. In a cultural milieu where spiritual values are relatively debased, one cannot expect to find as great interest, good leadership, and willing followers in the Holy Name Society as can be found in a parochial athletic program.

The factor of interest seems to require that a leader be active in the kind of group whose interests follow his. A very pious man, with good leadership qualities but with no interest in athletics, could hardly be successful in the youth clubs. A woman whose absorbing interest is in her children, and who also has good leadership qualities, may be very successful as a director of Girl Scouts, but she may be a relative failure in the Confraternity of Christian Doctrine.

It must be noted that these four elements are in a sense cumulative and overlapping. (1) The relations between the leader and the priest, (2) the relations between the leader and the members, (3) the function and goal of the group, and (4) the interests of the priest, leader, and members—all these must be properly combined if there is to be successful lay leadership. In the last analysis, it seems necessary to include also the two preliminary elements discussed above: (5) the general leadership qualities and (6) the peculiar aspects of parochial groupings.

Chapter Four

Social Solidarity and Modal Parishioners

THE modal parishioner is the "ordinary Catholic," the person who helps to constitute the urban Catholic masses. He is neither enthusiastic enough to be counted among the most active inner-core parishioners nor lethargic enough to be included among the marginal Catholics. In a sense, he is the most widely representative of the urban Catholic, because this category makes up about 70 per cent of the members of the city church. The modal parishioner is a sort of silent symbol which indicates to non-Catholics the meaning of the Church in human life and social relations. The objective observer cannot say that "this is the *best* of Catholicism," but he can say that "this is the *most* of Catholicism," and from these modal Catholics he can estimate the exemplification of the Church in the modern world.

This does not mean that the modal parishioner is exemplary in the sense that he represents the highest pattern of Christian living, in the way that the nuclear parishioner tends to be a model for others to follow. But in the social and cultural environment in which he moves the modal Catholic is actually the living model or "type" of Catholicism set before the great majority of non-Catholics. His behavior is interpreted as typical Catholic behavior; his beliefs and attitudes are considered those of the Catholic Church.

From this point of view, and because of their sheer numbers, the modal parishioners may be considered the most important category of lay Catholics to be studied by the social scientist. Their interpretive impact upon urban American non-Catholics is great because of frequent and continued contact. The masses of Americans do not learn about Catholicism by reading the carefully worded and clearly defined texts written by Church apologists. They have little contact with the trained clergy and with the relatively few theologically educated Catholic laymen who could explain the teachings of the Church. It is from modal Catholics that they become aware of the practical ideology and of the institutionalized patterns of thought and behavior characteristic of lay Catholics in the big cities.

Since the modal parishioner holds a position midway between the nuclear and the marginal Catholic, he may be said to live up to his religion in a "middling sort of way." He generally observes the Friday abstinence and knows the difference between Advent and Lent. His name is likely to be on the roster of the Holy Name Society at some time during his life, but he hardly ever attends a meeting. He attends Sunday Mass most of the time but has difficulty "catching Mass" when holy days of obligation occur during the working week. His children fill the parochial schools, and he has a kind of aloof respect for priests and nuns.

What is the "façade of unity" which these numerous and representative Catholics present to the world? A superficial view sees them as a close-knit and self-satisfied group of people who are perhaps a threat to the social and political integration of the larger community. "In the hands of the hierarchy they become instruments for the development of a militant and exclusive faith. The lay members are carefully guided by the hierarchy into ways of separatism and monopoly. They are segregated from the rest of American cultural and social life as much as possible in order to preserve their faith unsullied."[1]

An almost equally superficial view may result also in the opposite conclusion that the Catholic masses, the modal parishioners, are in no way united. This view holds that they have become so well integrated into American society that one must search closely for characteristics which distinguish the ordinary Catholic from the ordinary non-Catholic. "The parish as we know it now, particularly in big industrial cities and urban areas, is no more than an artificial, purely geographical group. It has no relation to the general social and economic life of its members; it is in fact no more than a haphazard collection and agglomeration of people."[2]

Limited scientific research in urban Catholic parishes indicates that the truth lies somewhere between these two extremes. The conclusions from this research do not flow either from the fears of religious apologists who decry the ghetto mentality of some Catholics

1. Paul Blanshard, *American Freedom and Catholic Power* (Boston: Beacon Press, 1949), p. 31.
2. John Fitzsimons, "The Life of the Parish," *Worship*, XXVI, No. 6 (May, 1952), 304–10. The author later tempers this remark by indicating some of the actual bonds of parochial solidarity.

or from the fears of non-Catholics who foresee the development of an organized Catholic power structure.[3] In other words, urban modal Catholics are not nearly so separatist or so solidaristic as opposing popular opinions seem to hold.

The concept of social solidarity implies a relatively high degree of morale and of consensus, a close adherence to a common value system, and is externalized in actual and measurable social co-operation among the members of the group. Newcomb summarizes the findings of other social psychologists when he says that "a group is most cohesive when its members (1) find membership in it attractive; (2) are motivated to take their roles, as assigned; and (3) share common understandings of the group norms." The sociological principles of shared task-involvement, social facilitation, and group reinforcement must be taken into consideration, as well as the cumulative interdependence of all of these factors. Observation of the group in action is the test of solidarity. "If it shows good teamwork, gets things done, and sticks together in spite of disruptive influences, we should probably assign it a high rating in cohesiveness."[4]

It may be supposed that the existence and expression of social solidarity among Catholics would serve a double function: first, to draw Catholics closer together in all their human relations and social activities and, second, to distinguish them from all other religious groups as well as from so-called secular organizations. The scientific approach to this question of the social integration of modal Catholics necessarily tests the assumption that there exists a distinctively Catholic bond of unity that can be recognized in operation *at the parochial level.*

The question of the social solidarity of the urban Catholic parish may be discussed in two other contexts. It faces us in the attempt to conceptualize the parish as a communal group held together by shared religious values. We note that the sharing of functions is a much more practical factor of unity than the sharing of common values. The same problem occurs in the attempt to establish criteria of membership in the parish, and it was seen that the lack of social participation on the part of all (or of a large segment) of the parishioners leaves us with the tentative conclusion that the parish is at best a social aggregate.[5]

3. See below, chap. 15, on the second "major issue."
4. Theodore M. Newcomb, *Social Psychology* (New York: Dryden Press, 1950), chap. xvii, "Group Solidarity." See, at the end of the present chapter, the discussion of the practical factors at work among small groups of parishioners who are highly cohesive.
5. See below, chap. 14, sec. *d*, and above, chap. 2, pp. 18–19.

If social solidarity, as technically defined, does not exist within the individual urban parish, we may assume that it is not likely to exist within the whole Catholic Church. But the test of the definition of solidarity and of the presuppositions about its presence or absence requires a careful study of social processes as they actually occur in the group life of urban American lay Catholics. The popular assumption that Catholics "stick together," and that this solidarity is based principally on the fact that they share the same religion, requires also an analysis of the various "kinds" of unity expected of Catholics. Briefly, this test and this analysis must consider the unity of Catholics (*a*) by human consensus, (*b*) by divine grace, and (*c*) by social virtue. The first two types are not easily susceptible of empirical study, while the third kind of unity can be observed and measured (1) on the general community level, (2) on the religious supraparochial level, and (3) on the level of parochial activities and groupings.

a) *Solidarity by consensus.*—For many centuries the apologists of the Catholic Church have stressed the fundamental importance of unity as one of the four distinguishing characteristics of the true religion. (The Church of Christ is *one*, holy, universal, and apostolic.) They have emphasized the fact that Catholics who are orthodox and who are united with Rome agree upon the truth of the same dogmas of faith all over the world and all through time. Catholics also accept the same code of morality, which is obligatory and applicable to all members of the Church who have reached the age of reason. Catholics everywhere agree to the same fundamental divine worship in the sacramental economy of salvation.

This form of solidarity is for the most part an intellectual unity, a consensus of the mind, concerning the abstract truths of Catholicism. The sharing of these religious beliefs and moral values and liturgical forms constitutes what might be called the theological explanation of Catholic solidarity on a supernatural plane. But this theological unity, this common agreement on the essentials of creed, code, and cult, is only by implication also a social communion. It means that all Catholics, as individuals, have a similar attitudinal relationship to God and the things of God and that in the aggregate they have a kind of "mental communion" among themselves. But it merely presupposes that there is also an *expected* social consequence.[6]

6. It may be argued that this expectation of Christian social solidarity is so forceful that it is almost an essential characteristic of the faithful Catholic. Max Scheler (who himself became an apostate) has emphasized the phrase, "Unus Christianus, nullus Christianus," to indicate that a "nonsocial" or antisocial Christian is unthinkable (*Vom Ewigen im Menschen* [Berlin, 1933], p. 557;

In other words, in the abstract order, the consensual and theological unity of creed, code, and cult can be conceptualized as a series of parallel lines leading directly from each individual to God. Thus, all Catholics may be said to have a similar relationship to God in the sense that they believe and worship in the same general way. Things that are similar, however, and persons who are similar are not necessarily closely associated with one another. Likeness of kind, though it may frequently beget "consciousness of kind," does not always lead to close relationship among those who are similar. Just as the greatest physical proximity of two persons may be accompanied by the greatest social distance between them, so also two Catholics side by side in a church pew may be theologically similar but have no observable social relations with each other.

b) Solidarity by divine grace.—The second type of unity among Catholics depends upon the functioning of sacramental grace rather than upon any mental activity of the individual participants. This too has been emphasized by Catholic apologists, and it has been discussed by those observers who are seeking evidence of its social effects.[7] One observer has bluntly remarked about Catholic parishioners that "the only union and the only common attachment to the parish is through their sacramental life. That they should all eat of the same Sacred Banquet is edifying, but it produces nothing more than spiritual community. It does not become incarnated in society."[8]

The spiritual community, of which Fitzsimons speaks, is in no wise synonymous with "community." It appears to be the kind of unity mentioned by St. Paul when he said that all are one in the baptism of Christ; there is no longer Jew or Gentile, male or female, bond or free (Rom. 10:12; Gal. 3:27–28). It is a kind of mystical (but ontologically real) relationship between and among Catholics. It is often described as a kind of sacramental bond of persons within the Mystical Body of Christ which ties together the members not only of the Church militant but also of the Church suffering and triumphant.[9] The obvious implication is that this unity should be-

---

quoted by Joachim Wach, *The Sociology of Religion* [Chicago: University of Chicago Press, 1944], p. 29).

7. This is further discussed below, chap. 15, pp. 207–9, as one of the major problems of the sociology of the parish.

8. Fitzsimons, *op. cit.*, p. 304.

9. The "Communion of Saints" is an essential dogma contained in the formula of the Apostles' Creed and includes all members of the City of God on earth, in purgatory, and in heaven. The present discussion is limited, of course, to the living members on earth.

come "incarnated in society" and should help to develop a community spirit among Christians.

Solidarity by divine grace cannot be tested by the tools of the social scientist. Granted that this supernatural bond really exists and that it really unites baptized persons as members of the social aggregate of which Christ is the Head, it is still primarily the work of God and not of men.[10] The sociologist is not in a position to question the fact that God intends that the sacramental unity which He produces should be accompanied by a social unity which man produces. Research in human relations reveals that this hidden bond is not necessarily recognized or put into practical operation by the very persons who are united by it. Mortal enemies, completely incompatible personalities, strangers who do not even know of each other's existence—these may all be in the same fellowship through this sacramental union; but they can hardly be said to exhibit the empirical and measurable solidarity of a human group on earth.

c) *Solidarity by social virtue.*—There remains, then, for our empirical study only the external manifestation of the virtue of universal love. Neither the unity of faith nor the unity of grace can be said to be a fruitful frame of reference in sociological research. Both of them may and do exist even where there is a lack of perceivable social solidarity, and both are necessarily presupposed in the operation of the fundamental principle of Christian solidarity: the social virtue of love. St. Paul exhorts: "And above all these things have charity, which is the bond of perfection" (Col. 3:14). In another place he says: "For all the law is fulfilled in one word: Thou shalt love thy neighbor as thyself" (Gal. 5:14).

The recognition of the supernatural virtue of charity as the peculiar social bond among Christians is not a recently discovered concept. The pagans themselves in the first century of our era had called attention to it when they said of Christians, "See how they love one another." This universal and supernatural love is both an internal motivation (not easily susceptible of measurement) and an external relationship (which must be observable in social actions). Presumably the Catholic's love of his neighbor is based upon his love of God, but this is also a supposition which the social scientist can neither measure nor prove.

But, even if we grant the validity of this supposition, there still

10. Of course, the alliance with God through Christ is volitional, or mentally guided, in the adult's first step toward joining the Church, but the theologians teach that even this first step presupposes the grace of God.

remains the task of observing the external practice of the virtue of love, and this is nothing more or less than the manifestation of social solidarity among modal parishioners. If the unity of faith and grace and love actually exists among Catholics, it may be supposed that there is (or ought to be) a realistic and recognizable social solidarity among members of the same Church. This returns to the double function of Catholic solidarity mentioned above and raises the double question: Can it be said that Catholics co-operate socially because they are Catholics? Can the social relations which they have among themselves be distinguished from the social relations among non-Catholics?

We have said above that the social virtue or practice of Christian love may be found on three levels: in the general community relations, in the religious relations of Catholics outside the parish, and in parochial activities. These three areas in which Christian love operates must be studied from the point of view of the typology of parishioners. In other words, since the four types of parishioners (nuclear, modal, marginal, and dormant) can be called Catholics in varying degrees, they must also be expected to differ in the practice of social virtue. Here, however, we are primarily interested in the display of Christian love by the modal parishioners.

1. Social virtue *in the general community* allows for several degrees of interpretation. The widest and all-embracing concept of Christian love means that the individual has universal good will toward all persons regardless of religion, race, or nationality. If Catholicism is the true religion of Christ, then it must demand that the Catholic love not only his fellow-Catholics but also Jews, Protestants, Hindus, Moslems, and even atheists. It does not demand that he must love non-Catholics in the same degree that he loves Catholics, just as it does not demand that he must love strangers as much as he loves the members of his own family.

Within certain limits of time and space, the test of universal love is found in the kind and degree of social relations in which the Catholic participates. In the big cities one may frequently note close social relations of dormant and marginal Catholics with people of other religions. On careful analysis this association is always based on nonreligious factors and must therefore be excluded from the present discussion. The nuclear parishioner, because of his deep religious interest, is most frequently attracted to associations of fellow-Catholics who are engaged in spiritual functions, but he is also the only type of parishioner who practices true Christian love to all persons and uses this virtue as a basis of social reform.

The modal parishioners, about whom we are most concerned in this chapter, associate with non-Catholics in occupational and recreational activities. In our research we have found very few who are actively engaged with non-Catholics in those organizations which work for civic improvement. The great mass of modal parishioners appears to be suspended between two polar expressions of social virtue: between those who are motivated in their broad social relations by the love of God and those who appear to be motivated by secular values and natural love.

It may be said in general that for the modal parishioner almost every other factor of social solidarity seems to have more practical effect in the quality of human relations than the religious factor for which we are searching. In our research studies the evidence has been overwhelming that so-called secular factors constitute common interest areas, promote close co-operation, and effectively unite people in a way that religious factors fail to do. This does not mean to suggest that a clear-cut distinction can always be made among motives and factors of human behavior or that in any given instance a single factor explains behavior.

2. It will be expected that social virtue among Catholics *on the supraparochial level* is of a different degree from social virtue between Catholic and non-Catholic on the level of the general community. But even here the same factors which tend to unite or divide people in the general community (class status, educational and ethnic background, etc.) tend to unite or divide these persons who profess the same Christian religion. This is true even though the religious bond of Christian love is intended to transcend all other factors of association and to be expressed in positive human relations among baptized Catholics.

The most impressive example of the external failure of this social virtue is noted in the traditional system of human relations across racial lines. This system has become institutionalized in every phase of human activity, and the caste line is found not only in education, business, and recreation but also in religion. The modal white Catholic unites more readily, more cordially, and more permanently with almost any other white person, whether Jew, Protestant, or atheist, than he does with his fellow-Catholic who is a Negro. Except for a small minority of nuclear and zealous Catholics of both races, the religious bond of charity is practically inoperative between these two groups of baptized Catholics.

The social analyst meets a kind of dilemma at this point. In spite of the canonical ideal of an integrated parish which includes all baptized Catholics living within a designated territory, the *de facto* situation in southern cities exhibits racially separated parishes. It may be said that in this system of socially segregated parishes, according to which the territorial boundaries of white and Negro parishes overlap, there can be little expectation of social solidarity based on Christian love across racial lines. The social bond of the Mystical Body which is presumed to unite baptized persons regardless of race is empirically insignificant in comparison with the practical day-by-day effect of racial separatism.

It is an odd sociological fact, however, that the present tendency to break down class, racial, and ethnic barriers among Catholics exists more on the supraparochial than on the parochial level. The lay persons who are active in Catholic organizations which cut across parochial lines are usually nuclear Catholics and only occasionally modal parishioners. In other words, at the present time the social solidarity of Christians based on the supernatural virtue of love seems to be best exemplified by the "better" Catholics in programs and functions which are not limited to the parish confines.

The present situation among these lay Catholics in the urban South appears to hold dynamic promise for the future. National loyalties and racial pride have in the past interfered with the practice of Christian love, but the gradual amelioration of these factors in our democratic culture has also had a positive effect upon the religious institutions. In some ways, the Catholic Church in the South, like other religious groups, has been strongly affected by the general social system of the region. On the other hand, the Church has been partially successful in resisting this system. As Myrdal pointed out ten years ago, "In the South, especially in southern Louisiana where the French and Creole traditions are dominant, the Roman Catholic Church is the only one where Negroes are allowed to attend white churches."[11]

11. This refers to attendance at services in white parishes, not to membership in the parish as a social unit (Gunnar Myrdal, *An American Dilemma* [New York: Harper & Bros., 1944], pp. 870 ff.). "But even here," Myrdal continues, "the dominant tendency is to keep Negroes in their own churches, to prevent Negroes from joining in interchurch Catholic meetings or celebrations, and to provide a separate set of white priests—who seldom mingle with other priests—for the Negroes." In 1953 there were fifty-seven American Negro priests, of whom nine were on the foreign missions and three had come originally from outside the United States. One of the latter, Joseph O. Bower, S.V.D., was raised to the episcopacy by Pope Pius XII on April 22, 1953 (see also Albert S. Foley, *Bishop Healy, Beloved Outcaste* [New York: Farrar, Straus & Young, 1954]).

In the last analysis it must be said that the modal parishioners of the urban Catholic Church do not demonstrate a specifically Catholic kind of solidarity based on supernatural love, even though this may not be called peculiarly parochial. If this were otherwise, the evidence would satisfy the criterion for a communal group (even above the parish unit) and would expect that Catholics co-operate socially because they are Catholics and that they demonstrate the virtue of charity in the practical human relations of everyday life. It might even be expected that the social scientist could then abstract and isolate certain patterns of social behavior which could be recognized as Catholic quite aside from the formal and institutionalized behavior at religious services.

3. The social virtue of charity *on the parochial level* would unite all parishioners into a strictly defined social group. A recognizable degree of social solidarity would then be achieved in the actual human relations of urban Catholics and would indicate that the Catholic parish is a communal group.[12] Our research has shown that this concept can be applied only to the nuclear parishioners, a relatively small group of faithful participants who constitute the inner core of the parish.[13] Our research has indicated also (as we shall see below) that the most manifest examples of social solidarity in small groups within the parish are not necessarily and primarily based upon the fundamental virtue of Christian love.

The white urban parishes which we have studied are made up of Catholics not only of different "religious types" but also of different occupational and class statuses. The professional and management class is easily distinguished from the category of semiskilled workers like truckers and bus-drivers and of skilled workers like plumbers and machinists. The professional and business people tend to have close, cordial, and multiple social relations with a circle of non-Catholics who are associated in the same general occupational category. The semiskilled and skilled manual workers have similar social relations with non-Catholics in their own occupations. As Catholics, however, and as members of the same urban parish, these two groups seem hardly aware of one another's existence. In other words, similar occupational and class status appears to constitute a more effective social bond between Catholics and non-Catholics than the same religion constitutes between Catholic and Catholic of different classes.

Besides the racial factor which in the segregated system must

12. See below, chap. 14, "Conceptualizations of the Urban Parish," pp. 187–88.
13. See above, chap. 3, "Nuclear Parishioners and Leaders," pp. 23–30.

be considered a supraparochial problem, the economic and class factor represents the most obvious example of lack of social solidarity based on Christian love; but there are others. The amount and kind of education seem to affect the solidarity of modal parishioners. College graduates have hardly more than a nodding acquaintance with those who have attended only grammar school, and this seems to be true even when there is a blood relationship between them. Modal parishioners, whether they have graduated from Catholic or secular universities, identify more closely with non-Catholic college graduates than they do with fellow-parishioners of less education. Their formal and informal group life is more often centered around the interests they developed in college rather than on any parochial or religious interest.

Many urban parish priests complain that the college graduate "is lost to the parish." This does not mean that the college graduate leaves the Church, fails to receive the sacraments, or becomes a dormant parishioner. As a matter of fact, the Catholic Church seems to be the only religion in America in which increased education is accompanied by improved religious observances.[14] But the point at issue here is social participation rather than religious practices. In so far as he participates in religious groupings, the Catholic college graduate tends to join interest and vocational groupings. His inactivity in parish societies is paralleled by his general lack of association with fellow-parishioners of less education.[15]

One more negative example may be cited even though it seems to be gradually disappearing among urban Catholics. Ethnic solidarity was at one time much more in evidence than religious solidarity. For example, Catholics of German and Irish ancestry[16] within the

14. George A. Kelly, *Catholics and the Practice of the Faith* (Washington, D.C.: Catholic University Press, 1946), p. 122. See also the review of this book by Everett C. Hughes, *American Journal of Sociology*, LII, No. 5 (March, 1947), 456, where Hughes points this out as a "rather less expected" finding.

15. Social solidarity may be partially indicated by the selection of marriage partners. Catholic college graduates have a higher percentage of marriages with nonparishioners than do the Catholics with grammar-school education. Kelly (*op. cit.*, p. 125) asserts also that better-educated Catholic women enter mixed marriages more than do Catholic men of better education. This conclusion requires further analysis. It may be that men (generally less faithful to religion) leave the Church in greater numbers when they marry non-Catholics and are thus not contained in the statistics derived from exclusively Catholic sources.

16. Irish parishes were not juridical national parishes because they did not administer to a foreign-language group. It must be noted further that conflict, or fear of conflict, was not always an important motive in the erection of national parishes.

same parish territory disagreed so violently that they maintained on two sides of the same street separate parish church, rectory, school, and convent. In situations of this kind the German Catholic had more friendly and intimate relations with the German Lutheran than with his fellow-Catholic who was of Irish parentage. These older ethnic differences are less obvious now, but they are being replaced by others. In some southern parishes, where large numbers of Mexican Catholics reside, the disrupting factor of ethnic dissimilarity largely offsets the presumptive solidaristic factor of Christian charity and a common religion.

One cannot speak of social solidarity in an empirical sense or of the principle of Christian love at work between two groups who simply do not have any relations with each other. But the statement is sometimes made that the "great leveler" is the parish organization or formal subgrouping. In other words, the normal urban parish is said to unite people of all classes, of different education, and of all ethnic backgrounds in its societies and organizations. The rebuttal to this claim is known by every experienced parish priest. The various organizations do not provide a locus of parochial solidarity except for the handful of dependable nuclear parishioners. Modal parishioners who are well educated, who are professional and business people, simply do not belong to these societies, and those who are from the skilled and semiskilled occupations often form at best a nominal membership.

This brief review of the various levels on which the concept of Christian love is expected to operate and of the racial, occupational, educational, and ethnic diversities among modal Catholics must not be interpreted as an indication of complete discord within the urban Catholic parish. From the historical point of view, the city parish in the South has made notable progress in its constant struggle against natural factors of separations and segregations of various kinds. This has been a history of gains and losses which must be measured and analyzed not only against the ultimate goal of Christian solidarity but also against the array of dysfunctional factors and situations which seem to be normal to our urban culture.

While the city parish, as a social aggregate, does not conform to the definition of a solidaristic social group, there are religious subgroupings within the parish which often exemplify a high degree of social solidarity. These various parochial societies are kept going by a relatively small number of people—and even some of these are nuclear only from the point of view of social participation and are modal from the point of view of religious observances. The normally functioning urban parish has fifteen to twenty formal organizations and fifty to seventy recognizable informal cliques, clubs, and groups of various kinds in which the parishioners participate. Modal parishioners frequently co-operate with fellow-parishioners in a positive way in all of them, but this social co-operation appears to be based on a dominant interest other than on shared religious faith or on the virtue of Christian love.

At the risk of oversimplification we may roughly divide these numerous subgrouping into two kinds: those which are secular in the sense that they are not under the direction of the parish priests and those which are officially listed as subunits of the religious parish. The latter are examples of associations doing "Church work," while the former encompass all kinds of congenial, recreational, economic, and other activities.

1. The small secular groupings in which modal parishioners participate frequently exhibit a high degree of social solidarity. On close analysis it appears that shared interest and common status are the most important factors which unite the members of these groups. For example, the participants in various informal bridge, poker, and bowling groups do not associate with just anyone in the pursuit of these recreational activities, nor do they limit the membership to Catholics. Furthermore, the common social status which they share in the community and neighborhood does not seem to depend to any great degree on a similarity of religious convictions. The same appears to be true of boys who play football, basketball, and baseball with the neighborhood teams rather than with the parish teams.

Social solidarity tends to be selective, and it is practically impossible to assert that Catholicism, or membership in the same Catholic parish, or even the virtue of Christian love, is the basis of selection in these secular groupings. Association in all these activities extends beyond the circle of parish membership to include non-Catholic whites who share the same interest and status. Roughly speaking, it may be said that this generalization applies in the pursuit of all secular and nonparochial functions (occupational, civic, political) and even to some philanthropic and charitable activities (the Community Chest, Red Cross, orphans' parties, etc.) for which modal parishioners co-operate in small local unity.

It is probably a valid generalization to assert that the ideal and real patterns of social solidarity never meet each other among the modal parishioners of the urban Church. Perhaps the arbitrary ideal has been set too high for attainment, or perhaps it is unrealistic to expect and to search for a clear indication of religious motivation in the so-called "secular" functions of modal parishioners. Perhaps, too, Christian social solidarity among them is simply the unity of faith and grace spoken of above, a subconscious acceptance of common religious and moral values for which God is providing supernatural aid.

2. Can it be said that the approximation of the real to the ideal is recognizable in the various subgroupings which do work for the parish Church? If we cannot discover the primary religious principle of social solidarity in the secular activities of these urban white Catholics, we may at least hope to discover it in those activities which are called "Church work." Two observations must be made concerning these groupings: first, they have various specific objectives and aims besides the generalized purpose of the parish,[17] and, second, we are concerned here with the informal "working core" of people and not with the total formalized and organized parish society.

Almost every normally successful urban parish contains one or more subgroups of highly active, well-integrated, and smoothly co-operating parishioners. These persons may be the directive and working force within a dramatic club, an altar society, a parents' organization, or any of the functioning groups which are found in the normal city parish. In every instance, however, the solidaristic group will be a relatively small segment of five to ten persons operating within the larger organization. We have made a detailed analysis of several of these groups and have found the following characteristics in all of them.

a) The most noticeable fact is that in each group these actively co-operating persons are also close friends outside the immediate Church function which they are performing. Some of them became acquainted through the Church work; some got into the work because they had been old friends. They visit one another's homes, have the same social interests, and are of the same economic class.

b) In each group these members are in approximately the same age category. Parishioners of sharply different age levels do not seem to co-operate well in Church work. This coincides also with

17. See the categories of these parish organizations below, chap. 14, sec. *f.*

the fact that their background in formal schooling is approximately the same. Those who are long-term residents of the same parish or neighborhood tend to co-operate better than those who are newcomers.

c) The Church work in which they are engaged is recognized as important by the persons (priests, nuns, and other parishioners) whose esteem they value. They are frequently reminded that they are "making a contribution to the cause," that the work "just wouldn't go on if it weren't for them," and that the success of the enterprise revolves around them.

d) The specific activity in which they are engaged is usually simple, concrete, and definite. When it entails an occasional complicated decision, the priest may offer the solution, or an individual member may take over the problem. The group which operates with a repetitive formula (the distribution of food tickets to the poor, the seating of parishioners by ushers, the teaching of catechism) tends to be more solidaristic than one in which the function has to be constantly redefined.

e) The work not only is the kind which they can do easily but is also one which they like to do. This usually means that they have become experienced in some specific pattern of action which has developed through an attraction to the particular function of the group. They enjoy the work itself—singing in the choir, sewing linens for the altar, taking care of children in the school nursery or cafeteria, coaching athletic teams.

These five characteristics appear to be minimum essentials for the exhibition of social solidarity in parochial subgroupings. The members are good friends of relatively similar age, education, and class status. The function they perform is appreciated by persons outside the group; they are able to do it, and they enjoy doing it. There may be other minor characteristics, but the one we sought for most seemed to be conspicuous by its absence. We wanted to know whether they were associating in this work because of some "higher" motive: their love of God, membership in the Catholic Church, parochial religious loyalty, etc.

We finally resorted to direct questions on this point and asked them individually the open-end question: "Why do you all work so well together?" Some of the answers were as follows: "Father asked me to help out"; "I have the time, and nothing much else to do"; "I just like to do this kind of thing"; "I get a lot of fun out of it"; "I enjoy being with these people." Perhaps these persons were motivated by high spiritual values in performing these functions and in associating with one another, but they may have had difficulty in verbalizing their motives.

An interesting aspect of the analysis of small-group activities on the parish level is that some of the people who co-operate best are not nuclear parishioners from the point of view of religious observances. The analyst is struck with the fact that a non-Catholic spouse of a mixed marriage, or a person who has not made his Easter duties, is as capable as any other person of demonstrating social solidarity in the parochial subgroupings. On the other hand, the faithful Catholic also exhibits solidarity with nonparishioners when they perform nonreligious functions together. As long as the several characteristics mentioned above are present in the group situation, it does not really seem to matter whether the members of the group share the same religious convictions.

In conclusion, it must be noted again that social solidarity is a relative concept. It differs in kind and degree from group to group and in relation to the rigor or leniency of the norms involved. Perhaps the norms of social cohesion, when based upon the complete ideology of Christianity, are too ethereal for the measurement of the human behavior of ordinary, modal parishioners. This seems to be the case in the American urban culture where functions, values, and objectives are strongly secularized. Our tentative generalization, based on the empirical studies so far made in urban parishes, is that specifically Catholic solidarity, motivated by Christian love and operating on the parochial level, is at best an ideal toward which priests and parishioners are struggling with varying degrees of success.

Chapter Five

The Marginal Catholic: An
Institutional Approach[1]

O<small>NE</small> of the primary functions of institutions is to pattern and standardize the behavior of individuals. The religious system, as institutionalized by the Catholic Church, is highly regulative of the conduct of its church adherents, and in the "ideal type" it is more or less personalized in the behavior of nuclear parishioners. But the facts of social life show that this ideal tends almost always to be exemplified by the exceptional individual and the minority category. People resist the standardization of the religious institution in many ways. This is exemplified to its greatest extent in the persons of dormant Catholics and to a lesser extent in marginal Catholics.

Bennett and Tumin aptly generalize this concept when they say that "in some cases an institution may play a negative function in the life of an individual in so far as the existing practices and rules serve as a hindrance to his actions and desires. His reaction to that institution then would be to seek means of avoiding the consequences of its operation. He can do this by making his own private adjustment, or he can accept the adjustment worked out by a group of similarly hindered individuals. But, even if this marginal adjustment is successful, it is clear that his life has been affected by the institution through the very necessity to adjust."[2]

It is obvious to the student of society that a dynamic process of adjustment and readjustment is occurring not only among the various institutions of a culture (especially between the sacred and the nonsacred) but also between the person and the institutions which surround him (especially between the "secular-minded" individual

1. See the author's article of the same title in *Social Forces*, XXXII, No. 2 (December, 1953), 167–73.
2. John Bennett and Melvin Tumin, *Social Life, Structure and Function* (New York: A. A. Knopf, 1948), pp. 169–70. On this problem see also Abraham Kardiner and Ralph Linton, *The Individual and His Society* (New York: Columbia University Press, 1939), and J. O. Hertzler, *Social Institutions* (Lincoln: University of Nebraska Press, 1946), chap. x, "Institutions and Individuals."

and the religious institution). It is neither necessary nor possible to examine this fluid process in relation to all the personnel involved with the operation of the urban Catholic parish, but it is a fruitful approach to the understanding of dormant and marginal Catholics.

This chapter is concerned only with the marginal, or "fringe," Catholic, and it takes into consideration the several facets of cultural and institutional marginality which have beguiled sociological thinking ever since Robert Park first introduced it and Everett Stonequist elaborated upon it.[3] We have employed the marginal concept in analyzing our data on 14,838 white Catholics, seven years of age and older, living in three ecclesiastical parishes of a southern city. In so far as we have been able to classify these parishioners, we estimate that a little over 1,800 of them may be placed in the marginal category.

The several important aspects of marginality have been combined in the present analysis: (*a*) the individual's internal psychological conflict, symbolized in the general term *value conflict*, which seems to have been paramount in the original discussions of the marginal man;[4] (*b*) the ´*imperfectly institutionalized role*, which implies a kind of ambiguity and inconsistency in both the behavior of the marginal man and the sanctions attending his behavior;[5] and (*c*) *socioreligious distance*, because a classification of religious participants requires a social stratification of the religious structure according to the behavioral and value norms employed.

It appears that all three of these aspects of marginality may be fruitfully combined in a basic "institutional approach" to the problem of the marginal Catholic parishioner. If the urban cultural system is conceived as a series of interlocking circles, each of which

3. The original contributions on marginality have become almost classic (see Robert E. Park, "Human Migration and the Marginal Man," *American Journal of Sociology*, XXXIII, No. 6 [May, 1928], 881–93; see also Everett Stonequist, "The Problem of the Marginal Man," *American Journal of Sociology*, XLI, No. 1 [July, 1935], 1–12, and *The Marginal Man: A Study in Personality and Culture Conflict* [New York: Charles Scribner's Sons, 1937]).

4. The oversimplified version of this cultural and personality conflict has been discussed in the following articles: Milton M. Goldberg, "A Qualification of the Marginal Man Theory," *American Sociological Review*, VI, No. 1 (February, 1941), 52–58; Arnold W. Green, "A Re-examination of the Marginal Man Concept," *Social Forces*, XXVI, No. 2 (December, 1947), 167–71; and David I. Golovensky, "The Marginal Man Concept: An Analysis and Critique," *Social Forces*, XXX, No. 3 (March, 1952), 333–39.

5. This aspect is competently analyzed by Walter I. Wardwell, "A Marginal Professional Role: The Chiropractor," *Social Forces*, XXX, No. 3 (March, 1952), 339–48.

represents a major institution, the human being may be said to occupy a position somewhere inside each circle. Conformity to the behavioral norms and acceptance of the goals and values of any particular institution may be measured along the radius of the circle. The more distant from the center, the less conforming and the less accepting would one be.

Two valid and accepted sociological generalizations concerning the major institutions underlie the present analysis. The first is that the major institutions are universal in the American culture in the sense that every individual is somehow affected by all of them. This seems true of the religious institution even in regard to those persons who disclaim any affiliation with organized religion. Cuber put this fact accurately when he said that there no longer exists the "either-or" proposition of church membership and affiliation and that the measure must be in degrees of participation rather than on clear-cut lines. "To the degree that a given person is observably controlled in his behavior by the institution in however slight a degree, he cannot be said to be wholly outside its 'culture.' He is a marginal participant, perhaps even with non-Church culture ascendant over Church culture—but marginal to the Church culture, nevertheless."[6]

The second generalization is the fact that the several major institutions in our culture are, at various points of comparison, inconsistent with one another. This is indicated when Golovensky remarks that American culture "is not a monolithic organism but rather a pluralistic mosaic, a congeries of conflicting and contradictory values."[7] As Williams points out, we do not find a neatly unified "ethos" or an irresistible "strain toward consistency" in our society. And in reference to religion he italicizes the statement that "American religious organizations are extraordinarily segregated from other institutionalized structures."[8]

While the culmination of institutional inconsistency which Lynd analyzed would be complete social chaos and would probably be accompanied by an almost culture-wide phenomenon of neurotic personalities which Horney described, the present concept of a "pluralistic mosaic" of overlapping institutional circles seems to be a necessary and useful instrument of analysis for marginality. With-

6. John F. Cuber, "Marginal Church Participants," *Sociology and Social Research*, XXV, No. 1 (September–October, 1940), 57–62. Cuber's concept of religious marginality would embrace also those whom we have termed "dormant Catholics."

7. *Op. cit.*, p. 335.

8. Robbin M. Williams, *American Society: A Sociological Interpretation* (New York: A. A. Knopf, 1951), p. 339.

out suggesting a complete fragmentation of the culture, we may say analogously that the division of labor, which Durkheim analyzed so brilliantly, has extended to a sort of "division of institutions." The functions of institutions have become compartmentalized as well as ritualized. Social values and goals have become functionally specific in each institution. Behavioral patterns, both expected and actual, differ according to the institution in which they operate. Again it must be said that, as these institutional divergences increase, the individual who attempts to perform his roles in the several major institutions tends to be pulled in different directions.

The marginal Catholic, the "individual" in question here, is not "all of a piece." He must be conceptualized as both dynamic and pluralistic and as a person who plays multiple roles and occupies a potentially shifting status. In other words, the persons measured by socioreligious distance are not held in permanently static positions. If they are Catholics who are "going away" from the central values of the religious institution and from the nuclear parishioners in the social structure, they probably are not, nor do they consider themselves to be, "institutional hybrids" or "split personalities." If, on the other hand, they are returning to the modal or nuclear status, they are probably experiencing the soul-searching and the psychological turmoil which seem to accompany the preliminary steps toward spiritual conversion.

The Catholic parishioner, like other church participants, is faced, in varying degrees of intensity, with the conflict of institutions which exists in the American culture. He, too, like other Americans, is subject to the "patterned evasions" which are found particularly in urban society. For example, certain values current in our capitalistic business system are incompatible with those of the Catholic Church. The Catholic's proximate conformity to the role demands and vocational values of the business institution may imply his growing distance from the ideals of the religious institution. His economic role may have little integration with his familial role and even less with his religious role.

The marginal Catholic is still under some influence and control of the religious institution, yet he may be very near its circumference because he is being pulled toward the center of one or more other institutions.[9] He may be said to be partially accepting the values of the religious institution, yet partially rejecting them,

9. Yet he often interprets this influence obversely as a "push" from the religious institution because the Church in its doctrines and practices refuses to "change with the times" or to "keep up with modern progress."

because of their disagreement with other institutionalized values. His religious role in the structure of the Church is ambiguous because in the relatively clear-cut formal institutionalism of the Catholic Church there seems to be no patterned status for the person who is "neither hot nor cold."

The concept of socioreligious distance among the members of a church implies that certain subjective and objective criteria can be employed to identify the marginal participant (as well as the nuclear, modal, and dormant Catholics). The generalized criteria of religious belief and behavior must be specified and graded in order to discover the number of persons to be included in each category. From the formal teaching of the Church we know that certain elements of religion are more important than others. From the observation of the persons in action relative to the religious structure we can learn the frequency with which they perform the more important functions. From personal interviews we can gain an approximate estimate of the attitudes toward religious doctrines, values, and practices.[10]

For example, *nuclear* parishioners co-operate with other lay persons and with the priests in parochial activities, exemplify Christian behavior in their personal lives, hold high relegous values, and fulfil the formal sacramental expectations of the Church. This combination of standards obviously cannot be employed to measure the number of marginal Catholics. On the other hand, certain criteria mark the *dormant* Catholic—a sort of outside limit, such as his baptism in infancy, probably his reception of the sacrament of matrimony, occasional attendance at a church service, and refusal to join any other church. He is quite likely also to follow the accepted custom of infant "christening" for his children. A person who is measured by this combination of norms is already beyond our definition of marginality.

Objectively we employed three criteria in order to determine the extent and percentage of marginal parishioners among the 9,052 white Catholics seven years of age and over whom we studied. These were Mass attendance, the paschal reception of the Eucharist and of sacramental penance, and the religious education of children. The statistics given here are combined from Church records, a house-to-house canvass, census questionnaires, and interviews. The territory in

10. For a rough example of an attempt to measure religious ideology see the chapter on "The Catholic Mind of the Parish" in the writer's *Dynamics of a City Church*, Vol. I of *Southern Parish* (Chicago: University of Chicago Press, 1951), pp. 259–71.

which these data were gathered comprised three urban southern parishes. In this area there lived 14,838 white baptized Catholics seven years of age and older. Since the large number of 5,786 dormant Catholics are really "outside" the Church, we exclude them also from our percentages in this analysis. We estimate that approximately one-fifth of the remaining 9,052 persons are marginals.

Mass attendance.—Unless they have a valid excuse, all Catholics above the "age of reason" are morally obliged to attend Mass on Sundays and on certain designated feast days of the liturgical year. We found that 1,792 persons (or 19.8 per cent) of the 9,052 Catholics did not even approach this standard of religious observance. As a matter of fact, more than half of this 19.8 per cent admitted that they did not go to Mass at all during the preceding year. Less than half of them attend Mass even so much as once a year, and the occasion on which they do attend is usually Christmas or Easter or a wedding or a funeral.

Annual reception of Communion and penance.—Every Catholic knows that he has the strict obligation to confess his mortal sins once a year and to receive the Eucharist at least once during the paschal time. This is commonly called "making one's Easter duties," and its symbolism is very strong in Catholic culture. We found that 1,946 persons (or 21.5 per cent) admitted their failure in this obligation during the preceding year. This percentage is somewhat higher than that given for the failure in Mass attendance, but the difference seems to be explained by the fact that there are some Catholics who go to Mass occasionally during the year but do not receive the sacraments.

Catholic education of children.—All these 9,052 Catholics lived in an urban area within easy reach of parochial and other Catholic elementary schools. We suspected that the marginal Catholic parent is most likely to neglect the formal religious education of his children and to permit them to attend the public schools of the community. Among the Catholics of this study there were 1,223 families with children of elementary-school age. Of these families, 283 (or 23.1 per cent) sent one or more of their children to the public school. While this criterion does not give us the total number of marginal Catholics in the universe of research, it indicates that the percentages of those who seldom attend Mass or receive the sacraments are roughly the same as the percentage of parents who neglect the Catholic elementary education of their children.

While there are some exceptions[11] to each of the three criteria of religious duties, we have found that for the most part the *same people* are negligent in all three religious obligations. This rough congruence makes it possible to assert that the marginal parishioner is marked by the same general negative characteristics. When a comparison is made between this category and the two others, it reveals, as a tentative estimate, that approximately 20 per cent of these Catholic parishioners are marginal, 70 per cent are modal, and 10 per cent are nuclear (out of 9,052 persons seven years of age and older).

It was relatively easy to arrive at these statistical conclusions, drawn from selected measurable norms of Catholic behavior. It was much more difficult to determine *the reasons why* approximately one-fifth of these people who "profess Catholicism" seem to hover near the fringe of the religious institution, neither completely inside nor completely outside it. We felt that the subjective attitudes of these persons would provide an important clue to at least a partial and tentative explanation of marginality among Catholics. We wanted to find out more about these marginals; for example, whether they considered themselves "not-so-good" Catholics, whether they showed symptoms of religious ambivalence, or whether their religious roles were more or less ambiguous.

We tried to relate the results of random interviews with marginals, their relatives, and with priests to the general theory of institutional inconsistency in urban culture. As noted above, this hypothesis states that the various major institutions tend to come in conflict with one another and tend to pull the participants in "different directions." The results of our interviews partially confirm the hypothesis of this institutional approach to religious marginality.

It is an axiom of social science that the value attitudes and the expectations of the social roles of the individual are patterned within the institutional framework of the community in which he lives. It seems quite clear also that the (secular) folkways and mores which have gradually accumulated in the recreational, economic, familial, and even political and educational institutions, and which form the major content of the social behavior and thinking of the urban Catholic, have an ascendancy over the (sacred) folkways and mores of the religious institution.[12] The lack of consistency and of integra-

11. As we have seen, some persons attend Mass but do not make their Easter duties; also, some parents who are otherwise modal Catholics send their children to the public school.

12. See, however, the discussion of the influence of urban secularism on religious practices, below, chap. 15, pp. 197–200.

tion among these basic institutions seems to be clearly reflected in the marginal Catholic.

The following are the four most frequently obvious generalizations which apply to the analysis of marginal Catholics. There are undoubtedly many others, but these appear to be the most influential factors in the formation of this type of religious participant. It must be noted, of course, that these factors are at work upon all Catholics—to a lesser extent among nuclear and modal parishioners, to a much greater extent among dormant Catholics.

a) *Contrasting assumptions.*—Among the marginal Catholics in this southern city there is a noticeable attempt to reconcile values and patterns of conduct which are contradictory. The most blatant example of this is the assumption that brotherhood and democracy are a practical ideal worthy of pursuit, coupled at the same time with another assumption to the effect that Negro Catholics are not fit persons to belong to the same parish or to attend the same school with whites. The norms of brotherhood and love which are deeply imbedded in religious ideology are not sufficiently strong to draw the marginal parishioner closer to the center of Catholic life. The traditional cultural patterns of "white" thought and behavior tend to weaken his adherence to religious teachings.[13]

Another example is current in the contrast between professed honesty and the demands of occupational roles. The religious ideal firmly asserts the doctrine that a lie is always a moral evil and that the virtue of honesty must be operative at all times. The religious institution is here in conflict with the known practices of the economic institution. The marginal Catholic tends to think that "you can cut corners" with small deceptions and minor dishonesties in the business world. "After all," he says, "everybody does it, and you don't want to be overscrupulous about these things."

It must not be implied that the marginal Catholic is morally more sensitive than other Catholics or that he is *always* conscious of the contrast between the assumptions according to which he behaves. While he is aware of the Church's teaching—at least in a general way—he may also feel that one has to be practical in everyday life. There are, of course, many modal parishioners who accept and fulfil all the rituals and formalities of religion and at the same time conform largely to the secular patterns and values of the culture. In

13. In some instances we found dormant Catholics who professed racial equality and used, as an argument against religion, the segregation policies and practices of churchgoers.

this respect the difference between the modal and the marginal Catholic seems to be that there is no general awareness of inconsistency, no psychological frustration disturbing to the modal parishioner.

b) Relative morality.—This moral phenomenon represents an attitude closely allied to the above concept of contrasting assumptions. In the latter case the individual is attempting to accept both of the contrasting beliefs and finds himself pulled in both directions. Relative morality here means that the goodness and the badness of social behavior depend upon the social situation in which a person is involved. It is reflected in the blunt statement of one interviewee: "Every man's ethics are his own, and they change with his circumstances."

Perhaps this concept of the relativity of morals is met most frequently in the difficult problems of sex, love, and marriage. Personal interviews with marginal Catholics show that birth prevention is often given as a reason for "losing interest" in the Church. The individual "wants to do the right thing" according to the teachings of religion, but circumstances make it impossible. "God understands my position. He will not hold me responsible, because he knows that in my case the Church's stand on birth control is unreasonable."

The marginal Catholic usually does not go so far as to deny the validity of the Church's doctrines on sex sins, birth prevention, divorce, etc.[14] In fact, he is likely to praise and defend the "high morality" of Catholicism in a society which seems to be losing its moral standards. He readily admits that the Church is correct in its general principles and that every Catholic should try to conform his life to these principles. But, even though sacramental absolution is refused to him because he is himself "unable" to follow the principles, he is sure that God understands his position better than any priest in the confessional. It is manifest that an attitude of this kind will tend also to diminish the appreciation for the other behavioral aspects of Catholicism.

c) Anti-authoritarianism.—A third important factor is a misapplication to the religious institution of the traditional American ideal of personal independence. The hierarchical structure of Catholicism shows the hand of Christ ruling His followers on earth through a formally stratified religious monarchy. The principal functionaries

14. The dormant Catholic, on the other hand, tends to deny large and important doctrines of the Church. In this sense, he is an informal and objective heretic. But even this seemed better to one fallen-away Catholic than the prospect of "being a hypocrite."

of the Catholic Church are arranged in a relatively clear-cut pattern of rank, based on appointment from above. To the marginal Catholic this often seems to be an arbitrary and authoritarian arrangement which conflicts with the American ideal of equal representation for all.

The apparent emphasis on rights and privileges (with a corresponding neglect of the concepts of duties and responsibilities) which is characteristic of American culture has helped to crystallize this spirit of religious anti-authoritarianism. Many of these marginal Catholics apparently fail to realize that they are already living under numerous forms of social control in the various social structures in which they participate. The laissez faire philosophy is expressed in a strange way in this southern urban culture when the same person, on the one hand, heartily indorses the authoritarian southern political demagogue and, on the other hand, resists the authority of bishops and pastors within the ecclesiastical structure.

The way in which priests and parishioners carry out their reciprocal social roles is also relevant in this particular attitude of marginal Catholics. The charge is often made by marginal Catholics that the priests tend to be "dictatorial" in those functions of the Church which are not primarily religious and which do not "require dictation." The marginal parishioner, like the dormant Catholic, is usually insistent that the priest should confine himself strictly to Mass, sacraments, and rituals. When the priest does otherwise—for example, when he speaks out on social questions— the marginal Catholic accuses him of interfering with the freedom of the parishioners.

d) *The dysfunctional parish.*—This fourth factor influencing the behavior of the marginal Catholic is more complex than any of the three others. The general hypothesis is that both the social structure and the cultural values of the urban industrial and commercial society have interfered with the functioning of the Catholic parish *as a community of persons.*[14] This is mainly a structural problem, but with functional implications, and it seems to influence both the attitudes and the behavioral patterns of religious participants.

The multiple functions of the old-fashioned, solidaristic, community parish have been attenuated. Like the functions of the

15. This is a variation of the basic sociological theme running through the writings of Suhard, Michonneau, Loew, Le Bras, Lebret, and Godding. The last-named thinks that the "fundamental cause of de-Christianization" has been the "extinction of all those basic communities which help men to develop" (see Maisie Ward, *France Pagan?* [New York: Sheed & Ward, 1949], pp. 178 ff.).

family, those of the parish have been largely absorbed by other institutions, and they have been partially replaced by the "escape mechanisms" of urban society.[16] This seems especially true in the so-called leisure-time activities of urban Catholics. Radio and television, the picture magazines, commercial movies, sports and dances, are now enjoyed outside the context of the parish. They are also generally outside (or at least indifferent to) the system of typical religious values.

From an empirical point of view, one may suggest that the higher values of the religious institution could offer psychological compensation for the person who is regimented and thwarted in the daily pursuit of economic goals. The materialistic and sensate functions of the working day could be balanced by the more humane and social functions of a highly integrated and active parish. Ideally, the religious institution might be placed in "balance" with the economic institution or at least provide an escape or outlet for social needs.

It seems, however, that the modern urban Catholic parish has been unable to cope with these institutional changes in American culture. Instead of a "balance of institutions" there has been a substitution of nonreligious institutions. The marginal Catholic leans toward secularized activities and the use of secular escape mechanisms. He claims that he "sees nothing sinful in this," but, because of it, he logically becomes more worldly in his thinking and thus marginal to the religious center. Whether urban priests and parishioners have generally failed by allowing the socially orientated functions of the parish to lapse, or whether the marginal Catholic has failed by a too-ready acceptance of secular substitutes, is a question beyond our inquiry at this point.

In broadest summary of the factors described above, it may be suggested that the marginal Catholic is largely a product of institutional inconsistency. Hertzler, in writing about organized religion, says that "its power to standardize behavior and exercise social control, either for groups or for individuals, *has diminished as that of various other institutions has been augmented;* its influence has

16. It is argued, of course, that the "entanglement" of religion in the various other social institutions formerly prevented these from attaining functional progress. Releasing the economy, the family, the school, etc., from the domination of religious institutions like the local parish has permitted spectacular and "professional" development. This is the hard core of the sociological argument of secularism.

evaporated from one department of life after another."[17] This does not mean that the moral responsibility of the individual to make choices among institutional values can be omitted as a factor of marginality.

Presumably, any marginal Catholic can at any time stop to meditate on his religious status and, with the help of divine grace, make the decision to return to the Church as a fully participating nuclear Catholic. The enthusiastic apologist of religion may say that "the grace of God is sufficient for him. The sacraments and Church services are available. He need but make up his mind." This presumption has validity, and it can never be denied by a religious believer, but it views the ordinary human being as though he were isolated from other persons and uninfluenced by institutional and cultural contacts. It by-passes the fundamental sociological fact of the cultural and institutional environment.

17. See J. O. Hertzler, "Religious Institutions," *Annals of the American Academy of Political and Social Sciences,* CCLVI (March, 1948), 13. (Italics mine.)

Chapter Six

Dormant Catholics and Leakage

Even though the urban Catholic parish is a social aggregate or a loose plurality of persons (rather than a tight communal group), it does maintain some outside limits. These boundaries are crossed and recrossed in both directions by those who enter the Church and by those who abandon the Church. Dormant Catholics in our day are seldom publicly expelled or excommunicated from the flock. In spite of its reputation for authoritarian procedures, the Church takes no drastic, recognizable action against the nonconformist but reluctantly allows the "lost sheep" to go his own way.

From an empirical sociological point of view, this departure of delinquent Catholics tends to function toward the improved internal social adjustments of the parish itself. Every social unit has to face the problem of unassimilable elements. "There are always kickers, cowards and shirkers who do not hold up their end of necessary joint undertakings of benefit to all; there are the socially ignorant and the socially infantile who are unconscious of or immune to any conception of their social obligations and responsibilities; some are callously indifferent and inconsiderate; many people are egoistic and selfish; some are downright predatory in their relations to others."[1]

On the other hand, it must not be thought that these discordant and nonconformist persons are always conscious and deliberate about the steps which separate them from the Church. We have come to use the terms "dormancy" and "leakage," which imply for the most part a kind of unobtrusive, unintended, and even accidental escape from the Church and the parish. Except for a few "professional" former Catholics who give lectures or write books against the Church, it is as unusual for a dormant Catholic to publicize his withdrawal from the Church as it is for the Church to announce publicly his dismissal. In our American cities religious

1. J. O. Hertzler, *Social Institutions* (Lincoln: University of Nebraska Press, 1946), p. 10.

68

dormancy is looked upon (indifferently or regrettably, according to the religious values of the onlooker) as a social situation which "just happens."

The dormant Catholic, unlike the marginal parishioner, does not really have a position within the parochial circle of the Catholic religious institution. His constant and practical patterns of thought and behavior are non-Catholic. By the three institutional criteria of baptism, place of residence, and race, he could be included among the participants of the urban white southern parish. By the personal criteria of intention, religious practices, and social participation, he must be definitely excluded from the parish system as a social unit.

The dormant Catholic is colloquially known as a "fallen-away" Catholic,[2] who continues to be an object of the evangelical and missionary concern of the Catholic clergy. He is usually Catholic "by birth" and has received the sacrament of baptism and probably the sacrament of matrimony with a priest officiating at the ceremony. He usually has his children baptized and may "ask for the priest" when he is about to die. But he does not join a non-Catholic denomination.[3] In almost all cases his family is or was Catholic, and these family relatives may deplore his defection from the Church. He is the type of person about whom the clergy and the nuclear parishioners will sometimes hopefully remark, "Once a Catholic, always a Catholic."

It appears that Bishop Navagh's description of a "bad Catholic" is approximately the same as that of the dormant parishioner. He tells priests that "you will find bad Catholics, those who do not practice the Faith. Here too you will find numerous divisions. Some were baptized but not raised in the Faith; others by deliberate sin have cast it aside; still others through matrimonial entanglements or through social seeking or for business reasons have abandoned it."[4]

At best, it may be said that the dormant Catholic has only an intermittent or sporadic contact with the Church. He may occasionally

2. The novel *Fallen Away*, by Margaret Culkin Banning (New York: Harper & Bros., 1951), depicts the marital difficulties of a Catholic woman which led to her abandonment of the Church. The story includes a zealous parish priest who insists that she must be a good parishioner in order to be a good Catholic (p. 81).

3. According to our categories, the person who joins another denomination is no longer a dormant Catholic. He is "dead" to the Catholic parish and "alive" in his new religion. He is, therefore, completely outside the sociological analysis of the parochial system.

4. James J. Navagh, *The Apostolic Parish* (New York: P. J. Kenedy & Sons, 1950), p. 22.

attend a Church-sponsored dinner, bingo party, or athletic contest, but this may be no more frequent than his attendance at similar functions sponsored by Protestant, Jewish, or nonsectarian groups. Even the most obdurate dormant Catholic must have reciprocal relations with active parishioners in the various nonreligious institutional structures of his community. These relations may be in business, political, civic, educational, or recreational activities which occur in the day-to-day functioning of every normal urban community.

In the recurrent patterns of human relations which constitute the social system of the urban Catholic parish there is no place for the dormant parishioner. From a sociological point of view, therefore, he must be considered an "outsider." The problem of tidy social categories is again here involved, because in one way or another the influence of the Catholic social unit is still exerted on most dormant Catholics. If he is a member of a Catholic family which strongly adheres to the practices of the Church, he should probably be included among the marginal parishioners, because the influence of the religious culture is still upon him. If, on the other hand, he belongs to a household in which the other persons are either similar to himself or belong to non-Catholic sects, he should definitely be included in the category of dormant Catholics.

A minimum working definition of the dormant parishioner is that of a person who was validly baptized, does not practice the Catholic religion, has not joined a non-Catholic denomination, and belongs to a household in which the other members are either non-Catholics or dormant Catholics. This cannot mean, in the particular urban area where our study was conducted, that the parochial religious culture has absolutely no influence upon him. There are extensive rural areas and many small villages in the South where this would probably be the case, because they contain neither Catholics nor parishes. In most southern cities, however, there are enough Catholics and parishes to keep the dormant Catholic from being totally oblivious of their presence. Either directly or remotely his former religion still has at least a slight influence upon him.

The problem of the dormant parishioner is frequently discussed in terms of "leakage from the Church."[5] As far as the present writer knows, there have been no complete studies which provide accurate

5. See Thomas F. Coakley, "Catholic Leakage: A Factual Study," *Catholic World*, January, 1942, pp. 418–25; see also his "Revelations of a Parish Census," *Ecclesiastical Review*, May, 1934, pp. 529–30.

statistics on the number or rate of Catholics who leave the Church. On the other hand, the number of conversions, that is, of persons received into the Catholic Church annually (exclusive of infant baptisms), is recorded in *The Catholic Directory*. In 1930 this number was 38,232 (or 1.9 per thousand), in 1940 it was 73,255 (or 3.4 per thousand), and in 1950 it was 118,347 (or 4.3 per thousand).[6] Any statistics which may be provided by non-Catholic denominations, showing the number of Catholics who have been converted to some non-Catholic religion, would not help to determine the extent of dormancy. Such persons are by definition excluded from the category of dormants.

It is probably true that Catholic propagandists tend to minimize the amount of "leakage" from the Church, while Protestant propagandists tend to maximize it by emphasizing the number of former Catholics who annually become Protestants. The difficulty in obtaining reliable statistics, however, seems to reside primarily in the definition of the "fallen-away" Catholic. If this problem could be settled, and if an ecclesiastical requirement were made whereby parishes reported the number of dormants, the use of propaganda would not obfuscate the issue.

In order to discover the extent of dormancy among three white urban Catholic parishes, we have combined several approaches.

a) The house-to-house census is the most burdensome and time-consuming, but at the same time it is probably the most dependable method for discovering the number of dormant Catholics. This means a visit to every dwelling unit in the territory and not only to those in which Catholic families are known to live. In our own survey, which involved 21,754 white baptized Catholics, we found that about 38 per cent fulfilled our own definition of dormant Catholics.

b) A comparison between the normal community birth rate and the parish's infant baptism rate is also a revealing method for verifying the extent of dormancy. It appears that most dormant Catholic parents still have their children baptized in the Catholic parish. This is a cultural pattern to which they adhere until they have definitely made the step of joining another religious denomination. If the pastor knows through his regular census information that he has about five

6. *The Catholic Directory*, published annually by P. J. Kenedy & Sons, New York, obtains these statistics from diocesan reports, which are compiled from the records which each parish is compelled by ecclesiastical regulation to maintain. The above statistics exclude Alaska and Hawaii.

thousand regular parishioners, he can expect that the infant baptism rate and the birth rate should approximately coincide. But if the normal annual birth rate in his community is 24 per thousand over a period of years, while his rate of infant baptisms is around 40 per thousand for the same period, he will undoubtedly find the discrepancy in the fact that dormant Catholics are having their children baptized in his church.[7]

c) A comparison between the number of infants baptized and the number of children in the corresponding age brackets who later receive the sacraments of the Eucharist and of confirmation is also an auxiliary method for checking the extent of dormancy. This method must be employed cautiously over a period of years and cannot be applied in a city parish which is either dying or rapidly increasing. Allowances must be made for both the mortality rate and the rate and kind of migration in the parish. When these cautions have been observed, each five-year age cohort shows a considerable loss at the time of First Communion and an even greater loss at the time of confirmation.[8] These absent persons are dormant Catholics and most likely the children of parents who have become dormant parishioners.

d) A comparison between the normal community marriage rate and the parochial marriage rate over a period of years is also a means of discovering the number of dormant Catholics. It is assumed that in the secular trend Catholic parishioners marry at about the same rate as non-Catholics. If a parish of five thousand people has an average of about eighty marriages a year, it may be tempted to boast that its rate of 16 per thousand is considerably higher than that of the general community, which may have a rate of about 11 per thousand. The difference seems to be accounted for by the fact that many dormant Catholics, in spite of their general dissociation

7. In the *Southern Parish* study we made a comparison between the number of infants baptized over a twenty-year period with the number of persons in the corresponding age brackets reported in the parish census. Making allowance for normal mortality, we estimated that about 36 per cent of the infants baptized are no longer members of the Church (see *Dynamics of a City Church*, Vol. I of *Southern Parish* [Chicago: University of Chicago Press, 1951], p. 39).

8. Further studies in comparable urban parishes have verified the conclusions made in *Dynamics of a City Church*, p. 95. The loss between baptism and First Communion is a little less than 30 per cent, which indicates that some dormant Catholic parents may still see to it that their children receive the First Communion. The loss at the time of confirmation is considerably greater, which may indicate that less importance is attached to this sacrament.

from the parish, want to have the blessing of the Church on their marriage.

e) The comparison between the community death rate and the parish funeral rate is also helpful for our purposes. It is sometimes said that the dormant Catholic seeks the last sacraments and Christian burial. This is a common opinion of priests, who do all they can to bring a person "back to the Church" in his last illness. Statistics are scanty on this point, but they indicate that a much smaller percentage of dormant Catholics ask for the priest at the end of life than are baptized or married in the Church. There should be no significant difference between Catholics and non-Catholics in the death rate. If the normal death rate in the community is about 9 per thousand, it should be approximately the same for Catholics. But the urban parishes which we have studied have normally shown a funeral rate about 30 per cent higher than that of the larger community, and this seems to be accounted for in the main by the Church burial of people who during their lifetime were among the dormant Catholics.

These various methods for discovering the number and proportion of dormant Catholics in any given territory depend largely upon the accuracy of the parish census. Unless the priest has a fairly reliable knowledge of the number of active parishioners (including nuclear, modal, and marginal persons), he cannot satisfactorily determine the required percentages and rates of dormant Catholics. The extent of dormancy probably varies considerably from region to region and between rural and urban parishes. Our own studies in a number of urban southern parishes, however, are fairly consistent in revealing that approximately one-third of the white baptized Catholics must be considered dormant.

The attempt to discover the causes of dormancy presents a much more difficult problem. As Brother Schnepp has said, "The factors behind leakage constitute a complex problem difficult to reduce to simple terms."[9] The definition of dormancy involves a certain degree of arbitrariness, and its extent can be determined by the cautious use of intelligent methods suggested above; but the much larger problem of "reasons" for leakage can be only tentatively and partially solved by painstaking observation and interviews.

9. Gerald Schnepp, "Leakage from a Catholic Parish" (Catholic University doctoral dissertation, Washington, D.C., 1938). See also "Three Mixed Marriage Questions Answered," *Catholic World*, November, 1942, pp. 203–7.

Why do people leave the Catholic Church even though they may not join any other religious denomination? From one point of view it may be said that each case of defection is unique, just as each case of conversion to the Church is the result of unique experiences. On the other hand, it is also true that there are certain similarities which may allow generalization in one or several patterns of causal experiences. Even when these causal categories are tentatively established, however, some of them overlap in the explanation of the individual fallen-away Catholic.

The quick-and-ready answer purporting to explain defection from the Church usually revolves around the question of faith and morals. It is said that people lose the faith because they have become enmeshed in habitual sin, or that a gradual weakening of the faith has paved the way for habits of immorality, or that neglect of prayer leads to either the weakening of faith or the weakening of morality and eventually to both. This kind of explanation cannot be accepted, because it does not explain anything. It simply states the problem in a different way. It is like saying that a person is a dormant Catholic because he no longer lives up to the moral and dogmatic values of the Church.

For the social scientist it seems necessary to study the causes and influences which exist outside the individual and which may in some way account for dormancy. It may be said that the dormant parishioner is simply one step further removed from the religious center than the marginal parishioner. If this is true, it seems logical to say that the same set of cultural influences have affected both types of persons. In the case of the dormant Catholic the conflict between the values of the religious institution and those of other institutions has been resolved. He is outside the Church. If he is more than a few years out of elementary school, he has most likely been influenced by the four factors mentioned above: contrasting assumptions, relative morality, anti-authoritarianism, and the dysfunctional parish.[10]

The question here takes us a step farther. What was the added push (or pull) which translated the marginal parishioner into a dormant parishioner? Since people and circumstances vary so greatly, there is no single answer to this question. Why do people quit the Catholic Church? Those who have left the Church give a variety of answers. If we combine these answers with the analysis of parish statistics, it is possible to set up several general categories which seem to

10. See above, chap. 5, on the marginal parishioner.

be relatively reliable. At the same time two cautions must be observed. First, all these "causes" of defection from the Church do not have the same relative weight, so that it is not easy to say which is the "most compelling cause." Second, since most of this material was gathered through interviews with dormant Catholics, the weight given by individuals to any particular reason may be largely the result of his own rationalization.

a) Parental neglect.—Our studies show that the greatest single source of loss from the urban parish is among baptized infants. This refers to the fact that large numbers of children "disappear" from the parish almost immediately after their baptism. They cannot be traced in the records of the parochial school or in the catechism classes conducted for Catholic children in the public schools. They are not listed on the census schedules made out by the Catholic families who are known adherents of the parish. These children, numbering approximately one-third of all baptized Catholic infants, cannot be directly blamed for the fact that they are lost to the Church from the very beginning. Perhaps it is too much to expect the parish priest to "follow up" every infant baptism to find out whether the parents intend to pursue the Catholic training of the child. Probably the parents, therefore, must bear the blame for this "infant leakage" from the Church, but this fact merely raises the question again: Why are so many of these parents dormant Catholics?

b) Lack of religious training.—This is a broad category which covers both formal and informal schooling in the meaning of Catholicism and in the patterns of Catholic thought and behavior. More than three-quarters of the dormant Catholics whom we studied had not received training in Catholic schools or had failed to learn about their religion at home, at Sunday school, or in the release-time catechism classes. From one point of view, this is another aspect of the previous statement that the fault rests heavily on parents, since the Catholic training of children is neglected by their dormant parents. But it is also true that in adolescence and adulthood these dormant Catholics failed to take advantage of the numerous channels of Catholic instruction available to them in urban areas. In this sense the failure to learn and practice Catholicism is their own responsibility.

c) Family disorganization.—While dormant Catholics are present at every level of the social structure, they appear in greater proportions on the very lowest social level. A study of Catholics living in "parochial slums" shows large numbers of families with low income. They receive help from the welfare agencies, and they are barely able to eke out a subsistence. But family disorganization cannot be discussed merely in terms of economic want. There are some extremely poor people who are also very pious and practicing Catholics.

Family disorganization here refers to a kind of demoralization of the relationships of the family members both within and outside the family circle. The institutionalized patterns which are expected of the "normal" families in the same urban area are not followed by the disorganized family. Among Catholics there appears to be a correlation between the familial and the religious institutions, and these seem to have a causal reciprocity. It is probably more often the case that the breakdown in family organization brings about a breakdown in religious practices. On the other hand, there are also cases in which the lack of acceptance of the Church's teaching on marriage has morally eased the dissolution of the marriage and family.

d) *Mixed marriages.*—Marriage between Catholic and non-Catholic is mentioned more frequently, perhaps, than any other factor as a source of defection from the Church. Much has been preached and written on this subject, but the conclusions drawn are still scientifically unsatisfactory. The facts seem to indicate that mixed marriages are as often a source of conversion to the Church as they are a source of leakage from the Church. This comparison is only tentative, because sufficient information is not available for dependable conclusions. We have found, for example, that marriage to a Catholic is in some way connected with about 75 per cent of all adult conversions within the limited area of twenty-three urban southern parishes.[11] We have found also that the Catholic spouses in mixed marriages are distributed among the various categories of parishioners—nuclear, modal, marginal, and dormant—in approximately the same proportion as the spouses in Catholic marriages.

On the other hand, a simple test of dormancy in mixed marriages can be made by any pastor who maintains relatively accurate parish records. We have compared the marriage record with the census reports in twenty-three urban parishes. We found that approximately 30 per cent of the marriages performed over a period of ten years in these parishes were mixed marriages. But, in studying the census

11. See *Dynamics of a City Church*, p. 40. The findings in the *Southern Parish* project in this regard were verified in other parishes in the same city, but this does not mean that the conclusions are similar in other regions and in rural areas.

reports, we found that only about 18 per cent of the couples actually living in the parish are cases of mixed marriage. The difference between these two percentage figures may be assumed to represent a loss to the Church of the Catholic spouses and the children born to them. These figures must be revised upward, because they do not include those Catholics who contracted invalid marriages with non-Catholics outside the Church. These invalid marriages are not contained in the parish matrimonial record or in the parish census, and they probably represent persons who were dormant Catholics before entering the formal marriage contract.

e) Personality of priests.—There is no doubt that the attitudes and behavior patterns of priests are closely scrutinized by many critical people. It is difficult here to separate fact from fiction. To what extent do priests "drive people away from the Church" and to what extent do dormant Catholics rationalize this as an explanatory excuse for their own moral and religious failure? In more than 40 per cent of our interviews with dormant Catholics there was mention of this factor. "The priest terrified me; we were afraid of him when we were kids." Others offered somewhat tenuous explanations, remarking on the priest's aloofness, his lack of cordiality, his boorishness, his autocratic methods, etc.

f) Traumatic experiences.—This is a general category which includes a variety of "reasons" given by dormant parishioners for their abandonment of the Church. Some of them refer to their alleged "disappointment" with official functionaries of the Church, priests in the pulpit or confessional, teaching brothers and sisters, even churchgoing lay Catholics who set them a "bad example." These experiences with other persons may be summed up in the statement of one interviewee who said, "If that's what the Church is like, I don't want any part of it."

But these "shock" experiences are sometimes expressed in nonpersonal factors. There is apparently at times a sudden realization on the part of these dormant Catholics that one or more of the Church's teachings are in direct conflict with their own desires and convictions. This shows up, for example, in the so-called intransigence of the Catholic Church on the question of artificial birth control and in the proclamations of bishops that racial segregation must be removed from the churches. The dormant Catholic "just never realized" what these teachings meant in terms of moral thinking and behavior.

g) Drifting.—This classification is meant to include all those persons who seem unable to present a reason for having left the Church. They are likely to say that they "just lost interest" or that they "gradually stopped going to Church." These statements are not really an explanation of their defection. They are similar to the statement that one is a dormant because he has "lost the faith" or has stopped praying or that he has become involved in habitual immoral or irreligious behavior. These are merely descriptions rather than explanations of religious dormancy.

In spite of this apparent overlapping, there are two types of persons who have difficulty in explaining their dormancy and who fit this category of "drifters." They are, first, the *very aged* who seem to have become wearied of all aspects of life on earth. Generic dormancy, rather than specific religious dormancy, characterizes these old people. Theirs is a physical and mental apathy which is apparently not capable of meeting the institutional demands of their society. A second type is constituted by the *social strainers* who have immersed themselves in the scramble for social status. Unlike the old folks, theirs is a specific religious drifting. They are alert, ambitious, and energetic in the nonreligious institutions of society and seem to have given major credence to secular values and practically no advertance to sacred values.

The religious indifferentism which is most noticeable among the "drifters" is present in some degree among all the dormant Catholics. As a matter of fact, "dormancy" and "indifferentism" are more or less synonymous terms. It must be noted again that the seven general categories of excuses or explanations which dormant Catholics provide are not mutually exclusive. Some of the persons interviewed gave several of these reasons for their defection from the Church. Thus it is impossible to classify the people themselves and to show what percentage of them left the Church under each separate reason. Since no individual parishioner fits exclusively into any of these categories, the best we can do is to find the type of factor which seems to predominate in any given case. And, above all, the caution must be made that even the skilled interviewer finds difficulty in sifting genuine reasons from mere rationalizations.

While it is possible to obtain fairly accurate statistics on the number of dormant Catholics in any particular parish or city, it is very difficult to obtain satisfactory knowledge concerning either the degree of or the reason for dormancy. Much more research is needed in the latter aspect of this problem. It will not suffice to say that "the Western community is a secular community in which religion is tolerated, but no longer gives the regulative principles for every kind of human activity."[12] This may be true, but it is not explanatory of the fact that in the same Western secular community there are also large numbers of nuclear and modal Catholics who do regulate their lives by religious principles.

12. A. M. Hourani, *Syria and Lebanon* (London: Oxford University Press, 1946), p. 81.

PART II

Social Correlates of Religious Participation

Chapter Seven

The Religious Life-Profile[1]

T̲HE attempt to classify all the members of a socioreligious aggregate into their various subgroups and categories, or to stratify them in a hierarchy from the nuclear to the dormant, tends to present a relatively static picture of religious life. The fact is, of course, that over a period of time these categories do not "stay put." This means that the member content of the categories changes during the years, that some of the nuclear parishioners may become modal or marginal, or vice versa. Religious experience is a dynamic experience, and this changing aspect may be observed whether the individual parishioner is traced throughout all the stages of his life or whether the whole parish is divided into its successive age groupings.

The concept of the religious life-profile, as here employed, refers to the fluctuations in certain religious observances which occur during the lifetime of white Roman Catholics in a southern city. It is not a direct life-history, because none of these individuals has been studied from birth to his present age status. It may, however, be cautiously employed as a projection of the future religious habits of this population, although no prediction can be made about any particular parishioner. The persons who serve as a base for the present statistical study are 8,363 Catholic parishioners, ten years of age and over, and do not include dormant Catholics.[2] Since there are significant differences between males and females in the practice of religion, some distinctions are here made between the sexes.

The caution must be repeated that this study represents a static profile of a Catholic population as it was statistically frozen in April, 1951. The tentative explanation of the differences in religious observance is taken mainly from a series of interviews with persons

1. This chapter is based on an article, "The Profile of Catholic Religious Life," *American Journal of Sociology*, LVIII, No. 2 (September, 1952), 145–49.
2. See above, chaps. 2 and 6; also the article, "What Is a Parishioner?" *Theological Studies*, XIII, No. 2 (June, 1952), 220–27.

from this actual population. A continuing presentation of the same phenomena would require a life-history of each individual which would have to be drawn from the relatively unreliable source of personal memory. Parishes which have preserved complete and accurate census schedules for more than sixty years could also provide the material for a dynamic presentation of this kind. But the data here provided cannot imply, for example, that the present age group, fifty to fifty-nine, had a record of religious observance in their adolescence similar to that of the present ten-to-ninteen-year group.

The practice of religion is a complicated experience involving attitudes and degrees of belief as well as formal and informal measurable external behavior. Empirical analysis, however, is necessarily limited by the measurable data at hand and also by the arbitrary selection of criteria which are to be employed. We have selected three criteria against which to measure the religious observance of these urban white Catholics. These are the performance of Easter duties, the weekly attendance at Sunday Mass, and the reception of Holy Communion once a month or oftener. Of these three observances, the first and second are morally obligatory; that is, a Catholic who does not receive Communion at least once a year during the paschal time, or who wilfully misses Mass on Sundays, is guilty of serious sin. The Church does not place an obligation on the Catholic to receive Communion once a month or oftener, but a practice of this kind may be accepted as an external index of greater appreciation for religious values and of closer affiliation with formal religion.

Data have also been collected on other formal religious observances by these Catholics, but they do not lend themselves to treatment by *specific* age groupings. They are external practices—confessions, attendance at the various evening services, Lenten devotions, etc.—on which we have a complete breakdown according to sex but only a general analysis according to age. It must be noted also that the valid religious life-profile includes fluctuations in the internal and imponderable spiritual experiences of Catholics as well as in the ethical and moral behavior of these people in their social relations.

The limited criteria here employed are therefore no more than a partial index of the religious life of these 8,363 white urban Catholics. Because of the limitations of these norms, we do not include in this "life-profile" the children under ten years of age. Catholic children are not morally obliged to attend Sunday Mass until they reach the "age of reason" (about the age of seven), and they do not usually receive their First Holy Communion until a year or two later. We did not attempt to employ subjective psychological criteria, like those used by Harms.[3] These would probably be helpful in understanding the development of religious experience from young childhood through the postadolescent period, but they seem of doubtful validity in the later decades of life.

The statistical arrangement of the data shows definite and interesting variations according to the different stages of the parishioner's life. When the sexes are combined in each age category according to the three selected criteria, a relatively consistent pat-

TABLE 9

Age Group in Years	No. (100 Per Cent)	Percentage Making Easter Duties	Percentage Attending Mass Every Sunday	Percentage Receiving Monthly Communion
10–19	1,668	92.1	92.8	71.3
20–29	1,994	84.8	77.6	40.9
30–39	1,987	63.4	69.3	31.6
40–49	1,462	75.0	74.3	39.3
50–59	737	77.5	77.2	38.4
60 and over.....	515	86.6	90.9	25.6
Total	8,363	78.9	78.6	43.3

tern emerges. Table 9 shows that the youthful category from ten to nineteen years of age exhibits the highest percentage of religious observance. There is a sharp drop in the ages thirty to thirty-nine, and a general upswing in the three remaining age groups.

No claim can be made that a similar religious life-profile will be found among Catholics in rural areas, in national or racial parishes, in other regions, or even among white Catholics in other southern cities. But, on the strength of the comparative figures given here, certain aspects of the modal Catholic's religious life may be traced.[4] He tends to be very religious during the adolescent and postadolescent stages but becomes somewhat careless in his twenties. In the following decade of life he reaches an ebb in these religious

3. See his interesting division of religious experience into the "fairy-tale stage," the "realistic stage," and the "individualistic stage" (Ernest Harms, "The Development of Religious Experience in Children," *American Journal of Sociology*, L, No. 2 [September, 1944], 112–22).

4. If it is assumed that few fluctuations occur in the external religious observances of nuclear Catholics, the dividing line here seems to be between the modal and the marginal categories. We have said above (chap. 5) that the marginal parishioners constitute about one-fifth of the total.

activities. Then he gradually improves during the remainder of his life, but he never quite regains the record achieved in his youth.

Are there any explanations for these statistical fluctuations in religious observance? What happens to the individual at various stages of his life which may account for these differences? In the ordinary course of a lifetime a kind of cycle can be traced which shows the variations of institutional influences, particularly of education, recreation, occupation, and marriage. Each of these is in some way involved in one or more of the age statuses of the individual. Since this institutional influence is obvious, one cannot suggest that age alone is a predominant factor in religious observance (except in the case of physical disabilities which naturally accompany old age).

The youngest age group has the best record of formal religious observance. When this ten-year group is divided into two five-year categories, the statistics show that those in the younger teens have a somewhat better record than those in the older teens. It may be suggested that "fresh, unspoiled, unsophisticated youth" is expected to be closer to God and to take its religious duties more seriously than other age groups. On the other hand, there is frequent allusion to the teen-age period as one in which delinquency, immorality, and antireligious attitudes flourish.[5] From this study it seems that the latter opinion is not true of the largest percentage of the young Catholics studied.[6]

The probable reasons why these Catholic youngsters have a relatively high record for external religious observance may be summed up in adult supervision of various kinds. There are 1,668 persons in this grouping, and 1,366 (81.9 per cent) are still in schools. Of those still in school, 780 (or 57.1 per cent) are in Catholic grammar schools, high schools, or colleges. There is no doubt that the teachers in these schools (as well as some in the public schools) remind their pupils of their religious duties, encouraging them to frequent Communion and to Sunday Mass.

5. Paul Weaver's study, "Youth and Religion," *Annals of the American Academy of Political and Social Science*, CCXXXVI (November, 1944), 152–60, shows that many American youths are hostile to all churches and creeds and revere no faith. This critical study, however, does not show whether youth is more remiss than other age groups in their religious duties.

6. See our discussion, however, concerning the influence of the institutional environment on the religious life of adolescents ("Institutional Environment and Religious Life," *Lumen vitae*, VI, Nos. 1–2 [1951], 165–72). Cf. also below, chap. 9.

A study made of a sample of Catholic families in this same area revealed the fact that the mother of the family often reminds the younger children of religious obligations. Parents in these families exhibit closer vigilance and control over their children who are less than twenty years of age than they do over their older children. Even those parents who are careless in their own religious practices tend to insist that their children should be faithful to Church duties.[7]

The persons in the age category of twenty to twenty-nine present a falling-off of religious fidelity. The institutional controls vary among them and tend to be more lax regarding religious expectations of people in this age group. These individuals have achieved a degree of emancipation from the school and home ties which previously exerted social pressure upon them. They must rely more on their own initiative to comply with the rules and practices of the Church. They also tend to have more social distractions in parties, dances, and week ends away from home.

If this decade of life is the occasion for the person's entrance into adulthood, it marks also an introduction to novel social experiences. Acceptance as an adult in the community, the assuming of responsibilities in occupational, social, and civic life, and the increasing importance of the decisions now made necessarily involve a change of behavioral patterns. The recurrent performance of religious duties was formerly done as part of school and family routine, but the regulatory pressures of this familiar routine have been lifted. The world of the twenties is not completely new, but it is different enough to result in changed patterns of religious behavior.

A more important factor in diminishing religious observances is marriage. There are 1,994 persons in this class, of whom 1,308 (or 65.6 per cent) are married. The difference in religious observance between the married and the single is quite noticeable among Catholics in their twenties. Single persons are approximately 4 per cent better in Easter duties, 13 per cent in Sunday Mass attendance, and 23 per cent in monthly Communion than married people in this age category. It is perhaps an oversimplification to say that this difference "probably reflects nothing more significant than the fact that youth who are married are usually more absorbed in home

7. To some extent this is shown even among dormant Catholics, most of whom have their children baptized, and some insist that they receive First Holy Communion (see above, chap. 6, pp. 71–72).

duties than youth who are not."[8] Whatever the reason may be, the fact is that marital status seems to have a definite correlation with formal religious practices.

The life-profile of these Catholics reaches its lowest point of religious vitality in the thirties. This age classification shows the largest percentage of individuals who fail to make their Easter duties. It shows also the greatest percentage of irregular Sunday Mass attendance. On the matter of reception of monthly Communion, only the people sixty years of age and older have a lower record than this group. In so far as we can judge from these external indexes, the period of the thirties seems to present the most serious religious problems to the individual. Past this age, external religious observance generally improves.[9]

The fact of marital status must undoubtedly be considered in relation to these Catholics in their thirties. There are 1,987 in this category, of whom 1,880 (or 94.6 per cent) are married. This is a larger percentage of married persons than occurs in the twenties. Of these married persons, 1,578 (or 84.1 per cent) have one or more children. The presence of small children in the home undoubtedly has a deterrent effect on the obligation to attend Sunday Mass. One of the parents must usually stay with the children while the other attends Mass. The same reason may to some extent affect the practice of monthly reception of Holy Communion; but it does not seem to account for their failure to fulfil the Easter duties.

Experienced parish priests point to another factor, that of birth prevention, as an influence against religious observance. After the young married couple has had two or three children, the economic and social problems of a growing family begin to absorb their attention. The "moral decision" whether to limit the size of the family while still enjoying the full sexual privileges of marriage has already been clearly made for Catholics by their Church. There is no moral alternative in this matter. The Church teaches very definitely that onanism is against the natural law and that the Catholic who practices artificial birth control cannot also receive

8. Howard M. Bell, *Youth Tell Their Story* (Washington, D.C.: American Council of Education, 1938), p. 198.

9. "For all married people, there is a certain falling off in religious observance between the ages of thirty and thirty-nine. Except for this decline, increasing age generally brings with it a more faithful observance of religious duties" (George Kelly, *Catholics and the Practice of the Faith* [Washington, D.C.: Catholic University of America Press, 1946], p. 197). See *ibid.*, Tables 11, 12, and 13 (for married people) and 16, 17, and 18 (for single persons).

the sacraments. At the same time the economic and social pressures of the urban, secular culture constantly urge that two or three children "are enough."

The persistent practice of artificial birth control bars the individual from the sacraments of penance and the Eucharist. It means also that the Catholic cannot receive absolution of his sins so that he may make the Easter duties. But it does not mean that he is barred from attendance at Sunday Mass. The comparative statistics within this age group show that 69.3 per cent attend Mass but that only 63.4 per cent make the Easter duties. In the comparison with the previous decade and with the next decade of life, the percentage making their Easter duties in the age group thirty to thirty-nine is significantly lower.

Do Catholics in their thirties "naturally lose interest" in religious values and practices? It is probably true that in our current urban occupational structure a man in his thirties is most preoccupied with his chances for economic success. In this age period of life he will probably discover whether his career has future possibilities or is a dead end. The wife and mother is also concerned about her husband's business prospects and tends to follow the institutionalized patterns of behavior which are helpful to him. The religious effect of this central occupational interest is not simply a matter of the clash of secular and sacred values. It has an influence on all the patterns of behavior, and it seems to affect especially the religious activities of urban Catholics.

The next two decades in the religious life-profile show a marked improvement on all three indexes of religious observance. The individual is likely to return to the practice of monthly Communion, attend Sunday Mass more regularly, and make his Easter duties. Perhaps this is the period when Catholic parishioners "settle down." They seem to have achieved a regularity of living, assumed the responsibility of giving example to their growing children, and are not so greatly affected by the recreational and occupational demands to which they previously acceded.

It is probable also that, in these middle years from forty to sixty, the individual realizes and appreciates his social stake in the community and parish. The sense of belonging and the psychological security of social relations probably fortifies the religious practices which are expected of group members. This seems a particularly valid assumption among the females, who show a marked improvement over the religious observances of the thirties and have a relatively stable record through both the forties and the fifties. In our society these two decades mark the age period of "full adulthood," and it is probable that urban parishioners from forty to sixty years of age could be scientifically studied as the "ideal type" of American Catholic.

The period from sixty years of age and over shows an interesting variation in the religious habits of this "statistical" parishioner. In the making of Easter duties and the attendance at Sunday Mass, he returns almost to the religious fervor of youth. The slightly lower percentage record for Sunday Mass may be accounted for by the physical disabilities of old age. The sick and the infirm are, of course, excused from the obligation to hear Mass. But the somewhat larger difference between youth and old age in the making of Easter duties is not so readily explained.

The fact that parishioners sixty years of age and older show a drop instead of an increase in the reception of monthly Communion seems at first a puzzling phenomenon. It is true that older persons cannot maintain the fast as well as younger persons can; they may have to take medicine or a drink of water after midnight. Thus they cannot receive the Sacrament at the morning Mass.[10]

A more likely explanation, however, seems to be in the fact that these older Catholics were forming their religious habits at the beginning of the twentieth century when the practice of frequent reception of Communion had not yet become the vogue. Before the decree of Pius X on this practice was published in 1905, Catholics were not widely encouraged to receive Holy Communion weekly and even monthly.[11] Some of these older parishioners are daily communicants, but approximately three-fourths of them fail to receive Communion even once a month.

The general conclusion we must make from this investigation of religious practices in relation to age does not bear out the axiom that "religion interests only the very young and the very old." Certainly the record for the two age extremes is significantly different from that of the people in the thirty-to-thirty-nine-year bracket. The percentages for Easter duty observance and Sunday Mass attendance for the ten-to-nineteen-year group and for the sixty-and-above group are high in comparison with those for the thirty-to-thirty-nine-year group. The fact that the other age groups hold percentages at almost regular intervals in between seems to indicate

10. The Apostolic Constitution, *Christus Dominus*, liberalizing the Communion fast, was promulgated since this study was made.
11. See *Decrees of the Holy Congregation of the Council*, December 20, 1905.

that factors other than age are most important in influencing religious behavior.

Since the religious observances of male and female Catholics differ considerably, it seems necessary to define separately the modal Catholic male and the modal Catholic female. Sex differences among these 8,363 people studied show the expected predominance of female observance in every age category. Table 10 clearly indicates the percentage domination which the female parishioners have

TABLE 10

Age Group in Years	No. (100 Per Cent)	Percentage Making Easter Duties	Percentage Attending Sunday Mass	Percentage Receiving Monthly Communion
10–19:				
Males	835	90.8	90.7	63.3
Females	833	93.4	95.0	79.3
20–29:				
Males	930	83.8	72.9	40.6
Females	1,064	85.7	77.1	41.2
30–39:				
Males	924	56.6	62.2	24.1
Females	1,063	69.3	75.5	38.3
40–49:				
Males	745	66.9	68.3	30.5
Females	717	83.5	83.5	48.4
50–59:				
Males	365	72.3	72.1	29.6
Females	372	82.5	82.3	47.0
60 and over:				
Males	216	75.5	83.3	16.7
Females	299	94.7	96.3	32.1
Total	8,363	78.9	78.6	43.3

over the males according to the three selected criteria: frequent Communion, Easter duties, and the regular attendance at Sunday Mass.

Concurrent studies of sex differences which we have made in other religious practices demonstrate also that the females are more active in every case. Our statistics show that the proportion of males to females is as follows: of every one hundred persons who go to confession, only thirty-six are males; of those who attend evening services, thirty are males; and, of those who attend special Lenten services, twenty-four are males.[12] These are religious ac-

12. The sex ratio in this universe of Catholics is 92.3, but this excess of females is not large enough to correct the appreciable difference in the religious comparison of the sexes.

tivities which carry no moral obligation in the sense that a person who neglects them is committing a sin. Nevertheless, these practices of supererogation seem to be fairly reliable indications of the inner, voluntary religious spirit of Catholics, and they demonstrate that females are more religious than males.

Are there any explanations for the fact that, generally speaking, the religious life-profile of females demonstrates at every age a greater faithfulness to the teachings and practices of the Church? The popular psychological suggestion that women are naturally of a more pious temperament is not scientifically satisfactory and has generally been abandoned by serious students of religion. At any rate, as an explanation it merely pushes the inquiry back a step further. Behind this questionable cliché there are certain sociocultural factors which may tend to explain the difference.

It is certainly true that the culture norms of this southern urban community expect women to be more pious than men. (And this is probably true throughout Western civilization.) The habits of religious observances are ecclesiastically defined in the same way for males and females, but institutionally they are defined in different ways. Priests, teachers, parents, and other adults themselves have grown up in a society where females are better churchgoers than males. Some of the oldest residents remember when this disproportion was much greater than it is today. They say that, fifty years ago, "you hardly ever saw a man receive Communion, except at Easter time."

It also seems true to say that in our culture the religious role is more compatible with the other roles of women than with the other roles of men. For example, both the family roles and the "culture-bearer" role of women in this society imply functions and values which are relatively consistent with the functions and values of religion. Women are still supposed to promote and exemplify the "higher things of life." On the other hand, the secular roles (occupational, political, recreational, etc.) of the male are more likely to be in conflict with his religious role.

This may be only another way of saying that females are culturally more "domestic" than males, while males are culturally more "secular" than females. This assumption must be joined with another assumption to the effect that, by the very nature of the functions and goals involved, religion seems to have much more meaning in the home and family than it has in business and the "outside world." A neat explanation of this kind must of course be taken only as a theoretical generalization which is incomplete and to which there are numerous exceptions.

In summary, it may be said that age and sex have a degree of influence upon the religious practices of urban Catholics but that neither of these factors can be taken apart from the various institutional patterns which accompany both. Even when these simple generalizations have been made, however, it must be noted that there are some Catholics who all their lives fulfil the arbitrary criteria of religious observance which we have selected. It cannot be said that they are completely unaffected by the factors which we have analyzed in this chapter. Thus, while their regularity in religious practices does not invalidate generalizations made about modal parishioners, it does indicate that their religious life-profile probably requires more refined instruments of analysis than those now provided by social science.

Chapter Eight

Urban Mobility and Parish Life

AMERICANS of the present age are reputedly the most mobile people on earth with the exception of the few remaining nomadic tribes and the migrant workers in various nations. In a most general sense this American mobility includes all types of internal migration, social and occupational mobility, local residential change, and even the so-called "fluidity" found in commuting from home to office and in making vacation and business trips.[1] As Quinn points out, "no universally accepted basis for distinguishing between migration and mobility exists in sociological literature. . . . Except for studies of migration, the literature on mobility is not voluminous. Most of the literature, moreover, deals with social rather than ecological mobility, or with the effects of mobility on social and personal organization and disorganization."[2]

In this chapter *urban mobility* refers to the changes of residence made by 2,972 white Catholic families in a southern city on whom data could be obtained for the decade 1942–51. All these people were living in three white Catholic parishes during the year 1951, and their record of mobility during the decade included some changes of residence in other cities and states and also some rural-urban movement. For the most part, however, it was made up of residential change within urban areas. Since this mobility is an urban phenomenon and since most American Catholics live in cities and follow the institutionalized patterns of their communities, it may be assumed that urban Catholics change their residence as frequently as urban non-Catholics.

If the urban Catholic parish is conceptualized merely as a church

1. See the definition of terms by Stuart A. Queen and Lewis F. Thomas, *The City: A Study of Urbanism in the United States* (New York: McGraw-Hill Book Co., 1939), chap. xviii, "Physical Movement and Social Mobility."
2. James A. Quinn, *Human Ecology* (New York: Prentice-Hall, Inc., 1950), chap. xvii, "Migration and Mobility," where most of the significant studies on this subject have been analyzed.

center to which lay Catholics come for the satisfaction of their religious needs, it may be assumed that the fact of their movement from one residence to another does not interfere with the parochial and pastoral functions. But, if the parish is thought of as an organized system of social relations and of numerous social substructures, this residential mobility may be a disrupting factor in the efficient operation of the parochial unit. It is a widely held thesis among parish priests in big cities that the mobility of their parishioners not only makes the pastoral function more difficult but also interferes with both religious practices and social participation.

It may be safely assumed that people who move from one parish to another with some frequency cannot structure a solidarity with the members of any parish. They do not stay in one place long enough to become known to the priests. They do not become active and interested members of the parochial societies, nor do they develop a spirit of parish-consciousness, much less one of loyalty to the parish. In contrast to this assumption there is another which holds that the lower-class people, who move the most, are also the best Catholics and the most loyal parishioners.

In order to reconcile and understand these assumptions, it seems necessary to make a scientific study of three variables: mobility, socioeconomic status, and religious participation. We do not necessarily argue for a clear-cut process of causation among these variables. Whether people are more religious because they are relatively poor, whether poverty and mobility are causally related, whether mobility actually interferes with the practice of religion—these are all questions which we must leave unanswered. There has not been sufficient and satisfactory research in the area of urban religious practices to allow definite conclusions concerning these problems.

The fact of residential mobility by their parishioners is often discussed by urban parish priests. It is one of the factors which makes it most difficult to maintain an up-to-date census of the city church of any denomination. But the extent of mobility is sometimes exaggerated and sometimes minimized because little effort apparently has been made to keep a careful record of it. The obligatory parochial records for First Communions and confirmations are a revealing, though partial, source of information on the movement of Catholic families. A study of the cumulative ten-year records of three urban white parishes shows that about 38 per cent of the children who receive First Communion were born and baptized in another parish. This means that their families moved *at least once* (and perhaps oftener) before these children were eight years old. Children who receive the sacrament of confirmation average eleven years of age. About 43 per cent of them were born elsewhere. The adults who were confirmed averaged twenty-one years of age, and about 52 per cent of them were born outside the parish in which they were confirmed. The marriage records also show that about 55 per cent of the spouses whose residence is in the parish at the time of marriage were born elsewhere.

These figures can be validly extended because they represent a kind of minimum estimate of mobility. Approximately one-half of the urban Catholic families change their residence from one parish to another at least once in twenty years. But records of this kind do not tell the whole story, because they do not reveal how many times the family has moved from one residence to another within the parish territory between the time of the child's baptism and the reception of the other recorded sacraments. To get a more accurate picture of mobility, it is necessary to investigate other sources of information.

In a previous study of a single urban parish we have shown that over a period of ten years there was an average of 3.3 moves per family for the 1,498 Catholic families who were studied. Approximately one-quarter (26.8 per cent) of the families did not move at all, while the remaining 73.2 per cent averaged 4.5 moves in the decade 1939–48. In that report we said that "if the pastor or his secretary diligently kept the register of his parishioners up to date, the change of address was made 3,289 times in the course of these ten years. This is an average of about twenty-seven times a month!"[3]

This appeared to be an enormous amount of residential mobility, and we felt that a separate and independent study should be made in the same general area to check its validity. We conducted a new survey of this problem in three white urban parishes for the ten-year period 1942–51 and were able to obtain data on 2,972 families which were formed before 1942 and in which both spouses were living together. The comparison of the results of this study with our previous survey of one parish in the 1939–48 decade seems to be remarkably close. We obtained our data from three sources: the people themselves, the retail credit association, and the public utilities company.

3. "Urban Mobility and Religious Observance," *American Catholic Sociological Review*, XI, No. 3 (October, 1950), 130–39.

The extent of mobility of urban Catholic families is indicated in the fact that 9,851 moves were made by these families in the course of the decade. This is an average of 3.31 moves per family for the 2,972 families studied and an average of 4.55 moves for the 2,164 families which actually changed their residence. Thus we find that 808 families, or 27.19 per cent, did not move at all, while the remaining 72.81 per cent moved one or more times during the ten-year period.

Table 11 shows that the largest category of those who moved is made up of those who moved three or four times. The extreme of mobility is found in five families which moved thirteen times in ten years.

TABLE 11

FREQUENCY OF FAMILY MOBILITY	2,972 FAMILIES		9,851 MOVES	
	No.	Per Cent	No.	Per Cent
None	808	.27.19	0	0.00
One or two	553	18.60	845	8.58
Three or four	676	22.75	2,353	23.89
Five or six	413	13.90	2,293	23.28
Seven or eight	333	11.20	2,456	24.93
Nine or ten	141	4.74	1,349	13.69
Eleven or more	48	1.62	555	5.63
Total	2,972	100.00	9,851	100.00

This total mobility may be divided into various kinds. For example, the parish priest wants to know whether his parish has gained or lost families over the period of ten years. Regardless of the mobility of families from one residence to another within the parish, if the total movement out of the parish exceeds the moves into the parish, it is likely that the parish is in a dying residential area. As a matter of fact, only 2,245 (or 22.8 per cent) of the total moves were either into or out of the parishes studied. There were 1,654 moves into the parish and 591 moves out of the parish, leaving these parishes with a net gain of 1,063 families at the end of the ten-year period.[4] These families migrated from two directions: from rural areas into the city and from downtown parishes into

4. This is the gain from mobility alone and does not include the numbers of new families formed after 1942, either within the parish or moving into the parish after that date. Nor is this an index of the true growth of the parish, because it does not consider the numbers of families broken by death or separation during the period.

the relatively better residential areas repesented by these three parishes.

It is obvious that these families which move back and forth across parish lines present a problem of social integration. Only in exceptional instances do those with the record of frequent moving become personally acquainted with the priests or form more than casual acquaintance with parishioners. Only rarely do they participate in the extra-sacramental functions of the parish or join any of the parish societies. While residential mobility is not the single simple explanation for the relative lack of solidarity of the urban parish, it is probably the largest single factor for those families which move frequently.[5]

The turnover of pupils in the parochial schools is accounted for almost completely by these families which cross parish lines. Some of their children remain in the same school for as little as three months. The same is true of the Catholic children who are enrolled in the public schools and who are expected to participate in the released-time program for religious instruction. The records of First Communion classes for children in the Catholic school show a slightly higher rate of mobility than those of the Catholic children attending the public schools.

If these families which move into and out of the parish do not have children of school age, they usually come to the attention of the priests only when there is a sick call or some other emergency requiring pastoral consultation. Because of their mobility they usually do not receive the Sunday collection envelopes which are distributed annually and of which a record is kept in the parish rectory. Short of an all-embracing and continual census-taking, there seems to be no efficient way for the priests to make and keep contacts with them. The present possibility of integrating them into the parish as a social unit seems remote.

These generalizations have certain exceptions. Our statistics include some families which moved into the parish at the beginning

5. The best studies in this field have been made of rural Protestant churches. Their general conclusion is that "oldtimers rather than newcomers participate more in churches." See especially Harold F. Kaufman, *Religious Organization in Kentucky* (AES Bull. 524 [Lexington, Ky., 1948]), p. 33; Indiana Congregational Christian Conference and Town and Country Department of Board of Home Missions, *Hoosier Churches* (1943), p. 23; N. L. Whetten and E. G. Devereux, *Studies of Suburbanization in Connecticut* (AES Bull. 212 [Storrs, Conn., 1936]), pp. 110–11. See also the summary of research studies by John Hostetler and William Mather, *Participation in the Rural Church* (Paper No. 1762 [State College: Pennsylvania State College, 1952]).

of the ten-year period and have not since changed their residence. There are also some who have what the priests call "good parochial training" which they exhibit by visiting the rectory on their arrival, announcing themselves as new parishioners, and even asking for the series of collection envelopes. Occasionally the priests announce from the pulpit at Sunday Mass that new parishioners should assume the responsibility of making themselves known to the priests and of offering their services for parochial activities. Unlike those Protestant congregations which have "letters of membership" in their files, the urban Catholic parish seems to include only a small percentage of persons who voluntarily proclaim their membership in a new parish.

Besides the residential changes which cross parish boundaries, there are two other types of mobility. The greatest number of moves, 7,606, or 77.21 per cent of all moves made during the ten-year period, was made either outside the parish or from one house to another inside the parish. These families moved 3,469 times outside the parish (35.21 per cent of all moves) in which they had their residence in 1951. These moves must be taken into consideration when one is studying the total volume of mobility, even though they do not affect directly the social structure and relations of the parish of present residence.

The remaining 4,137 changes of residence (or 41.99 per cent of all 9,851 moves) were within the present parish boundaries. These represent a kind of "internal flux" of parishioners and indicate the difficulty which the parish priests have in "keeping up" with changing addresses. Family units which move from one address to another within the parish limits do not, however, present so great a problem as those which move across parish boundaries. Their relationships to the priests, the school, the parish societies, and other activities and to their fellow-parishioners are not seriously disturbed. As a matter of fact, the records show that the 808 families which stayed in the same residence for ten years are not better social participants in the parish than those families which moved from one house to another (or others) within the parochial territory.

It is quite obvious that the mobility of urban Catholic families must be considered a normal phenomenon of city life.[6] The de-

---

6. This generalization seems true even though the decade here under consideration had a higher than normal rate of mobility because of war-induced changes.

gree to which this mobility interferes with the social aspects of the parish structure cannot be determined until reliable comparisons can be made with parishes in which the families are relatively stable. Other factors which tend to decrease the social solidarity of the parish must also be considered. It seems safe to conclude, however, that, as long as a family remains within the same parish, its movements from one part of the parish to another part do not seriously affect its participation in the parochial center. Local residential mobility does not interfere with the web of social relations in so far as this is maintained in the urban parish; the same social and religious functions continue with the same participants.

TABLE 12

RENTAL VALUE CATEGORIES

FREQUENCY OF FAMILY MOBILITY	763 Families $20 or Less	1,471 Families $21–$40	534 Families $41–$60	204 Families $61 and Above	2,972 TOTAL FAMILIES
None	29.88	22.09	32.02	41.18	27.19
One or two	28.96	12.65	16.67	27.94	18.61
Three or four	20.45	24.00	24.53	17.65	22.74
Five or six	9.96	17.47	10.68	11.27	13.90
Seven or eight	6.82	15.16	10.11	1.96	11.20
Nine or more	3.93	8.63	5.99	0.00	6.36

It is generally surmised that persons in the lower-income brackets are both more mobile and more religious than those with higher incomes. We were interested in the relation between frequency of moving and the economic status of these 2,972 urban Catholic families. Table 12 uses the categories of rental value as the only measure of economic status and shows the percentages of families in each category according to the frequency of mobility.

This comparison shows that the lowest and the highest economic groupings change their places of residence less frequently than the two middle groups. The category of rental $61 and above has the largest percentage (41.18) of stable families which did not move at all in the ten-year period. On the other hand, the rental category $21–$40 shows the largest percentage (41.26) of those which moved five or more times during the decade. There are undoubtedly many factors at work which account for the differences in mobility in the various economic categories. More detailed correlations must be made before any conclusion can be drawn concerning the reciprocal influence of religion, mobility, and economic status.

Since the primary purpose of the Catholic parish is the sanctification and salvation of human beings, all activities of parishioners must somehow be analyzed in relation to this purpose. A central question therefore is the relationship between mobility and religious behavior. Does the frequent change of address have any effect upon the religious and sacramental practices of parishioners? In order to answer this question, we have selected five criteria: the validity of marriage, the performance of Easter duties, attendance at Sunday Mass, the reception of Holy Communion, and the attendance of children at the Catholic schools.

Since all the spouses in these families are Catholic, we have a total of 5,944 persons whose religious behavior we are able to compare. The group of 808 families (1,616 persons) which did not move at all during this ten-year period serves as a basis of comparison with the remaining 2,164 couples (4,328 persons) who changed their residence one or more times. This classification was made on the basis of the *number* of moves without regard to the *kind* of mobility (i.e., whether they remained within the parish or crossed parish lines). In order to keep our statistics comparable, we analyzed the religious practices of only the husband and wife and not of children or other occupants of the dwelling unit. In measuring the fifth criterion, we considered only those parents who had children of grammar-school age in 1951.

1. The first criterion employed here is that of valid marriages. The assumption is that people who identify themselves as Catholics will generally be concerned about the validity of their marriage according to the regulations of the Church. Invalid marriages are those which were entered into by two baptized Catholics before some official who is not a Catholic priest.[7] This norm of judgment is used popularly as one of the basic ways of distinguishing between "good" Catholics and "bad" Catholics. Spouses who are not validly married are not permitted to receive the sacraments even though they may sometimes attend Mass and other church services, rear their children as Catholics, support the parochial organizations, etc.

These comparative figures show that the percentage of spouses who are validly married decreases as the amount of mobility increases, but they also show that the percentage for stable families is approximately the same as that for families which have moved five

7. It is possible, of course, to find an invalid marriage between a Catholic and a non-Catholic, but in this study of mobility both spouses in every case were Catholic.

or six times. The two lowest percentage figures are found for those which have moved seven or more times during the ten-year period, but the difference between these families and the stable families is hardly large enough to be attributed to mobility as the main factor.

2. The second criterion of religious observance is that of the Easter duties. This is a minimum obligation imposed upon all Catholics who have reached the age of reason. The Church precept commands the annual reception of the sacraments of penance[8] and of the Eucharist during the paschal season. It is generally assumed that only the most lax Catholic would fail to perform this duty. Table 13 gives the percentages of spouses who fulfilled this duty in the paschal season of 1951.

TABLE 13

Frequency of Mobility	Per Cent of Valid Marriages	Per Cent Making Easter Duties	Per Cent Attending Sunday Mass Regularly	Per Cent Receiving Communion Monthly or Oftener	No. of Spouses
None	87.8	65.1	71.8	33.5	1,616
One or two......	94.2	71.7	73.6	35.2	1,106
Three or four....	89.3	71.2	74.5	36.6	1,352
Five or six......	87.4	70.6	75.3	34.2	826
Seven or eight....	85.3	64.3	70.0	30.1	666
Nine or more....	84.0	65.7	73.3	36.2	378

Here again the statistics show that the mobile families have a slightly better percentage record for this religious practice than the families which have not moved during the decade. There is, however, a gradual and almost regular decrease from those which moved least to those which moved most often.[9] Since the Easter duties are made only once a year and since they can be performed in any parish church, it does not seem that mobility would be an important factor in the failure of this obligation.

3. The next index of Catholic religious observance is that of Sunday Mass attendance. Every Catholic above the age of reason is obliged under pain of mortal sin to attend Mass every Sunday unless he has a legitimate excuse which makes attendance impossible. Table 13 gives the percentages only for those who attend regularly

8. That is, he must confess his mortal sins at some time during the year.

9. This comparison differs from that of our previous study, where it was seen that those families which moved the most had also the best record for Easter duties (see "Urban Mobility and Religious Observance," *American Catholic Sociological Review*, XI, No. 3 [October, 1950], 136).

(unless excused) every Sunday during the year and ignores the various possible subdivisions of those who go to Mass "a couple of times a month," occasionally, or not at all.

Generally speaking, the record of mobile families is slightly better than that of stable families in this regard. As a matter of fact, there is a gradual improvement in the three categories from those families which move once or twice to those which move five or six times, and then a drop in the last two categories. All the people who have moved, with the exception of those who changed residence seven or eight times, are better than the nonmovers. The percentage differences, however, are so slight that they reveal practically no important influence of mobility upon the attendance at Mass.

TABLE 14

Frequency of Family Mobility	Families with Children of School Age	Percentage with Children in Catholic School
None	502	65.4
One or two	381	62.6
Three or four	467	64.3
Five or six	259	69.2
Seven or eight	205	74.0
Nine or more	99	77.8

4. A further criterion of religious practices among Catholics is found in the frequency of reception of the Eucharist. People who receive Holy Communion once a month or oftener may be esteemed among the "better" Catholics in so far as external observances are an index of their religious fidelity. This is a "positive" practice in the sense that there is no obligation placed on Catholics to receive Communion frequently, and the persons who do so appear to have a deeper appreciation of the supernatural and sacramental life.

Here again the percentage differences among the various categories are almost negligible; at least they do not indicate that mobility can be considered a serious factor. The mobile persons have in general a slightly better record than the stable persons, and those who moved the most (nine or more times) have one of the highest records of all.

5. The final index of religious observance cannot be applied to all the married people studied above, because many of them did not have children in grammar school in the year of the study. This index is found in the choice of a school for the children of Catholic families. It is an almost universal assumption that the faithful

Catholic who is integrated into his parish unit will send his children to the Catholic school. There were 1,913 families with children of grammar-school age. Table 14 shows, in each category of mobility, the number and percentage of families which sent their children to the Catholic school.

All Catholic parents have the obligation to provide for the religious instruction of their children. Parents who send their children to the public school are expected to make use of the released-time program or of some other method of catechetical instruction. Table 14 includes only those families with children in the Catholic schools and does not imply that the other parents are failing completely in teaching religion to their children. Here again the record shows that those families which move most frequently also send their children to Catholic school more faithfully than the others. The lowest percentage is among those which move only once or twice, while those which move three or four times are only slightly lower than those which did not move at all during the ten years.

In summary of all the above statistical information several generalizations may be made concerning the relation of mobility to parish life. Frequent change of residence seems to have an adverse effect upon the social participation of the parishioner in the parochial unit only when this is a mobility across parish lines. In other words, the social relations of the parishioner to the priests, the other parishioners, the parochial school, and the parish societies is not affected merely by the fact that he may move from one residence to another within the parish territories. The urban family which moves often from one parish to another, however, is moving into different social situations with different social participants, and, if this happens frequently, the family is not able to structure positive and permanent relations in the new social units.

In the matter of religious practices generally we cannot find a significant factor of change in residential mobility as such, whether it is interparochial or intraparochial. If frequency of mobility can be demonstrated as a symptom of personal and family instability, it may also have an effect on the degree and kind of religious practices, but this would be the interpretation of mobility as an effect rather than a cause. As a matter of fact, however, the comparison between nonmovers and movers shows that the latter have a slightly, but consistently, better record on all five indexes of religious observances than do the nonmovers. Even those families which move the most (nine or more times in ten years) show up better on every index (except that of valid marriages) than those which did not move at all.

One final observation must be made concerning the record of religious practices by the persons studied here, all of whom are married Catholic couples. We have shown above that all the parishioners ten years of age and older have a percentage of 78.9 for making the Easter duties, 78.6 for Sunday Mass attendance, and 43.3 for receiving monthly Communion.[10] Thus the record for the parish as a whole is higher than that of the persons studied for mobility. The difference seems to be accounted for by the fact that the latter are married and that most of them are between the ages of thirty and fifty years. As we have seen above, married people, par-

TABLE 15

RENTAL VALUE CATEGORIES

FREQUENCY OF FAMILY MOBILITY	763 Families $20 or Less	1,471 Families $21–$40	534 Families $41–$60	204 Families $61 and Above	2,972 TOTAL FAMILIES
Nonmovers	29.88	41.27	32.02	41.18	27.19
Less than five	49.41	36.64	41.20	45.59	41.35
Five or more	20.71	22.09	26.78	13.23	31.46

ticularly those in the age bracket of the thirties, are less faithful to religious practices than are single persons and those in younger age periods. It appears, therefore, that age and marital status are much more significant than mobility as factors in the religious observances of urban white Catholics.

There appears to be some connection between mobility and economic status in so far as the latter can be measured against the single criterion of the monthly rental value. This is not a simple comparison which affirms that the poor move most and the rich move least. In Table 15 we divide these 2,972 families into three categories: the nonmovers, those who moved less than five times, and those who moved five or more times. Percentage-wise, the families in the second rental category are highest (41.27 per cent) among the nonmovers; almost half (49.41 per cent) of those in the lowest rental category moved less than five times; while those in the third rental group had the highest percentage (26.78) for those moving

10. See above, chap. 7, "The Religious Life-Profile," Table 9.

five or more times. The reasons for these variations may be found in the type of dwellings available for the various rental values, or it may be found in a number of other factors. Within this limited study, however, we cannot definitely assert a causal relation between religious observance, on the one hand, and economic status and mobility, on the other hand.

These tentative generalizations may be drawn from the fact that, even though urban Catholic families move around both within a parish and across parish lines, their residential mobility does not seem to affect their religious practices. For example, marriage is a single act, and the decision to marry validly or invalidly does not appear to depend upon residential mobility or stability. The annual reception of the sacraments at the paschal time, the weekly attendance at Mass, and the frequency of reception of Holy Communion are religious practices which may be performed in any Catholic parish church. These practices can hardly be affected in any direct manner by place of residence or by change of residence in big cities where there are numerous Catholic parishes. The same may be said of the criterion of elementary-school attendance. Since grammar-school education is compulsory and since Catholic schools are usually available, there seems to be no reason why mobility should be a factor in choosing a public school over a Catholic school.

The present study of mobility fortifies the generalization that the two elements, social participation and religious observance, are relatively independent variables in the parish life of the city Catholic. In the definition of the parishioner we have used them as separate criteria, and in the discussion of the nuclear parishioner we have seen that they do not necessarily coincide in the same person.[11] It is probably safe to assert that the urban American Catholic tends to think of Catholicism in terms of a universally operating spiritual agency through which he can satisfy his religious needs rather than in terms of specific parochial structures to which he is an integrated social adherent. This means that he thinks of himself more frequently as a member of the total Catholic Church rather than as a member of this or that particular parish. It is probably also safe to assert that, from the point of view of parochial participation and religious practice, the residential mobility of Catholics causes more difficulty for the parish priest than for the families involved.

11. See above, chaps. 2 and 3.

Chapter Nine

Social Status and Religious Behavior

THE sincerely religious person, especially the nuclear parishioner and the dedicated lay apostle with subjective religious experience, tends to emphasize the personal elements of religion. He speaks of conformity to the Will of God, of co-operation between the Divine Mind and his own human mind, of the part which is played by supernatural grace in his own soul. To belittle this personal aspect of the divine-human relationship would be to destroy religion in its essence, because religious behavior is nothing if it is not human behavior guided by the norms of divine revelation.[1]

The fact is, however, that the individual is pursuing his religious goals on earth in human society. He is in the world, if not of the world, and it is doubtful that even the anchoretic saint can withdraw himself completely from human society. Religion is essentially social. "Unus Christianus, nullus Christianus," so that the unsocial Christian and the unsocial saint are contradictions in terms.[2] This may be another way of saying that the human person works out his salvation not only in a concrete physical and geographical environment but also in a definite social and cultural environment.

It seems scientifically awkward to suggest that there is an institutional environment as well as a physical environment. The former penetrates the personality of the conscious individual in a way in which the latter cannot, so that it seems to become a part of him. The institutional environment, however, is psychologically both

---

1. This is, of course, in opposition to the positivistic assertion that religious truths and values are illusory myths. It is not in opposition to the area of knowledge called natural theology, which teaches that religious behavior is guided also by norms to which the human intellect can attain by reason alone.

2. "Vital religion, by its very nature, must create and sustain a social relationship" (Sidney Dimond, *The Psychology of the Methodist Revival* [London: Oxford University Press, 1926], p. 208). See also *Dynamics of a City Church*, Vol. I of *Southern Parish* (Chicago: University of Chicago Press, 1951), p. 5, where it is asserted that creed, code, cult, and communion are all essential to religion; and the discussion above, chap. 4.

subjective and objective in the sense that, while the individual is developed in, and socialized through, institutional patterns of behavior, he himself also accepts and exemplifies these patterns. He is influencing his own and others' behavior by the very fact that he has become an "institutionalized creature" of his own cultural environment.

Lewin had perhaps gone farther than any social scientist in attempting to conceptualize the individual and the situation as practically mutually continuous.[3] This is, of course, an ontological exaggeration and a scientific error, but it is almost necessary in order to counteract the opposite error of completely divorcing the individual from his environment and in order to emphasize the tremendous influence of institutionalized patterns on the social behavior of the individual. Hertzler says that "the dominance of institutions is so effective and subtle that the individuals may flatter themselves that they are exercising their own sovereign wills, whereas, in reality, they are reflecting institutional fiat. They are so conditioned by institutional stimuli that they do not realize how their thinking, their will, and their overt behavior is controlled and fabricated."[4]

It is perhaps unnecessary to belabor the concept of reciprocity within social and cultural systems. While it is true that institutions shape and direct human behavior, it is also true that people modify and create institutions. People change the mores and folkways and are changed by them. Because of this dynamic reciprocity in society, it is practically impossible to hold any of the variables constant long enough to make *precise* conclusions concerning the *degree* of influence of one or another. In other words, we are dealing with elements and factors which are not subject to satisfactory quantitative analysis.

In spite of this inherent shortcoming of social science and of the fluid character of social life, it seems possible to make a sociologically valid analysis of the mutual influences of institutions and religious behavior. A culture may be analyzed from a variety of conceptual frameworks. It is defined operationally as "the sum total of the historically developed, transmitted, and cumulated ideas, emotional

3. It was apparently Lewin's horror of "mere classification" which made him insist on "interdependent topology" in the field-theoretical approach (Kurt Lewin, *Principles of Topological Psychology* [New York: McGraw-Hill Book Co., 1936]).

4. J. O. Hertzler, *Social Institutions* (Lincoln: University of Nebraska Press, 1946), p. 180.

responses and ways of action."[5] Its units are the commonly shared and repeated patterns of social behavior and thought which are relatively integrated and have some permanence among a people. These component parts logically fall into a series of major institutions which grow out of and satisfy the basic needs of human beings in society.

The religious role, like the other roles played by individuals in society, has been institutionalized because the social patterns of which it is composed have been constantly repeated by many people. These patterns have become the expected and customary ways of thinking and acting in the pursuit of religious values and goals. In the dynamic social interaction of everyday living the religious role may be relatively integrated and reciprocal with the other social roles of the individual.[6] But the individual lives with other people in society who are also pursuing various roles institutionalized in the same culture.

The social role may in a rough way be considered the dynamic aspect of social status. As Hiller remarks, "each status is a place or position in the scheme of social relations, and consists not only of norm-prescribing privileges and obligations but also of the comparative esteem and disesteem in which these social places are held."[7] The status is contained in the institutional or cultural environment. Each status is not only an extrinsically evaluated position in the social structure; it also involves a web of reciprocal relations and is a vehicle of function and a container of social values. Thus one may be said to have numerous statuses which correspond to the relevant roles of the individual and influence his other roles. For example, the marital status of a parishioner seems to have an almost measurable influence upon his or her religious role.[8]

Thus, when we speak of the institutional environment, we mean the various customary ways in which people think and act when they pursue their principal roles and attempt to maintain their key status in the social structure. Persons think and act largely as a result of the way in which the expectations of their status influence them. This does not mean that human beings are mere automata, but it does mean, as Le Bras remarks, that their "liberty suffers pres-

---

5. E. T. Hiller, *Social Relations and Structures* (New York: Harper & Bros., 1947), p. 20.
6. For an example of an exception to this generalization see the discussion of the marginal Catholic above, chap. 6.
7. *Op. cit.*, p. 330.
8. See above, chap. 7, on the relation of age and sex to religious behavior.

sure."[9] Briefly, the institutional environment works through the status upon the role of the individual so that he tends to conform to the expectations of the culture.

This appears to be an involved description mainly because we are speaking of an abstract construct. The recognition of social values may tend to clarify it, since these are implied in the whole cultural and institutional system. The cultural patterns, which combine in various ways for the social position, relations, and functions of people within a community are a definite guide to the values and interests current in the community. From this point of view, statuses are both a result of and a vehicle for the culture values. In other words, the moral level of a community can be roughly judged from an analysis of the kinds of patterns which have become institutionalized into statuses. In a society with a spiritual or supernatural ethos they will differ greatly from those in a society with a secular and materialistic ethos.

Our study of urban American parishes provides adequate evidence for an analysis of some aspects of the influence of institutional environment on the religious behavior of parishioners. These persons are agents in a very complex network of institutionalized relationships. This vast complexity and the tremendous detail involved in patterned behavior makes it obviously impossible to give a lengthy account of several statuses. Nor is it possible even to outline all the statuses in a parish, the manner in which they are patterned, and the reciprocal influences which they involve. It is likewise impossible to include complete evidence for each statement made.

We shall select three examples of statuses among the many which are present in the average urban parish and attempt to delineate both the values they express and the manner in which they influence religious life. This is a brief review of the content of the institutional environment as it is displayed in (1) the adolescent status, (2) the occupational status of the male adult worker, and (3) the class status of the adult married female. In each case we shall note how the peculiar expectations and actions of the status affect different phases of the religious life of the urban parishioner: (*a*) the participation of adolescents in parochial organizations, (*b*) the sacramental activities of the adult male, and (*c*) the practice of the social virtues by the female.

1. The *status of adolescence* is seldom thought of in terms of a

9. Gabriel Le Bras, "Influence of Environment on Religious Life," *Lumen Vitae*, III, No. 1 (1948), 6.

value construct, but it is actually a fruitful source for the interpretation of cultural values. Ideally speaking, the adolescent is preparing himself for his future roles in the various social groups in which he will participate. In this sense, adolescence itself has a function, and the adolescent is pursuing a role made up of institutionalized patterns. Practically speaking, a youth sees little connection between his present and future social roles and seems to structure his status around this purposelessness.

In the urban parishes which we have studied, the young people, aged thirteen to sixteen years, follow certain conventional patterns of behavior. Most of them are attending high school and tend to follow expected and similar ways of acting, and they repeat the thought patterns of the local youth culture. For example, companionship within each sex category and between the sexes can be plotted and gives rise to both the gang pattern and the dating system.

Boys and girls in this age category seldom co-operate sucessfully as a combined group in the religious or recreational program of a parochial organization. The two sex groups do not play cards, dance, or carry on common recreation with each other. If a sodality sponsors a dance, most of the boys tend to come in a group, stand around the walls for a while, make belittling remarks about the girls (most of whom are forced to dance with each other), and then leave early to hang around the drugstore on the street corner. Other boys come with their steady girl friends who are not local parish girls and with whom they dance exclusively during the whole evening.

When a boy and girl "go steady," they seem to lose interest in all parochial group activities. This is not (nor is it intended to be by the participants) a companionship preparatory to the more permanent union of marriage. The individuals tend to be alone a great deal of the time, to keep late hours, and to place themselves in what appear to be the occasions of sin. In some extreme cases which we have discovered in our research the couple spends as much as fifty-five hours per week together. Many parents do not object to this pattern of behavior; as a matter of fact, some mothers seem to expect and urge their young daughters to enjoy this youthful dalliance.

On the other hand, the girls form friendship cliques among themselves, and the boys form gangs. These groups are small, but their internal social interaction is frequent and intense and devoid of any serious purpose. When they have enough money, they may attend the movies where the individual sometimes slips away from the group and sits with one of the opposite sex. This usually happens when parents have forbidden their children to have dates or have restricted the permissible number of dates per week.

These adolescents are frivolous rather than immoral. The young parishioners do not for the most part become involved in juvenile delinquency,[10] and they have a very good record for attendance at Mass and the reception of the sacraments. The dating system and the gang system have become institutionalized apparently because there is no "better" way of spending their time. This is symptomatic of the almost functionless role of adolescence in urban American society. If they do not follow these customs, they lose status among their peers, and the adolescents are influenced much more by their companions than by their teachers or parents. They are horizontal conformists even when they appear to be vertical rebels.

Adolescents participate in parochial youth organizations only on their own terms. They can be induced to take part in athletic programs but not in religious and spiritual programs. A reputation for piety gives little prestige in the secularized culture of adolescence. This does not mean that no youth defies the patterns. There are some who do, and they are recognized immediately as exceptions. They seem to lose whatever influence they might have had for changing the mores of the whole youth group. It is these exceptions who are usually the most faithful members of parochial youth organizations, and their refusal to conform to the institutionalized patterns is a partial explanation for the failure of the organized parochial groups to attract membership.

The way in which the youth status has been institutionalized helps to account for the fact that these youngsters from thirteen to sixteen are neither serious nor responsible. Any pretensions they may make for mature consideration are ridiculed by adults. Parents complain that these young people are irresponsible, that their ideas are silly, and that their behavior is erratic; but at the same time the parents will not trust the youths with responsibilities or discuss serious problems with them, and as often as not they set an example of erratic behavior themselves. It appears also that the priests and teachers tend to belittle any serious or radical idea by which the youth may seem to threaten the cultural status quo. These young people are thus persuaded to live up to the expectations of the culture as expressed also by adults.

10. This does not mean that there are no Catholic juvenile delinquents in the parochial areas studied. The observations of this chapter are based on the study of youthful parishioners who were mainly from modal families.

The role of adolescence is a difficult one in a society where adolescents are not socially esteemed or really needed. The transition from childhood to adulthood is unnecessarily prolonged, and the rites of passage which clearly distinguish the arrival at manhood and womanhood in primitive cultures are missing in our urban society. The so-called revolt of youth in the face of this social situation is not always a question of morality. The young people simply feel that they do not "fit in," that they are not wanted by adults. For example, they may like to gamble in an innocent way, but they hesitate to participate in the bingo and keeno parties organized by the parish. They shy away from any program which is organized by the priests and other adults of the parish, because they feel that the older people do not understand them.

The absence of adolescents in the organized societies of the parish probably indicates that they are marginal to the adult culture.[11] They seem to question subconsciously the kind of culture for which they are supposed to be preparing themselves. They have little appreciation for the values expressed by the parish societies; they are not interested in their activities; they are uncomfortable with the people who compose them. Standing on the threshold of these groupings, they are highly critical of them, and this may well be the reason why so many of them remain marginal to organized parochial programs when they grow older. Older parishioners with insight sometimes appreciate this fact and give suggestions for interesting and involving younger people in the parish societies.[12]

2. The *occupational status* of adult male parishioners is a second source for the interpretation of the cultural environment. The main function of the occupational role is personally interpreted as the provision of material essentials for the individual and his family. In the practical economic order, however, this function is culturally translated into one which emphasizes the contribution of the worker to the whole productive economy. The apparently simple goal of working for a living by producing economic goods and services is also surrounded by various and complex institutionalized patterns of thought and behavior which the individual is expected to follow. These patterns are relatively compulsive and cannot be ignored.

11. Youth is in some respects "an outsider," does "not take the established order for granted and has no vested interests either in its economic or in its spiritual order" (see Karl Manheim, *Diagnosis of Our Time* [London: Kegan Paul, 1943], p. 36).

12. See above (chap. 3) for the suggestions made by lay parochial leaders for the development of their successors, p. 32.

After all, the man must make a living in the milieu in which he lives, and he cannot segregate himself from its expectations.

In the urban white parishes which we have studied, the majority of employed males are wage-earners in the lower middle class. Whether they are in white-collar positions, service jobs, skilled or semiskilled work, they are subjected to relatively similar "demands of the job." They are regimented according to hours, place, and conditions of work, and, since most of them are not organized in labor unions, they have little voice in establishing the obligations and privileges of their occupations. They exchange their labor for money wages roughly in proportion to their productive capacity. They are culturally orientated to think of their working hours as much more important than their leisure hours and of their occupational role as paramount to their familial, religious, political, and other roles.

Attitudes toward the material standard of living are culturally related to this economic emphasis. The institutionalized patterns of thought and behavior in this urban society tend to exaggerate the importance of an increasing material standard of living. The "latest" and the "most improved" commodities, utensils, and furnishings are purchased (or at least desired) to replace others which may be perfectly serviceable but not so up to date. Economic emulation subtly and powerfully replaces spiritual or intellectual processes. The "success ideal" which is widely current in the American urban culture does not escape Catholic men, and all the channels of social control (radio, television, movies, newspaper and magazine advertisements) tend to keep this ideal before them. Anything which goes contrary to this idea—as the fulness of Christianity certainly does—is not widely and *practically* acceptable in the urban neighborhood.

It may be said, therefore, that the expected behavior of the employed adult male is largely fixed for him by institutionalized forces outside himself. In so far as he accepts them and exemplifies these, he is also an influence on his fellow-workers. The more successful he is in his occupation, the more likely he will be to believe in these material economic ideals and to urge them upon others. The values contained in the successful fulfilment of the occupational role are shown also in the kind of example which these male adults provide for their children and other members of the family. The exaggerated importance of economic success in this commercial milieu influences fathers to send their children to business colleges rather than to liberal arts colleges and to convince their sons and daughters that they must prepare for well-paying occupations and must cultivate friends who will be helpful in an economic rather than a spiritual sense. Thus the norms of the properly functioning paternal role are influenced—and largely evaluated—by the standards of the occupational role.

The connection between the occupational and the sacramental activities of the adult male may at first glance appear to be a tenuous one. But the fact is that the men who are pursuing this economic ideal by following the expected patterns of their status have neither the time nor the interest to participate in the genuine spiritual life. It is no mere accident that Catholic male parishioners between the ages of thirty and forty-five years have a lower record in the reception of the sacraments of confession and Communion than any other age-sex category. Other partial explanations for this negative phenomenon have been noted—the complications of a growing family, the possibility of birth control, etc.[13]—but the involvement in occupational demands seems to be one of the principal factors.

Except for those men who work on Sunday mornings, it cannot be said that employment activities directly and immediately interfere with the reception of the sacraments. This is precisely why it is so important to analyze the content of occupational status as a composite of institutionalized ways of thinking and acting. The excuse for infrequent reception of the sacraments is not immediately attributable to the man's occupation, and so the explanation must be found in the status and role surrounding the actual work. The cultural expectation is that the worker will be too tired, too preoccupied, or too busy about "important" things to give much time and thought to the sacramental life. Voluntary, time-consuming, spiritual activities are not consonant with an ethos which develops gainful occupation as the key status of the adult male.

These generalizations are more or less confirmed by the example of the very men who appear to be exceptions to them. The relatively few male Catholics who are actively engaged in parochial societies and programs are also either relatively unsuccessful in their economic pursuits or will participate only in those parochial activities which have a commercial aspect. They are found, for example, in the ushers' societies, which usually have as their main function the collection of money, and in the special committees which may be occasionally formed by the parish priests to meet some financial crisis of the parish. They consider these activities to have a "real

13. See above, chap. 7, "The Religious Life-Profile."

value," and they esteem the priest who can successfully direct them as a "real businessman," the highest accolade they can bestow upon a member of the clergy.

This state of mind allows little room for the appreciation of those liturgical practices in the home which extend and enrich the whole sacramental economy of the Church. These practices seem to be reviving gradually and sporadically in the families of professional people and of apostolic persons who take a serious interest in the refinement and development of various forms of religious behavior. Families which "go in" for Mass preparation, communal recitation of grace at meals, the expression of seasonal moods, and the celebration of specific religious festivals are not headed by the type of adult male worker we are here describing. These practices seem to him somewhat odd, even suspect, because they are not contained among the formalized patterns of religion with which he has been acquainted. To his mind they are not realistic, worth while, useful, or important.

3. The *class status* of adult women is a third matrix of institutionalized patterns of thought and conduct which affects the religious life of parishioners. The class structure of the city parish which we have studied is almost identical with the class structure of the urban white secular community in which the parishes exist.[14] It is no exaggeration to say that the same cultural values exist in both and that the same criteria are employed to establish the position of people in the structure. This refers to the way in which people think about social strata and not to the classification which might be made through the use of spiritual and religious norms of behavior.[15] Thus there is a fairly large segment of the adult female population among urban Catholics who accept and exemplify the institutionalized patterns of the larger society. The class status of these married women is of course the same as that of their husbands, and the women under consideration here are the wives of the lower-middle-class male workers mentioned above.

Women, for the most part, are the culture-bearers of any society. Because of their numbers, their class status, and their strategic position as wives and mothers, most of the women we are here discussing may be said to be representative of the culture in which

14. For example, the rough scheme of four socioeconomic classes which we employed in the previous chapter can be duplicated in the general white community.

15. We are not using here the stratification of Catholic parishioners into the categories nuclear, modal, marginal, and dormant.

they live. An analysis of their social behavior and relations reveals the fundamental value system of the community in which they live. They express the ethos of a community in ways related to, and in support of, the status which their family enjoys.

At the same time the behavioral content of the class status is largely formed and influenced by the cultural environment. For example, the aspiration for a higher standard of living is one of the most forceful motives for the conduct of women in this group, and it is one which is commonly approved and promoted in the larger society. The women tend to form social cliques which help them to maintain their class status and which may be a springboard for higher status. Certain expectations of the status are easily recognized and are almost unconsciously followed. The woman must have sufficient leisure to demonstrate that she is not of the lowest working class; and this means that there must be a Negro maid or cook at least for part-time work in the home.[16] Having a telephone and radio is taken for granted, but the family should also possess a television set and various household appliances and, if at all possible, an automobile. These are all symbols of a rising standard of living and are not necessarily objects which of themselves give enjoyment and utility.

The cultural environment has been so thoroughly impregnated with the value of upward social mobility that many of these women are not even aware of its impact upon their religious beliefs and practices. It would probably be difficult to convince them that there is anything morally questionable in their attitudes or that there could be any significant connection between ideal Christian values and these real cultural patterns. The influence of prevalent culture norms on their status, and consequently on their behavior, may be seen in the manner in which the social virtues of charity, neighborliness, and justice are practiced. These are certainly important components of religious life, even though they are not so formal and measurable as organizational participation by adolescents and the reception of sacraments by adult males.

In the first place, the presence of a lower caste, the Negroes, and the traditional white attitude toward them, have almost institu-

---

16. This pattern is gradually changing as the housewives acquire labor-saving household devices and as the wages of domestic servants increase. But it is still largely true, and any socially aspiring family must at least have a "girl" to take care of the smaller children.

tionalized a social habit of injustice.[17] With hardly a conscious awareness that they are doing so, these women can "take advantage" of the situation and exploit their own social status. The caste line prescribes certain institutionalized modes of conduct between whites and Negroes, so that the social status of the white woman is protected. Their refusal to consort "socially" with Negro women, or to allow their own children to play with Negro children, implies a culturally established attitude of superiority which is hardly consonant with the personal belief in universal Christian charity.

The demands of class status include the fact that the woman knows and maintains her own place in relation to other groupings. According to this evaluation, there are also certain white people who are not "nice." They may live in the same block, and they certainly live within the territory of the normal urban residential parish. These neighbors may have achieved a high degree of spiritual perfection, but sanctity is a seldom-used criterion in the interpretation of social stratification. Strangely enough, the woman of whom we speak may be willing to act as an emissary from one of the parish eleemosynary groups to a needy lower-class family, but the thought of spontaneous, familiar neighborliness to the poor does not occur to her.

Even when the neighbors are of the same social class, these adult females do not spontaneously offer assistance. Nor do they expect any in return, except, perhaps, in instances of extreme necessity, as accident or sudden death. Generally speaking, their attitude is that, if the neighbors have sickness in the family, they should hire a nurse; if they need someone to watch the children for a few hours, they should hire a baby-sitter. The fences between the adjoining properties should be kept in good repair, and everyone should "mind his own business." In fact, the concept of a willing neighbor always ready to assist others is interpreted in one of two ways: either the woman is an inquisitive interferer or she is a foolish person unacquainted with the standardized habits of the community.

In a broad sense this lack of Christian charity, justice, and neighborliness may be said to be a function of the so-called process of atomization and anonymity which seems characteristic of urbanization.[18] The insistance on the "right to choose one's own friends"

17. This is analogous to the so-called subconscious pattern of illegality which persists in a selective manner wherever a community includes large numbers of underprivileged persons.
18. This is, of course, an oversimplification of a very complex trend which involves the rationalization, opportunism, economic avarice, sensate satisfactions, as well as the shift in social relations, functions, structures, and values.

is an expression of class status and a means of maintaining it. The inhabitants of large, long-established cities multiply social strata much more rapidly than the people of small villages and towns. Urban Catholic parishioners, especially the women with the greatest stake in social status, have not escaped this influence. Only the relatively static woman who is unwilling or unable to follow the expectations of her class position may be found trying to pursue the Christian social virtues to their fulness. Some of these do exist in the urban parishes, but they are the exceptions. The general fact is that the large majority conform to the institutionalized class patterns and neglect the social virtues which are implied in the Christian religion.

In conclusion it must be noted that a complete analysis of the institutional influence of social status upon the religious behavior of individuals is much more complex than it may seem from the above discussion.[19] It involves a conflict between the religious institution and a series of secular institutions, between the perennial Christian value system and the volative 'secular value system, as well as between the individual Catholic and the various institutional complexes in which he exists.[20] In this area of social research, where the social facts are so numerous and involved, there must necessarily be a selection of the pertinent facts to be discussed. This process of selection may result in a distorted picture so that the actual reciprocal relation between environment and individual may appear to be one-sided.

The popular belief that the individual is the complete dominator of his environment is also a one-sided misinterpretation of the social facts. The institutional environment has a much greater impact on human behavior than most Christians seem willing to admit. On the other hand, unless resistance to this environment were possible on the part of individuals, there would probably be very little social change. The interesting fact of American urban life is that there is also a conformity to change, and this social change seems to be proceeding in the direction away from religious patterns toward secular patterns of behavior. For this reason, the holy and intelligent lay persons in the urban parishes who recognize the influence

19. See my article, "Institutional Environment and Religious Life," *Lumen Vitae*, VI, Nos. 1–2 (1951), 166–72, of which the present chapter is a further development.

20. It would be absurd to deduce a theory of laissez faire inactivity from the emphasis which has been placed on institutional influence in this chapter. A central thesis of Christianity is that people *can* be agents of social reform and personal perfectibility.

of the institutional environment are compelled to go against a lively trend. The difference between the static and the dynamic conceptualization is analogous to the difference between the man who pushes a heavy weight off his chest and the man who swims against a strong current.

The study of urban parishes suggests that the individual lay person can be greatly helped in his religious behavior by the reformation and repatterning of the various social statuses and roles. At the present time personal resistance to cultural environment as contained in these statuses almost demands the price of idiosyncracy. Status resistance means the development of new cultural patterns that are shared in each category by at least a few adolescents, a few male workers, and a few adult females. Any intelligent program which aims at religious and social reform can hardly escape this sociological reality.

PART III

Social Relations and Structures

Chapter Ten

Social Roles of the Parish Priest

THE priest is the key person in any Catholic parish, and his role in the functioning of the parochial system is so important that without him the parish would cease to exist. From the sociological point of view, he is the most essential of the four elements in the canonical definition of the parish.[1] The concept of a "religion without a priesthood," or of a religion in which the ministers of God are merely employees, directors, or supervisors of congregations, is completely alien to the religious institution of Catholicism. All parochial activities, strictly so called, directly or indirectly depend upon the priest. They touch upon him in some way even when they do not completely revolve around him.

The number of priests assigned to any parish varies according to its size and needs and according to the availability of priests in the diocese. The normal city parish in America usually has three or four priests, although there may also be one or more in residence whose chief function may be nonparochial but who occasionally "help out" by celebrating Sunday Mass, going on a sick call, or hearing confessions in the parish.[2] It must be noted, however, that there is only one designated pastor, who bears the heaviest and ultimate responsibility for the operation of the parish. The other priests are his assistants, or curates, ranked by seniority, according either to their date of ordination or to their date of appointment to the parish.

In this analysis of the priestly roles in the parish system we omit the distinction between pastor and curates and base our generali-

1. See above, chap. 2, pp. 18–20. Cf. also *Dynamics of a City Church*, Vol. I of *Southern Parish* (Chicago: University of Chicago Press, 1951), chap. 2, "What Is the Parish?"

2. These priests may be primarily engaged in any of a variety of extraparochial tasks; they may be staff members of the diocesan newspaper, hospital chaplains, directors of youth movements, superintendents of education, university students and teachers, etc.

zations on the composite activities of many urban parish priests. We exclude here the role of part-time assistants whose principal priestly function is nonparochial. The status of the parish priest is quite different from that of the priest who teaches in a seminary, gives missions and retreats, edits a paper or magazine, or acts as a military or institutional chaplain. The parish priest is in a traditionally stable position, whose status is fixed by canonical prescription and whose function is regulated by traditional usage and by synodal decrees. The fact that he has closer relations with a larger number of people over a longer period of time tends to make his position sociologically more significant than that of the nonparochial priest.

This does not mean to attribute a lack of importance to the social and religious function of the extraparochial priest. We shall see later[3] that the urban Catholic laity associates for religious purposes in interest groups and in vocational groups, as well as in parish societies, and that priests participate actively in these various forms of social relations. Cardinal Suhard seems to appreciate this fact when he points out the immense complexity and wide variability of the priest's position in contemporary society. While all priests share a common, sacrament-orientated function in that the two central sacerdotal powers are the celebration of Mass and the forgiving of sins, they perform also many other nonsacramental functions.

The Cardinal writes that "the sacerdotal function, always in essence the same, can take, and has in fact taken in the course of the ages different forms and functions, in which stress is laid in turn on its royal, prophetic, or sacrificial character. Thus it is that a priest, and more particularly a bishop, has become at different times paterfamilias, ruler, defender of the city, regent, judge, and so on."[4] This indicates a historical pliability in the sacerdotal role, not limiting it to the sacraments, the sanctuary, and the sacristy. The same interpretation, from a wider historical perspective, is given by Wach. "Through his regular dealings with a group of people or individuals who come to him, rely on him, and depend on him for the performance of necessary cultic acts, the priest becomes a guide, adviser, comforter, 'pastor,' and 'confessor.' Through this immediate and intimate contact the priest exerts the tremendous influence to which the history of civilization bears witness. This influence was originally

3. See below, chap. 11, for the discussion on lay associations.
4. Emmanuel Cardinal Suhard, "Priests among Men," in *The Church Today* (Chicago: Fides Publishers, 1953), p. 282.

primarily religious but extended soon into the moral, social, cultural, and political spheres."[5]

The present dynamic situation in the urban American parish seems to require not so much the emphasis of one role more than another as a simultaneous co-ordination of multiple roles. Sociologically, a social role is a combination of institutionalized patterns, that is, of recurrent uniformities of thought and behavior centering around a social need.[6] These patterns are formed partly by historical ways of doing things and partly by the exigencies of the particular circumstances. In the case of the parish priest they are strongly influenced by the culture of the local community as well as by the wider doctrinal and empirical culture of the Catholic Church.

Since the main objective of the Church on earth is the sanctification and salvation of souls, it is obvious that the primary and all-embracing role of the parish priest must be a religious one. In his relationship with parishioners, the priest plays this religious role by the fulfilment of two predominant functions: that of mediator and that of father. Certainly these two functional and transcendental characteristics are expected wherever priests are at work, and nowhere so much as in the modern urban parish.[7]

The concept of the priest as a *mediator* has most commonly signified his pivotal function as the spiritual pleader between God and the people, a kind of channel through whom supernatural life flows to the laity, a sort of distribution center for sanctifying grace. This factual situation does not merit the naïve interpretation sometimes given to it—that the Catholic laity "is not permitted to pray directly to God"—but it does mean that the laity requires the

---

5. Joachim Wach, *Sociology of Religion* (Chicago: University of Chicago Press, 1944), p. 366. He adds that, in spite of all these external roles, "the parochial work of the parish priest, however, and the quiet and profound influence of this type of spiritual leadership have always been more far-reaching than all his 'official' activity in public affairs" (*ibid.*, p. 367).

6. See Ralph Linton, *The Study of Man* (New York: Appleton-Century Co., 1936), p. 114, where he says that "a role represents the dynamic aspect of a status"; and John Bennett and Melvin Tumin, *Social Life, Structure and Function* (New York: A. A. Knopf, 1948), p. 52: "The behavior expectations which attach to the various places or statuses an individual occupies are collectively described as the role." The role is also a container and expresser of cultural values (see above, chap. 9).

7. There are many wider roles than that of the parish priest. Young offers the following interesting roles which the religious functionary may follow, according to the activity performed: teacher, missionary, religious executive, mystic, prophet (Kimball Young, *Sociology* [New York: American Book Co., 1942], pp. 488 ff.).

spiritual ministrations of the clergy.[8] After all, the parish priest is the minister of the sacraments, the celebrant of Masses, and the voice of God in the pulpit, and it is for this that he was ordained by the bishop.

The *fatherliness* of the parish priest is the pastoral attitude in the care of souls; it is the concern of the shepherd for his flock. It is connoted in the "fatherly" counsel and assistance which the priest provides in the moral and personal problems of his parishioners. Besides sacramental confession, which is a completely confidential relationship, the priest's paternal function is characteristically thought of now as that of a "trouble-shooter." He is expected to "do something" about the drunken husband, the delinquent boy, the unchaste wife, the girl in trouble. These are sporadic problems involving for the most part parishioners whom the priest hardly knows. Each of them stresses a person-to-person relationship on the basis of an individual problem.

The individualization, or "atomization," of urban social life has extended to the Catholic parish, so that the old-fashioned concept of the parish as "one big happy family" is now practically extinct. The ordinary day-by-day routine of the big-city parish has now become largely formalized, with office hours in the rectory and a schedule of appointments to facilitate the multitude of priest-parishioner contacts. Paradoxically, while the influences of religion have been dwindling in the family life of parishioners, the number of functions have been multiplying in the official life of the parish priest.

The two principal functions of mediator and father seem to have become subdivided and specialized in the quickened modern life of the urban Catholic parish. In the more leisurely era of the past, and in those places where the neighborhood and the community were a social reality, it was comparatively easy for the priest to fulfil the "social" implications of his role as mediator and father. The *mediator* role was centered in the larger liturgical programs, elaborate processions, Sunday vespers, frequent Solemn High Masses, and evening devotions, which the parishioners willingly attended in large numbers. In his role as *spiritual father* the parish priest had closer contacts with families and neighborhoods. He knew the social back-

8. The ways in which the central religious functions are performed by priest and people in the normal parish are described in *Dynamics of a City Church*.

ground of individual parishioners. He could "stay with" a problem case until the wayward boy or girl was reintegrated into the family. He could personally help a husband to find a job, and meanwhile he could provide economic assistance to the family. All this has changed, and the priest's influence on the moral and social behavior of Catholics has greatly diminished since his relationship with them has become relatively depersonalized.[9]

The modern city priest is challenged by a whole complex of functional demands which appear to require a corresponding complexity and expansion of the basic transcendental roles of mediator and father. For purposes of analysis we have selected two generic roles and seven specific roles out of this total complex which undoubtedly contains many more. Usually, these cannot be allocated to the different curates serving in the parish but must be shared by all, with the heaviest weight of responsibility resting upon the pastor. It need hardly be added that this process is an analytical abstraction consonant with the elaboration of parochial functions. It does not suggest that these "newer" roles supplant the basic and transcendental function of the priest.

Throughout the discussion of these various roles two generalized factors must be assumed as constantly present. The first is the peculiar social structure of the modern city with its predominantly associational and secondary types of group relations. The second is the development of the patterns of the sacerdotal roles in the midst of two conflicting value systems: the ways of the world as accepted and practiced by the parishioners and the ways of God as taught and striven for in the Church.

a) For want of a better term we here use the phrase "the *communal* role of the parish priest" to describe the generic concept according to which the priest-parishioner relationship becomes socialized. While the priest realizes that many of the social bonds which once held the parishioner to the local Church have been weakened, he knows also that this has not diminished the status of the parishioner as a social person. In pursuing his communal role, the priest attempts to accept the parishioner for what he is in the community: a social being with all kinds of *related* bonds and functions and needs. In other words, in order to know and assist the *whole*

9. "Counseling" is still a large part of the priest's function, but the "cases" have multiplied so greatly and other demands on the priest's time have so increased that the "follow-up" is now almost impossible.

person, he tries to know the parishioner in his social context as a member of a family, of a neighborhood, and of occupational, recreational, and other groups.

Regardless of the so-called atomization of modern industrial and urban society, the individual must necessarily be involved in a matrix of social relations. This factual observation belies what Mayo calls the "rabble hypothesis" which for many years "has bedeviled all our thinking on matters involving law, government, or economics."[10] It bedevils also the priest who thinks of his parishioners in terms of so many Communions, or so many confessions, as well as the parishioner who thinks in terms of purely "personal" religion to the neglect of its communal aspect. Sociologists and anthropologists have everywhere found that at the very bases of society are innumerable small formal and informal groupings of people. The parish priest cannot allow himself to accept what Wach calls the "rationalistic hypothesis of the isolated individual which formerly played a considerable part in social and political philosophy" and which now has been abandoned.[11]

From this point of view, the components of the Catholic parish are not primarily its individual parishioners but its subgroupings. That is to say, the parish priest plays a communal or group role toward his parishioners. He participates in a definite *social* relationship with the parishioner as a member of various groups and not merely in an *individual* relationship with him as an unattached person. In the modern urban parish the parishioner too, like the priest, is faced with a complex of roles which he exercises by virtue of his character as a social being.

It is beyond the scope of this present chapter to study in detail the part which priests play in all the informal cliques and groups of the urban parish. No individual priest can participate in all of them, but three or four priests in the same parish can have collective knowledge of, and contact with, almost all of them. Each of the priests is closer to some families and friendship groups than to others. Some of these social relationships are within the parish; some are in other parishes. Through these informal contacts the priests' knowledge of the parish and of its problems is broadened. This is not in

10. Elton Mayo, *The Social Problems of an Industrial Civilization* (Cambridge: Harvard University Press, 1945), p. 44.
11. *Op. cit.*, p. 58. See also below, chap. 12, on the social structure of parish organizations.

every case merely a matter of visiting for the sake of the priest's relaxation and recreation. Theoretically, the parish priest is "always on duty," and the extent to which this generic communal role is utilized toward supernatural objectives depends largely upon the priest's own insight and his enthusiasm for God's service.

The performance of this communal role has been institutionalized in various ways. Immigrants from rural to urban parishes express regret that the priest seldom visits their home or stops to chat with them on the street or at the church door. Some indicate that the priest "plays favorites" in his social contacts; others complain that class selection is the basis of the priest's visits to homes. Very few large urban parishes can boast of a conscientious biannual census, in which the priests themselves call on every family in the parish.

It is obvious that informal contact with city Catholics outside the rectory is limited not only by the many other demands on the priest's time and energy but also by the relatively irregular habits of the urban family. On Sundays and on weekday nights the parish priest is likely to be busiest with duties about the church and rectory, but these are also the only periods when the family is likely to be at home together. In spite of these limitations, however, the priest cannot successfully exploit his communal role if he comes to be known as simply a "rectory priest" or a "sacristy priest."

b) The *administrative* role of the parish priest here refers to the fact that he must be an organizer and manager of the social relations and structures which center in the parish. This active interest in the innumerable social groupings of parishioners may be more sharply analyzed when it is focused on the formal subgroupings of the parish. In the power structure of the Catholic Church the appointed priest must exercise a supervisory functional relationship with all the parochial societies. This duty of the priest is not so haphazard or indefinite as his generic social role toward informal cliques and groupings seems to be. Since the rules, norms, practices, and goals of these societies are relatively well known among the parishioners, the part which the priest plays in them can be quite clearly defined.

From the structural point of view it does not suffice to say that the pastor "runs the parish." He is also ex officio a sort of superpresident and supertreasurer of all the official constituted societies of the parish. These societies are usually "divided up" among the priests of the urban parish, but the pastor may step in at any time, take over any meeting, and change any plans as he sees fit. The experienced, successful pastor seldom does this but delegates authority to the curate in charge and allows a wide range of autonomy and responsibility to the lay members of the groups.

But even the fairly simple supervisory concept of the administrative role is complicated by several social facts: the societies have different immediate objectives, varying degrees of successful participation, membership of sharply differing personalities, and peculiar traditional patterns of action. Thus, the administrative or organizational role of the priest cannot in every instance be fixed and simplified by his own decisions. It is largely determined by the type of society in which it is employed. For example, the priestly role approach required by the Boy Scouts is quite different from that needed in the Ladies' Altar Society.

It may be said of course that the administrative role must operate in practically all the activities in which priest and parishioner participate together. Exceptions are found in the person-to-person relationship of the confessional, counseling, and advice. But even these, in a sense, have to be organized. Because of the variety of demands made by the formal subgroupings of the parish, the priest's administrative role must be further defined. The analytical specification of the administrative role which seems most logical is probably that which coincides with the general goals of the various parochial groupings. While the communal and administrative roles are generic, the further subdivision of priestly roles is specific.

c) The *businessman* role is an example of the "newer" demands on the priest's time, ingenuity, and patience. The minimum requirement here is the raising and administering of funds for the maintenance of the parish plant. Bishops no longer accept slipshod financial reports that have been carried around under the pastor's hat. While it is true that a pastor has the assistance of two lay trustees and usually seeks the advice of bankers and brokers, it is he (and not the laymen) who has the ultimate financial responsibility of keeping the parish solvent. Every expenditure for the church building, rectory, school, and convent, all the salaries of workers, and the disbursements for charitable and other activities must be checked by him. This responsibility extends also to the treasuries of the various parochial organizations under his charge.[12]

The patterns of behavior in the businessman's role have been set in the predominantly commercial culture of the large city. The

12. See below, chap. 14, for the discussion of legal and financial limitations on pastors.

priest is strongly tempted—in fact, is often forced—to follow these patterns almost exactly. Some parishioners consider it high praise of the priest when they concede that "he's a good businessman." This is probably what Cardinal Suhard had in mind when he wrote that "the parish in a large community is supposed to constitute a spiritual community, but this spiritual community is weighed down by out-dated practices, and paralyzed by administrative cares with little or no relation to the spread of the Kingdom of God."[13]

The priest is here in the midst of the old dilemma of God or mammon. The large urban parish requires that he be a financier; he must be a money-gatherer; he must pay the debts. Many a priest has been dismayed by the inroads which the business role has made on the spiritually more important priestly roles. Not only is it time-consuming but it is worrisome; and, worst of all, it obtrudes on the spiritual values and the supernatural goals of the whole religious institution. Success in this role, as measured by the standards of the commercial world, is almost never achieved except at the expense of higher personal and spiritual values. As one priest has remarked, "Matthew may be the businessman's saint, but he became a saint only after he stopped collecting money."

d) The *civic* role of the priest is also a necessary distraction from his more immediate parochial concerns. As a respected and influencial citizen of the community, the priest is sometimes expected and at other times forced to play a large part in the community activities. He may be called upon to co-operate with mayors' committees, rotarians' projects, and voters' leagues. He may be asked to sponsor every kind of program from new playgrounds to better street lights, from patriotic parades to garbage-disposal plants.

There is no question that the priest is the symbol and interpreter of Catholicism to the various nonsectarian groups in the community.

13. Emmanuel Cardinal Suhard, *Growth or Decline?* (South Bend: Fides Publishers, 1948), Appendix A, p. 107. This appendix does not appear in the 1953 edition of his writings, *The Church Today.* In his provocative chapter, "The Clink of Money round the Altar," Michonneau says that the chief obstacle in bringing Christ to the people is "the firmly-rooted belief that religion is nothing but a business affair. . . . Almost everyone believes that priests are after money, that religion is a 'racket' " (G. Michonneau and H. Ch. Chéry, *Revolution in a City Parish* [Oxford: Blackfriars Publications, 1949], p. 120. In another place, Cardinal Suhard remarks that "the temptation, however, can be great for the priest, to assume functions other than his own, and for which the laity havé a special vocational grace. He will have to resist it, even if, for the moment 'efficiency' is somewhat reduced. For his specific role never involves the running of temporal order. There his competence ceases" ("Priests among Men," in *The Church Today*, p. 292).

He has the difficult task of being a reformer without being a "busy-body," a congenial citizen without being "one of the boys"; in other words, he has the task of preserving the dignity and charity of the priesthood in a situation which is frequently charged with acrimony and distrust. Sometimes the moral choice is easy, but the voice of a pressure group may be insistent. He may find himself torn between the property interest of landlords who demand restrictive zoning laws and the human interests of the underprivileged who need low-rent housing.

The priest's off-the-cuff remarks about political leaders and political situations may have unexpected repercussions. The bosses of political machines frequently like to do "favors for Father," with the more or less subtle expectation that Catholic votes will be thereby influenced. The involvement of the priest with these openhanded political figures may be a source of embarrassment to the Church. Because of such connections, the priest may have difficulty in speaking publicly about civic conditions which need to be exposed and reformed.

e) The *recreational* role does not refer specifically to the priest's personal relaxation in bowling, golf, or handball but to the fact that the priest has an organizational function toward parish groups which are recreational or athletic in their objectives. In a much broader sense, of course, the parish priest is interested in the physical welfare of all his parishioners and not merely of those who are formed into teams and clubs. He has more definite obligations toward the playground activities of the school children, their physical education periods, and their organized school teams.

It usually falls to the lot of the youngest curate to guide the athletic and recreational groups of the parish. If the parish has competent scout leaders and den mothers, lay coaches and trainers, this task of the priest is considerably lightened. But there is the further risk that competently directed sports programs become exceedingly successful and that this very success may tax the time and patience of the priest. The importance which parishioners often place upon these activities is usually out of all proportion to their value in the general supernatural functions of the Church.

This is a basic problem of relative values which constantly permeates the priest's role in parish athletics. To what extent are they worthy of his time and energy? To what extent do they act as a channel for attracting and holding the youth to the parish and for leading them to higher functions and aims? Parochial athletic programs tend to become standardized according to the attitudes of the priest in charge. This is not a question of understanding or appreciating sports. Most priests have had some early player experience on athletic teams and have a tempered evaluation of sports. The problem for him is a reflection of the general problem of recreational institutions in urban culture, wherein sports have become almost an end in themselves.

f) The priest's *ameliorative* role is considered here in relation to his organizational duties toward the groups which perform the corporal works of mercy. Of course, the priest operates also in a wider field through his personal charities to the needy and through his co-operation with diocesan and civic fund-raising drives for a large number of worthy causes. In most of these latter instances, however, the priest is merely a channel or contact between the extraparochial organizations and the people of the parish. This tends to be a function of the civic role discussed above.

There are usually two main parochial groups for the amelioration of needy cases; the men operate through the St. Vincent de Paul conference which exists in most urban parishes, while the women may belong to any one of a number of charitable societies. It is true also that all the other parish societies occasionally contribute to the poor, help orphans or old people, or come to the assistance of their own members in need. Depending upon the type of parish, whether it is in a better residential neighborhod or in a slum area, these groupings will have more or less work to do.

In one sense the manner in which the priest pursues this ameliorative role is the key to his own attitudes and interpretations of Christian social ethics. Patterns of behavior toward the poor and the destitute vary greatly in the business and commercial milieu of the American city. The priest is a constant target for "panhandlers." He may be softly gullible or toughly cynical. He may take the attitude that every case should be thoroughly investigated, or he may insist that openhanded generosity is the only Christian answer to poverty. Most priests seem to develop an intermediary pattern which avoids both extremes.[14]

g) The *educational* role of the parish priest is very broad in scope and in its larger aspects includes the teaching of Christian doctrine in the pulpit, in private counseling, and in the operation

14. For a discussion of this problem and a series of amusing anecdotes see *Roman Collar*, the true story of a New York priest, by Robert Moore (New York: Macmillan Co., 1950).

of the parochial school. It may be said that the priest is always the teacher of Christianity and that his essential evangelical activities are centered around the task of bringing the truth of Christ to the people. Both the long-term and the immediate preparation for the sacraments of Communion and confirmation must be supervised by the priest in the parochial school as well as the released-time program for public-school children.

The content of this role includes the whole range of techniques which have been devised by modern educators. The curates in a city parish usually do some teaching in the parochial school, and one of the priests is the moderator of the Parents' Club. The patterns of thought and behavior for the pursuit of these functions have become institutionalized by other existing schools and organizations in the city, and a certain degree of standardization comes also from the regulations and suggestions of the diocesan supervisor's office. The extent to which the priest can pursue the expectations of this role is limited mainly by the demands of his other roles.

The teaching abilities and educational success of the priest are popularly judged from his performance in the pulpit. The sermon at Sunday Mass is the only regular relationship which exists between the priest and most of the parishioners. It is a major source of esteem or disesteem for the whole status of the priest, because it is the single large aspect of the priest's behavior about which the parishioners talk the most. The good preacher is a good educator, and the good preacher attracts and influences the largest number of parishioners. This does not mean that the instructional functions in the confessional, the school, and the rectory are less important in any individual case. But, from the point of view of a social function, preaching is the principal test of the educational role of the priest.

b) The *sociospiritual* role is arbitrarily named here to specify the functions the priest performs with those groupings which are primarily spiritual in their goals. Large, formal organizations like sodalities and Holy Name societies, as well as small, informal Catholic Action clubs, are included under the priest's direction. Ideally, the members of these groupings may be viewed as people who want to "do something over and above" either the obligatory attendance at church services or the voluntary participation in the liturgical activities of the parish. Their primary spiritual aims are meant to be achieved through corporate action, and, because of this, the priest's participation is essentially a social role.

The priest's role in most of these organizations is mainly standard-

ized from outside the parish in the sense that plans and programs
are frequently supplied by diocesan and national headquarters.
There is a tendency, however, to wander away from the general
prescriptions and norms and to make local adaptations. This devia-
tion is most easily noted when a change of curates occurs, and
some of the membership remark that the previous priest director
"did not do things this way." The degree of spiritual vitality which
each priest brings to the group is an important factor in this role.

Since many other factors must be taken into consideration, it
would be unrealistic to assert that the degree of success achieved
by each of these spiritual groupings is proportionate to the functional perfection of the priest's role in each of them. This relation
between the priest's role and the group's success could be valid
only if the priest restructured the organizations according to the
operational principles of social science, for example, by multiplying
active nuclei in the Holy Name Society, by adapting and utilizing
the complete program for the sodality, by encouraging and obtaining lay responsibility in internal organizational activities, etc. Even
when all this has been done, however, spiritual lethargy must still
be considered a relatively constant factor in the modern urban
culture.

i) The *liturgical* role of the priest is primarily centered around
the religious services conducted in the parish church. These services,
unlike those of some non-Catholic religions, require the priest as a
functionary and are the public example of his role of mediator between God and man. But the assistance and participation of lay
people must be structured around this central priestly function,
directly by the acolytes and choir members, indirectly by the ushers
and the members of the Altar Society. To obtain this assistance, to
maintain and perfect it, the priest must be the supervisor of group
effort in the liturgical activities.

This functional role is not quite so simple as it may at first appear. Voluntary service is being contributed by human personalities
whose interests and motives must be guided and sublimated. The
choir member may be more intent on demonstrating his vocal
prowess than in singing praise to God; the usher may be so intent
upon filling the collection basket that he forgets to kneel at the
Consecration of the Mass. The priest's problem is also one of getting
people to work together, and this is often more difficult than the
problem of arranging beautiful church services.

The expectations of the parishioners are probably more influential on the liturgical role than on any other which the priests exercise. This is particularly true in a long-established parish where traditional customs take on almost a dogmatic force in the minds of the laity. The priest who has tried to inaugurate the Dialogue Mass or the use of missals in place of the singing of hymns or the recitation of the Rosary is sometimes looked at with suspicion by the older members of the congregation (not to say also by some of the older members of the clergy). The older altar boys may not like the way in which the new curate is training them. The problem of church music is still unsettled in many parishes in spite of the definite regulations from the Holy See. Thus the institutionalization of the liturgical role is derived not only from the direction of prescribed Church norms but also from the direction of the actual practices of the people.

Although we have said above that the priest is the key person in the parish, it is obvious from the discussion of the various priestly roles that the co-operation of the laity is essential. It cannot be said that the success or failure of the various aspects of parochial activities rests solely upon the manner in which the priests fulfil their roles. These roles always imply reciprocal relations of rights and duties, of patterns of thought and behavior, on the part of both clergy and laity. They also imply that the goals of organized effort in the parish are considered worthy of attainment by both priests and people. This is sometimes a source of psychological and social conflict especially when there is a contrast between the sacred and the profane functions of clergy and laity.

The multiple needs of the parish, as an aggregate of persons who are serving God and trying to save their souls, are therefore roughly correlated with the multiple-functioning roles performed by the priests. Throughout this whole analysis it is obvious that the personality and the abilities of the priest must be taken into consideration. While the ideal pattern may be a correlation between the priest's interest and competence and the specific roles assigned to him, it is often true that this ideal alignment does not exist. In parishes where there are three or four priests there may be some juggling of roles and persons so that the best results can be obtained. But no priest can do all things well. Some are excellent administrators; others are liturgical experts, youth leaders, preachers, builders, or public relations experts.

Two facts, however, stand out. The first is that each priest must have some minimum adeptness in each role. The second is that the priest must conform to the needs of the parish rather than insist upon doing only that for which he is best trained or in which he has the greatest talent and interest. It is a striking anomaly in an age of specialization that the parish priest (unlike trained personnel in other professions and occupations) is forced to maintain an adaptive readiness to be "all things to all men." The relatively simple functional specificity, which involves the performance of sacramental and liturgical rites, and which appears to be the primary focus of sociological attention, is the role which gives the least trouble to the priest. His sociologically complex problem arises when he is expected by the needs of parishioners to be expert in all the other functions, even while he is expected by the demands of the organizational structure to emphasize the technical managerial functions which maintain the parish as a going social concern.

In spite of these various difficulties, it is probably true to say that institutionalization on the parish level has made the priest's roles operative. In other words and in the ultimate analysis, these roles operate smoothly relative to the degree to which they have been systematized and regulated by repeated action. This does not mean that they must be (or even can become) wooden and immutable. As a matter of fact, it is a mark of well-functioning human relations between priests and people in a parish when a newly appointed priest can easily fit into the patterns set by his predecessor and when the priestly roles can easily adapt themselves to the changing needs of parochial groups.

Chapter Eleven

Social Relations of the Laity

THE conceptual approach employed in the *Southern Parish* study considered the Catholic parish as an instrument of social engineering. It discussed only briefly other instruments, such as radio, the press, and the collegiate system, which are successfully used by the Church in its evangelical mission. The hypothetical assumption there was that the local parish is the most important agency for stabilizing and re-Christianizing American urban culture and society.[1]

Without abandoning or minimizing this hypothetical approach,[2] it is possible also to think of the whole Catholic Church as a congeries of social groupings. This basic approach is introvert rather than extrovert; it looks at the internal fact that Catholics associate with one another rather than at the external objective that Catholicism "will bring others in the fold" and will influence Western civilization. We are here interested in the fact that, while the local parish may remain the primary type of association among lay Catholics, there are also several important nonparochial forms of association. In combination they constitute a kind of social typology of religious groupings for lay Catholics.

The literature of social science has become familiar with a re-

1. See *Dynamics of a City Church*, Vol. I of *Southern Parish* (Chicago: University of Chicago Press, 1951), chap. 1. The present chapter is based on an article, "Lay Social Relations," *Social Order*, II, No. 4 (April, 1952), 170–74.
2. Cardinal Suhard, the late great proponent of "new forms" of religious institutions, did not abandon the traditional approach. "All should be convinced that the parish is the best site for the apostolate. This institution—the first cell in the life of the diocese—is providentially commissioned to unite souls to the Body of the Church. In addition it is provided with the required organization for penetrating the masses. From which it follows that a living, active parish community, which is coherent in its activities, and strongly united with the diocese in which the plenitude of the priesthood and apostolic ministry resides, is the incomparable instrument for the expansion of the Christian life" (Emmanuel Cardinal Suhard, *The Church Today* [Chicago: Fides Publishers, 1953], p. 26).

ligious typology set up by Ernst Troeltsch and extended by Howard Becker and others. It started with the classic distinction between the church type and the sect type of religious association. The former tends to be catholic, compulsory, and conforming, in the sense that it tries to embrace everyone, to institutionalize its procedures, and to find a *modus vivendi* with the total society. The sect type tends to be small, voluntary, and spiritual, in the sense that it includes only the highly religious person who freely follows the promptings of the Holy Spirit and who tries to regain the original enthusiasm of Christianity.[3]

Howard Becker has added two more stages in this typology. He defines the denomination at a point somewhere between the ecclesia (or church) and the sect, saying that its members are less fervent than those of the sect but that its patterns are not so highly institutionalized as those of the church. He includes also the cult, which is smaller, more personal, and more mystical than the sect. If there is a chronological evolution in this typology, it is from cult to sect to denomination to ecclesia. There can be no doubt that under each of these headings many varieties of religious association may be subdistinguished.[4]

The social theorists who have constructed or who employ religious typologies recognize the fact that there is much overlapping among these classifications. "Cults frequently are much like sects, and it is extremely difficult to draw a line between the two—just as it is difficult to draw a line between the sect and the denomination."[5] This difficulty multiplies tremendously when one attempts a historical and universal approach to the problem, as was done by Wach in his *Sociology of Religion*.[6]

The investigation with which this chapter is concerned is much more modest than any of these. It confines itself only to the urban

3. Ernst Troeltsch, *The Social Teaching of the Christian Churches,* trans. Olive Wyon (New York: Macmillan Co., 1931), I, 331–36. See also H. Richard Niebuhr, *The Social Sources of Denominationalism* (New York: Henry Holt & Co., 1929), pp. 17–21, for a discussion of Troeltsch's distinction.

4. Leopold von Wiese and Howard Becker, *Systematic Sociology* (New York: John Wiley & Sons, 1932), pp. 624–28. See also the theoretical application of this typology to a research project by Liston Pope, *Millhands and Preachers* (New Haven: Yale University Press, 1942), pp. 117–40, and by J. Milton Yinger, *Religion in the Struggle for Power* (Durham, N.C.: Duke University Press, 1946), chap. ii, "A Typology of Religious Groups."

5. Von Wiese and Becker, *op. cit.,* p. 628.

6. Joachim Wach, *Sociology of Religion* (Chicago: University of Chicago Press, 1944). See especially his chap. v, "Specifically Religious Organization of Society," pp. 109–204.

laity of the Catholic Church in this country and suggests a typology of social groupings within those limits. It excludes the numerous religious orders, congregations, and societies of clerics, nuns, and brothers, who are canonically separated from the laity. It excludes also, on the other hand, the many groups and organizations to which Catholic lay persons belong but which are not primarily religious in their functions and objectives. Catholics are active in the Elks, chambers of commerce, country clubs, garden clubs, bowling teams, and many other secular associations, but they can hardly be said to belong to these qua Catholics.

Even when the problem under discussion is limited in this way, the basic difficulty of valid sociological classification still remains. What "principle of association" can be employed for the arrangement of a logical typology? On what norms may the groupings of urban Catholics be differentiated? If one sets up his norm of groupings on a continuum from the most fervent to the least fervent, or from the loosely structured to the highly structured, or from the smallest to the largest, he encounters the same difficulties which are found in the cult-ecclesia continuum.

In other words, the degree of religious fervor, the type of social structure, and the size of the group are not always correlated. Just as one finds fervently religious individuals in either ecclesia or cult, so also will he find loose structuring in both small and large groups. It is probably true that the small, informal, close-knit group can most effectively maintain its zealous and charismatic tone. But even here it seems that there are two further considerations: the time element and original impetus. Every pastor has noted with regret that the enthusiasm of the original founders of a group gradually wanes with the passage of time. The problem of "renewal of spirit" must be faced by all social groupings regardless of their values and goals.

Canon law indicates various types of lay associations by focusing on objectives toward which they may worthily strive. These associations may be constituted by the Church "either to promote a more perfect Christian life among its members, or for the undertaking of works of piety and charity, or finally, for the advancement of the public cult."[7] By specifying these acceptable objectives

---

7. Canon 685. The meaning of "public cult" is given in Canon 1256: "The cult which is exhibited and offered to God or to the Saints and Blessed, in the name of the Church by appointed ministers, in the form and manner prescribed by the Church, is called public, otherwise private."

and functions, the Church appears to be classifying lay organizations among Catholics.

These objectives specify the three types of lay associations which have their *ordo praecendentiae* as follows: (*a*) in the first place are the *tertii Ordines saeculares*, made up of lay people who live under the direction, and according to the spirit, of a religious Order, in the pursuit of Christian perfection.[8] (*b*) Second, there are *confraternitates*, which do works of piety and charity and have been established for the furtherance of public worship.[9] (*c*) Third, there are *piae uniones*, established to carry out some work of piety or charity.[10] (*d*) A fourth type of grouping, the *Secular Institutes*, was given canonical status in 1947 by Pope Pius XII in the Apostolic Constitution *Provida Mater*. The members profess the evangelical counsels, work full time in the Christian Apostolate, and have community headquarters.[11]

There is also a great variety of groups under each of these general headings, but all are characterized by highly formal organization, detailed norms and regulations, a carefully regulated system of communication and authority, and an official institutionalization. Because they differ so greatly in both the contemplative and the active aspects of their functions, these official groupings of lay persons can probably be measured and graded by different sociological norms: solidarity, values pursued, structure, function, etc. Furthermore, this typology is not all-inclusive. There are numerous groupings of Catholic lay people in urban America which do not fit into the canonical categories. For these reasons it seems useful to attempt another typology, or classification, of lay associations.

The three most general types of religious groups to which American lay Catholics belong are the following: (*a*) *parochial* groups, the basis of which is the fact that a person resides within a certain arbitrarily designated territory called a parish; (*b*) *interest* groups, which freely cut across parochial and even diocesan lines and for

8. Canon 702.
9. Canon 707, n. 2
10. Canon 707, n. 1.
11. See *Secular Institutes: A Symposium on the Modern Lay Community* (London: Blackfriars Publications, 1952), which contains the official papal documents; also the *Proceedings of the Conference on Secular Institutes, Held at Notre Dame University, January 26–27, 1952* (Chicago: Fides Publishers, 1952), which gives some American experiences of these institutes. Cf. the excellent discussion and bibliography in T. Lincoln Bouscaren and Adam C. Ellis, *Canon Law: A Text and Commentary* (2d rev. ed.; Milwaukee: Bruce Publishing Co., 1951), chap. xi, pp. 332–44.

which the lay person has a personal preference; and (*c*) *vocational* groups, to which the layman belongs because of a particular function and role he performs in the larger society.

There are three preliminary observations which must be made about all these groups. The first is that they are completely voluntary. Membership in the Catholic Church does not imply or demand affiliation with any of the numerous lay associations functioning within the Church. Second, it is probable that much less than half of all lay Catholics above the age of reason are in any way affiliated with these groupings. Active participation is limited to a much smaller percentage of the laity. Third, although membership is voluntary and relatively small, all the groups are subordinate directly or indirectly to the clergy and ultimately to the hierarchy of the Church.

a) The *parochial* principle of association among the Catholic laity seems to stem from the fact that all lay Catholics must necessarily live in a designated parish and that their most frequent social contacts are within the family and the neighborhood. It is a basic expectation that "the beliefs, the behavior, and the worship of the Catholic faith are exhibited here in the parish, or they simply are not exhibited at all."[12] Because of this residential necessity, the lay Catholic lives his faith, practices the Christian virtues of love and justice, and exemplifies Catholicism to his neighbors within the parish territory. But this is quite different from saying that he is an active and dedicated member of the parish as a social group or of any of the subsidiary groupings of the parish.

In another place we have also surmised that "the parochial system of the Church is the most likely sociological factor for strengthening the inner structure of the Church and for channelling the influence of Christianity to the larger community and nation." This was not meant to ignore the numerous other social structures within the Church or the other types of lay association, but it did suggest the hypothesis that "a vigorous parochial system bespeaks an internally strong Catholic social structure."

The principle of parochial association seems to indicate that a parishioner must first be a "local" Catholic before he can be a "universal" Catholic. From a chronological point of view this is probably correct, since most Catholics have their first childhood contact with the Church through their local parish. But in its application for adults the underlying persuasion seems to be that just

12. See *Dynamics of a City Church*, p. 8.

as charity begins at home so also loyal Catholicism begins in the parish. An extreme view is that the lay person must restrict himself completely in his Catholic activities and associations to his own parish. A moderate view is that he may indulge in supraparochial activities only if he has energy and enthusiasm left after having participated satisfactorily in the parochial activities.

Aside from the legalistic argument that the Church has through canon law assigned every lay person to a particularly designated parish, the strongest argument in favor of the principle of parochialism within the ecclesiastical structure is its analogy with the principle of familism within the total social structure. It is said that, since the family is the basic unit of society, "as the family goes, so goes the nation," and "if the family system is strong, the society is sound." Similarly it is said that, since the parish is the basic unit of the Church, "if the parish is well-integrated, the whole Church will be strong."

These aphorisms appear to be sociologically valid if they are understood to mean that face-to-face, multiple-functioning relationships and primary groupings form the basic network of the larger society. They are sociologically acceptable so long as they are not rigidly exclusive, or in so far as they do not lead to the conclusion that other forms of association are unnecessary, unimportant, or even somewhat "suspect." In the sense that the family and the parish can (or should) be the locus of socialization of the young and the laboratory of day-to-day social relations of adults, these units are undoubtedly basic to their respective social structures.

Because of the proximity and convenience of parochial organizations, and also because of a feeling of loyalty to the local parish, most lay Catholics who associate with one another in voluntary religious groupings do so on the parish level. They are drawn from the ranks of "nuclear" and "modal" parishioners,[13] and they are frequently encouraged by the pastors to participate in the various subsidiary functions of the parish. Besides the numerous groupings in which these functions are performed, there is always a solid inner core of Catholics in any parish who form a recognizable social group.

The limited sociological research in the urban parish system in this country reveals that the parish can no longer be conceived realistically as an *ecclesiola in ecclesia*, a sort of total Church in miniature. Nor can one say that only the layman who continuously

13. See the explanation of these terms above, chaps. 3 and 4.

and exclusively lives as a parishioner is "a truly living member of the visible body of Christ." Even if this were a desideratum for all lay Catholics, the fact is that it does not (and probably cannot) exist in our urban and industrialized society.

This is a point of crucial importance for an understanding of the distinction between the ideal and the real order of parochial relationships. What Falardeau says of Canada seems true also of our country: "The parish can fulfill its function ideally where it is superimposed upon an isolated community whose whole population not only is Catholic but can be easily held, without outside interference, under the complete control of the Church ministers. In a city, the parish church remains the locus of religious services, but the pattern of parochial relationships assumes new characteristics. . . . The parochial churches tend to become enterprises competing for a critical clientele, while their attending ministers become anonymous functionaries with whom only casual contacts are made."[14]

It is probably true, as Werner Schollgen points out, that the Christian ethos is not associational (*gesellschaftlich*) but communal (*gemeinschaftlich*). But this is like saying that the Christian spirit is in essence "cultic" rather than "ecclesiastic." In the urban areas, where the sense of communiy and of neighborliness on a territorial basis has largely vanished, the parish has become a secondary, associational type of social structure. Perhaps the social ideal may still be held that the parish should be communal, but our empirical studies clearly demonstrate that it is now largely associational.[15]

Priests and lay persons who are proud of their own parish, fiercely loyal to it, and jealous of their parochial prerogatives may insist upon the principle of parochialism in either its extreme or its moderate formulation. This insistence will probably be socially advantageous if they can restore their parish to a communal type of social structure. Meanwhile, however, two facts must be recognized: first, the urban American parish does not now fit this description and, second, the Church recognizes, urges, approves, and makes provision for other types of social relations, functions, and structures.

b) The *interest* groupings of lay urban Catholics may be called "preferential" groups brought together on the principle of free as-

14. Jean C. Falardeau, "Parish Research in Canada," in *The Sociology of the Parish*, ed. C. J. Nuesse and Thomas J. Harte (Milwaukee: Bruce Publishing Co., 1951), pp. 331–32.
15. This is indicated in the discussion below, chap. 14, secs. *b*, *c*, and *d*.

sociation rather than on the principle of parochial residence. The interest involved here is, of course, a religious one. While it is true that an individual Catholic may have a voluntary interest only in parochial societies, and join them freely and exclusively, it is also true that he may freely cut across the territorial, parochial lines and join groups which are not "parish-based."

The Third Orders, confraternities, and pious unions of which the canon law speaks are in some instances parochial and in others supraparochial. For example, a territorial parish which is administered by the Benedictine Fathers may attract nonparishioners to its Third Order. There is also the situation, envisaged in canon law, wherein there are two churches, one the parochial church, the other proper to the confraternity or pious union. The membership of the latter groups may be drawn from outside the parochial territory, and their functions must always be nonparochial in the technical sense.[16] "The confraternities and pious unions which have been erected in churches of their own, have the right, with due observance of the law, to exercise non-parochial functions independently of the pastor, provided they do not injure the parochial ministry in the parish church."[17]

The interest groupings of lay Catholics on a supraparochial level are not limited to these lay ecclesiastical societies which are erected or approved by the formal exercise of ecclesiastical jurisdiction.[18] The diocesan newspaper in any large American city can be scanned for news about Third Orders of Dominicans, Franciscans, Carmelites, and Benedictines and about various sodalities and confraternities. But it also contains accounts of other supraparochial associations of lay Catholics like laymen's retreat leagues, Catholic information centers, interracial councils, Cana conferences, Young Christian Workers, high-school and college alumni and alumnae groups, and many others.

16. "Parochial functions," reserved by law to the pastor, are listed in Canon 462 as follows: conferring solemn baptism, bringing Holy Communion publicly to the sick, administering the last sacraments, announcing the banns for ordination and marriage, assisting at marriage and giving the nuptial blessing, burying the dead, blessing homes on Holy Saturday or another day according to custom, blessing the baptismal font on Holy Saturday, holding outdoor processions, and giving certain solemn blessings outdoors.

17. Canon 716, n. 1. Thus, the canonical term "non-parochial functions" does not mean functions that are open to nonparishioners. But the sociological fact is that the membership and the program of these ecclesiastical associations are open also to persons who reside outside the immediate parochial territory.

18. See the canonical categories given above, p. 141.

Even though the functions of these groupings are strictly and technically nonparochial, objection is sometimes made to them on the score that they do harm to the parish ministry, the ordinary care of souls. They are charged with taking the most zealous people away from the parish, lessening parish loyalty, and disrupting the orderly social structure of the Church. This is, of course, a negative restatement of the positive principle of parochialism, which tends to insist that parochial associations are both necessary and adequate for all Catholic lay persons.

On the other hand, the lay Catholics who join these supraparochial organizations appear to have positive motives for so doing. Motivation is, of course, a complex psychological phenomenon which does not lend itself easily to analysis. Parishioners frequently give as their first reason for joining these groups the feeling that they do not obtain a sufficient satisfaction of their spiritual needs within the parochial unit. Many parish priests reject this reason on the apparently legitimate ground that there is always plenty of spiritual work that can be done right in the parish without joining an outside organization. The argument runs thus: "If the person is really spiritual and zealous, he will gladly do what needs to be done rather than what he simply wants to do."

It seems necessary to make a double classification of lay people in these supraparochial groupings: those who are already active in the parish societies but want a further outlet for their zeal and those who participate in religious group life only outside their parishes. This second type adds a number of further reasons for joining the supraparochial groups. They have "tried out" membership in the parish organizations but were impatient with the officers, the other members, or the spiritual directors. They came to the conclusion that the societies "never do anything." They found the other members uncongenial, or they felt that their own talents were neither recognized nor utilized.

Perhaps the more influential motive is not the negative one of dissatisfaction with the parochial subunits but the positive attraction of the directors, members, interests, and activities of the supraparochial groups themselves. For example, young unmarried female parishioners may dislike the program of the parish sodality, but they are interested in Catholic broadcasting programs, in teaching Catechism to orphans, in family aid in the slums, etc., where they can co-operate with young women of similar zeal and talents from other parishes. College graduates find that supraparochial groups give an outlet to their interest in the interracial aposolate, Catholic Action groups, and various study clubs and liturgical groups. Their former school loyalties and friendships provide social background for spiritual communion of an active sort.

It is true that the various Third Orders, attached to traditional religious communities, draw lay people away from their home parishes because of their deep spiritual programs. But the attraction also seems frequently to lie in the personality of the priest, brother, or nun who directs the organization. This personal "leadership appeal" is present in the numerous auxiliaries, or "helpers' groups," of people who attach themselves to some of the convents of the urban places. The women's circles help the nuns at the Good Shepherd convents, orphanages, homes for the aged, and hospitals for incurables. The lay woman receives extra attention, sometimes personal spiritual guidance, and an opportunity to display initiative and to utilize special talents in interesting programs.

From this point of view, it appears that the directors of the supraparochial groups of all kinds have to expend more effort to integrate these voluntary interest groups than the parish priests in the formal parochial organizations. While all organized spiritual activity of Catholic lay people is voluntary, there is a subtle distinction between the *parochial* and the *interest* groupings which sometimes escapes detection. The parish priest is likely to think of his parochial societies as a "duty" for parishioners. The supraparochial director,[19] on the other hand, realizes that his program is "beyond the call of duty," and he takes a more spontaneous and enthusiastic attitude toward his recruits. The lay persons themselves often seem unconsciously influenced by this difference between "dutiful" activity and "supererogatory" activity.

It may be said that the religious activities of these interest groups are both more personal and more universal than those of parish groupings. The spiritual satisfaction an individual obtains is placed in a setting which transcends the local and immediate problems of the parish. As one man remarked: "You get a broader outlook of the Church when you join up with these groups. You begin to see the work of the Church in a diocesan, regional, and world-wide perspective." The parochial horizon is extended, and the all-em-

19. The directors of interest groups are often specialists, even crusaders, in the supraparochial organizations and are left free to develop their "specialties." The parish priests, on the other hand, share the difficult task of overseeing a variety of groups within the parish which are sometimes at cross-purposes with one another.

bracing missionary, or universal, function of the Church comes into focus.

This is not meant to imply that only the most spiritual person obtains this broad view of Catholicism or that only the holy parishioners join supraparochial interest groups. It is abundantly evident from the study of the external practices of religion in any urban parish that the laity is at various levels of spirituality. From a subjective point of view, it is also clear that there is a complex assortment of spiritual needs among the people. Some persons have reached the point where they wish to practice nocturnal adoration or read the daily Divine Office; others may simply wish the spiritual uplift of a different kind of novena service. Religious needs differ in kind and degree; and it is a mark of the adaptive cultural genius of the Catholic Church that it can satisfy any orthodox spiritual requirement of its individual adherents.

The exclusively parochial basis of lay association cannot satisfy all these needs. Furthermore, the universal outlet of the parishioner's religious zeal gives to the Church at large a corps of willing lay workers without whom the far-flung operations of Catholicism could not be so successfully conducted. Every Catholic is a parishioner somewhere, but his participation in these interest groups is not a mere extension of his function as a parishioner any more than certain social structures and groupings in the Church are merely an extension of the parish. Hospitals, seminaries, universities, and missions constitute social organizations that are different in kind from parishes. They could not be adequately staffed and operated unless there were numbers of people whose interests lie beyond their immediate local parishes.[20]

Perhaps the most persuasive argument of intelligent Catholics in favor of supraparochial interest groups is the fact that the Church has traditionally approved innumerable nonparochial groupings for pious purposes. The various Third Orders of lay persons have received the highest approbation, and have been richly indulgenced, by the popes. Secular Institutes have also achieved the highest papal approval. Sodalities for school alumni and alumnae, lay organizations in support of hospitals and orphanages, social action committees for industrial relations, housing problems, and interracial activi-

20. The personal effort of these lay persons does not belittle the generous financial aid which parishioners and priests give through the *parochial channel* to the wider projects of the Church.

ties, and many other groups have received the blessing and encouragement of bishops.[21]

These voluntary associations with a fundamental religious inspiration seem to be multiplying among lay Catholics in our modern urban society. They are not parochial, nor are they religious congregations which escape the status of lay persons, nor are they vocational groupings. The gradual development of Secular Institutes provides a good modern example of the "full-time" type of lay interest group. On the national scene these groupings are sometimes called "movements" like that of the *Catholic Worker*, Friendship House, Grailville, and even the Christopher movement. In the local community they may even include the Knights of Columbus, the Knights of St. Peter Claver, study clubs, and special interest groups of various kinds.

The Roman Pontiff, Pius XII, has spoken with approval of supraparochial and supradiocesan religious interest groups. He pointed out that lay persons in these organizations are instruments in the hands of the hierarchy and that ecclesiastical superiors should use these instruments "with a consciousness of their grave responsibility; let them encourage them, suggesting enterprises to them and welcoming with good will the enterprises which they suggest, approving them in broadmindedness according to their opportunities. In decisive battles it is often at the front line that the most useful initiatives arise."[22]

In the light of this high approbation and recognition, it is improbable that one can condemn the lay members of these organizations as "parochial delinquents" or assert that "they should first be active parishioners and then, if they have a surplus of time and energy, they may join other Catholic groups." From both a sociological and a religious point of view, these people are functioning within genuine social groupings and pursuing relevant social goals. While the expectations of some ecclesiastics and parishioners may demand actual social participation in the parochial organizations, it must be remembered that the Church precept specifically obliges the

21. The most adequate discussion with which we are acquainted concerning supraparochial interest groups is given by two German Jesuits, Rahner and Nell-Breuning (Karl Rahner, S.J., "Friedliche Erwägungen über das Pfarrprinzip," in *Pfarrgemeinde und Pfarrgottesdienst*, ed. Alfons Kirchgässner [Freiburg, 1948]; Oswald von Nell-Breuning, S.J., "Pfarrgemeinde, Pfarrfamilie, Pfarrprinzip," *Trier theologische Zeitschrift*, LVI [1947], 257–62).

22. Address to the World Congress of the Lay Apostolate, October 14, 1951.

lay Catholic only to "contribute to the support" of the parish but leaves him free to associate with Catholics above the parish level.

c) The third general type of lay Catholic association is the *vocational* grouping. These groups represent a principle of association which seems quite distinctive from those of the parish societies and the interest groups. In this kind of association there is a "functional solidarity" in the sense that people are drawn together for religious purposes on the basis of their similar pivotal role and status in the larger society. This concept has grown out of the theory of occupational groupings explained by Durkheim[23] and proposed to Catholics by Pope Leo XIII in his encyclical *Rerum Novarum*. In practice it evolves around the "natural order" of the various functional categories in the economic structure. It has been more fully developed by the theorists of specific Catholic Action techniques.

With this in mind the late Pope Pius XI, in his encyclical *Quadragesimo Anno*, recommended highly the organization of people, not according to the status they hold in the labor market, but according to the functions they perform in society. Thus a man would not be integrated into society on the basis that he is rich or poor, employer or employee. He would associate in a systematic and organized way with those who are making the same type of economic contribution to the larger society. Durkheim even suggested that political representation should be arranged according to these *groupements professionnels* instead of according to regions and territories.[24]

The elaboration of the papal recommendation for professional groupings in the economic system is based on the hypothesis that persons who perform similar functions (not merely economic) are "naturally and spontaneously" likely to associate with one another. Similarity of interest and values develops with similarity of functions (and vice versa), so that social integration becomes relatively high among the participants. This notion of association based

23. See his famous Preface to the second edition of *The Division of Labor in Society*, trans. George Simpson (Glencoe, Ill.: Free Press, 1947), pp. 1–31.

24. A segment of the American Catholic Sociological Society led by Gerald J. Schnepp has for several years been absorbed in the theoretical study of the "Industry Council Plan" (see Schnepp's address, "A Catholic Industrial Program," *Catholic Mind*, XLVII, No. 1040 [August, 1949], 489–99, and "A Survey of Opinions on the Industry Council Plan," *American Catholic Sociological Review*, XII, No. 2 [June 1951], 75–83; cf. William J. Smith. "The Catholic Viewpoint on Industry Councils," *American Ecclesiastical Review* CXXII, No. 2 [February, 1950], 107–20; see also *Social Order*, III, No. 4 [April, 1953], 174–88).

on "like to like," which is encouraged in the encyclicals, appears to have sound sociological support from our empirical research.[25]

The "cell technique" of specialized Catholic Action, which is not only an apostolic instrument of the Church but also a form of lay association, insists upon this vocational approach to social grouping. The proponents of these lay organizations like to quote the words of Pius XI in 1934, when he said that workers must be apostles to workers, farmers to farmers, sailors to sailors, students to students.[26] In so far as the lay person's associates in his profession are non-Catholics, this advice must be considered an attempt to win converts to the Church. Our discussion here does not include the participation of the Catholic laity in nonsectarian groups of all kinds but limits itself only to groups made up of Catholics.

Catholic trade-unions, lawyers' guilds, doctors' guilds, nurses' sodalities, and adult committees in the Boy Scout and Girl Scout movements are examples of urban social groupings on the basis of functional similarity. Pope Pius XII also calls these a form of the lay apostolate and lists numerous other possibilities: in public opinion, games and sports, intellectual and cultural life, missions, work for migrants, charity and aid, etc.

Within the concept of the multiple-role theory, according to which a person participates in the activities of numerous institutionalized groups, it is possible that the lay urban Catholic may belong to several vocational groupings. For example, as the father of a family he may function with a neighborhood group interested in improving family life; as an engineer he may co-operate for a study of the moral problems of his profession; as a citizen he may join with fellow-Catholics for the purpose of political reform. In this sense the principle of vocational association may overlap that of interest grouping discussed above. Within his various roles, however, he usually has one that must be considered his pivotal or principal role. It is especially in this social role that he will associate with fellow-Catholics in vocational groupings.

In a highly specialized industrial society it is evident that this type

---

25. See above, chap. 6, "Parochial Solidarity and Modal Parishioners."
26. See James Cunningham, "Specialized Catholic Action," in *The American Apostolate*, ed. Leo Ward (Westminster, Md.: Newman Press, 1952), chap. iv, pp. 47–65. See also John Cogley, "The Professional Approach," *Commonweal*, LIV, No. 15 (July 20, 1951), 350; A. S. Foley, "Cell Technique of Specialized Catholic Action," *Review for Religious*, II (May, 1943), 164–75; Francis X. Mayer, "Method for the Lay Apostle," *American Ecclesiastical Review*, CXXIV, No. 2 (February, 1951), 119–23.

of association among lay Catholics is both logical and necessary. The modern multiplication of these groups in our urban centers indicates that they are required as an intelligent approach to the problems existing in the various institutions of our culture. The "division of labor" has carried over from industry, not merely as a technique of getting things done, but as a form of social organization.[27]

One can hardly conceive that this kind of social relationship must be confined only within the parish territory. Except in some large urban parishes which may be composed for the most part of a single social stratum (made up, for example, of workers from the same factory or industry), the lay Catholics must cross parish boundaries in order to find other members of their vocational group.

This discussion on the three general types of lay associations, the parochial, the interest, and the vocational, is not meant to indicate that either the common sociological typologies or the official canonical classifications are out of date and useless in urban America. This has been mainly a *de facto* discussion in which it was shown that urban American Catholics actually associate with one another not only because they are members of the same parish but also because they share supraparochial interests with some and nonparochial vocations with others.

One of the by-products of this type of discussion, and particularly of reliable empirical research in the different types of lay relationships among Catholics, will be the avoidance of the kind of controversy which engaged the German-speaking Catholic social scientist over the course of more than forty years. They argued about the "principle of association" of lay Catholics. The controversy raged between those who seemed to exaggerate the "pastor-principle" and the principle of parochialism, on the one side, and those who seemed to think that modern society demands an extreme of "free association."[28]

The sociological approach to religious institutions and groups is a relatively new venture among Catholic social scientists in the United

27. Peter F. Drucker, *The New Society* (New York: Harper & Bros., 1950), pp. 1–17, lucidly describes the way in which the "economic idea" has invaded all of the modern institutions.

28. See the contribution on parish research in Germany by Nikolaus Monzel, in *The Sociology of the Parish*, ed. Nuesse and Harte, pp. 333–40. For an adequate bibliography on this problem in the German literature see Karl Rahner, "Betrieb und Pfarrei," *Stimmen der Zeit*, CLIII, No. 6 (March, 1954), 401–12.

States. Some partial studies have been made on problem areas like "leakage," mixed marriages, birth rates, and differential religious observance, but the larger generalizations and hypotheses have hardly been touched. If parochial sociology is something of a "new movement" in this country, it may fall into the snare of enthusiastic overemphasis. The experienced social analyst realizes that the parish is not the only social structure of the Church and that American lay Catholics often associate on supraparochial and even on supradiocesan lines. A one-sided emphasis may tend to ignore the realities of Catholic social life and to obscure the total sociocultural system of the Church.

The facts in the case show that an exclusive insistence on parochial loyalty, while perhaps inspirational, is not realistic. It does not conform to the kind of society which is evolving in our American cities. On the other hand, an exclusive insistence on the nonparochial type of lay association seems to sacrifice the valuable and basic experience of primary relationships and groupings. In so far as there may be serious controversy about these various "principles" of lay relationship, it appears to revolve around the traditionalism, localism, and resistance to change so frequently encountered in conservative religious institutions.

These questions are intimately relevant to the whole conceptual scheme from which we view the total structure of the Church and the position of the parish within it. A static and rigid interpretation may simply suggest that the Church is made up of dioceses and that each diocese is made up of parishes. A loose and fluid interpretation may suggest that territorial limitations are outmoded in American cities and that voluntary social interaction is now the pivot of the Church's social structure. The Church as a social structure is both dynamic and static. To understand both aspects, it seems important that research and analysis be conducted to unravel the network of actual social relations in which Catholic lay persons are involved within the Church.

The clarification of this conceptual problem seems necessary for the benefit of the social researchers, the sociological theorist, the parish priest, and the parishioners themselves. By our continued empirical research in the Catholic social and cultural system in urban America (not limited merely to the parish) we are able to test the various hypotheses which have been discussed in this chapter.

Chapter Twelve

The Structure of Parochial Societies[1]

I<small>T</small> IS traditional in the Catholic Church in America that every parish develops a number of "societies," or formal subgroupings, through which the more zealous and interested parishioners may carry on the general and specific functions of the Church. These must be distinguished from various supraparochial and extraparochial organizations in which Catholic lay people participate and also from the relatively informal groupings which are not organized under Church surveillance. Technically defined, parochial organizations have canonical status, and all are under the authority of the local pastor.[2]

There is undoubtedly a variety of personal and social motives for the maintenance of formal parish organizations. The lay people may want to intensify their religious practices, assuage their loneliness, develop their parliamentary abilities, or simply "do something to help out the Church." The motives and objectives of the individuals who join parish organizations do not necessarily and always coincide with those of the teaching and administering Church (the bishop and the parish priests) fostering these organizations. Motives of individual members are often personal and noninstitutional, while official objectives tend to be the "stated ideals" as found in the written constitutions and as expressed on occasion by the priests and lay leaders. This does not necessarily imply conflict or antagonism between leaders and followers in parish societies. In so far as these parochial groupings *function* successfully, there is a tendency to by-pass, or to compose, the differences between official objectives and personal motives. Hence, it seems important to analyze the actual functions of these societies (i.e., what the group actually does co-operatively).

1. See article of the same title, *American Ecclesiastical Review*, CXXVII, No. 5 (November, 1952), 351–59.
2. See the general discussion on parish groups above, chap. 11; the various categories of subgroupings below, chap. 14; and the corresponding roles of the priest discussed in chap. 10.

In briefest form it may be said that the function of a formal parochial grouping is twofold: (*a*) it achieves various group goals and (*b*) it expresses various personal values. These goals and values may range in kind and degree from the high spirituality of a Nocturnal Adoration Society to the secular competitiveness of a sports group. This is perhaps another way of saying that all organized social activities in the parish may in some remote or proximate manner be directed to the ultimate purpose of the religious institution: the sanctification and salvation of souls.

In this chapter we are concerned with social structure as an aid to social function. This may be put in the form of a question: Does the form in which a parochial society is organized have any effect on the manner in which the group actually functions or operates? It is obvious, of course, that parishioners do not do things together unless there are group objectives and personal motives. But in the present discussion these may be taken for granted and are mentioned only in so far as they are related to the structuring of the group. Bishop Navagh makes the obvious comment that the mere inception or formation of a parish society "does not insure its continuance."[3] It may be added that the mere continuance of organized social relations is neither the objective of a parish society nor a proof of its effectiveness; and it may be suggested here that the *form* of the organization is as important as the fact of its inception.

Although there is some empirical evidence to the contrary, Americans are supposed to be quick organizers and quick joiners.[4] Whether or not this is an accepted generalization of urban Americans, it seems to be true of urban Catholics when they are nuclear participants in the parochial system. They find that establishing a new parish society or appointing a new committee within the existing society is a relatively simple procedure. Frequently they seem to think that they have "taken care" of a problem by setting up a committee, but at a subsequent meeting they "discover" that the problem still exists. This implies an almost naïve faith in mere organization as a means to ends.

3. James J. Navagh, *The Apostolic Parish* (New York: P. J. Kenedy & Sons, 1950), p. 117.
4. Studies show that less than half of the adult urban dwellers belong to one or more voluntary formal associations (see W. Lloyd Warner and Paul S. Lunt, *The Social Life of a Modern Community* [New Haven: Yale University Press, 1941], pp. 323 and 339; F. A. Bushee, "Social Organizations in a Small City," *American Journal of Sociology*, LI, No. 3 [November, 1945], 217–26; Mirra Komarovsky, "The Voluntary Associations of Urban Dwellers," *American Sociological Review*, XI, No. 6 [1946], 686–98).

Studies of parish societies in the United States have brought out the following social facts. (1) In any given parish the formal societies are relatively few in number. (2) They are mass organizations in the sense that they have considerable nominal membership and rather tenuous enrolment requirements. (3) But the active membership in each society is very small, and the repetition of office-holding by the same persons relatively frequent. (4) They are formalized in the sense that they have carefully worded constitutions and by-laws, especially when they are affiliated with a metropolitan, diocesan or national organization. (5) They adhere for the most part to a pattern of traditional categories by age, sex, and marital status.[5]

These social facts of organized parochial structures indicate that there is a tendency toward artificiality in the formation of parish societies. The lay parishioners are arranged in clearly defined groupings (according to tidy norms of age, sex, and marital status) which have been previously and formally structured, with constitutions and by-laws and with an emphasis on the administrative machinery. There is apparently a wide faith among both priests and parishioners in the neatness and balance of paper plans of organizations. This formality extends also to the planned functions of the groups, so that the corporate activities of the lay parishioners might follow a previously arranged pattern. But all this is at best a tentative preliminary to the successful operation of a parish society.

Of course, parochial societies do exist all over the United States, and they do function more or less successfully. There seems to be danger, however, that organization may become an end in itself. This happens through an overemphasis on the formalized and institutionalized structures and procedures. The active leaders tend to develop perfunctory patterns of behavior and thought, because it is easier to maintain the structure than to pursue the function. In other words, the ideal goals of both clergy and lay leaders may often be frustrated by overinstitutionalization. This is another way of saying that traditional and systematic procedures do not meet the socio-religious needs of contemporary urban culture.

From our study of lay societies in various urban parishes, we have formulated two general and tentative conclusions. The first is that the attempt to include all lay, voluntary, parochial activity into relatively few formal artificial organizations minimizes both effective-

5. See Frances S. Engel, "Parish Societies," in *The Sociology of the Parish*, ed. C. J. Nuesse and Thomas J. Harte (Milwaukee: Bruce Publishing Co., 1951), pp. 178–205.

ness (achieving purpose) and efficiency (getting people to contribute effort). The second is that the neglect of informal small groupings (sometimes called "natural groups") constitutes one of the greatest social wastes in the apostolic potential of the parish.

In a comparative study of twenty-three urban southern parishes we found that each parish had an average of 13.2 societies for lay people. These included groups of every kind and description which could in any way be identified as *parochial* and which were listed as such by the parish priests. All of them had relatively large numbers of names on the membership rolls, and this was particularly noticeable in the groupings of elementary-school children (Scouts, altar boys, Children of Mary, etc.).

Assuming that the parochial school children were not representative of responsible lay participation in parish societies, we omitted them from our study. Thus we were able to estimate the average numerical membership of societies in proportion to the number of parishioners fourteen years of age and older. We then went through the roll calls and the minutes of meetings of these organizations and eliminated the names of those who attended less than one-third of the meetings or who participated in no way in their society during the previous year. By this procedure we arrived at a definition of the practical and active membership of the parish societies. They averaged a little more than 142 persons per parish, or approximately 3.6 per cent of all parishioners who are fourteen years of age and over.

Priests interviewed in these parishes recognized and deplored the small numbers of active parishioners. Some of them remarked that "there is only a handful of lay people in every parish who do all the work," a statement which seems to be true of most voluntary groupings, whether religious or secular. There appears to be also a handful of families which supplies the core of people around whom the lay parochial organizations revolve. In a separate survey we found that the greatest proportion of younger members of parish societies are found in families where the father and/or the mother are also active in the parish societies.

Often the parish priests realistically and resignedly accept this fact of minimum lay participation as a universal, natural situation about which little can be done. They had concentrated much thought and energy on the various formal organizations and had "built them up" at one time or another during their parochial experience. But the groups do not remain "built up," nor do they flourish simultaneously. When asked why they continue to maintain the present system of relatively few formal organizations, the priests reply that this is the only way in which parochial unity can be preserved and proper direction can be given. In other words, they feel that a multiplication of societies would cause disunity among the parishioners, dissipate their apostolic energies, and probably make it impossible for the priests to moderate the lay activity.

These appear to be valid reasons for maintaining the traditional forms of the parish societies, but it seems also that the unity of the parish is sometimes threatened by overorganization. The priests—probably subconsciously—tend to regard organization members as first-class parishioners, the loyal and faithful few on whom they can depend. By contrast, those lay persons who were unwilling or unable to join the parish societies are relegated to a kind of second-class status.[6] This does not imply that the parish priests are ever unkind or brusque with people who are not participants of these groups. It seems to be a lack of attention, rather than any positive attitude, statement, or action, which brings about this feeling of discrimination between members and nonmembers of parish societies.

Another disruptive factor may be pointed out in the present system. In a quiet, subsurface way there seems to be rivalry among the various organizations existing in any particular urban parish. This is to some extent due to the priests' demonstration of interest (or lack of it) in one group rather than in another. The young assistant priest may take a more active part in the altar boys than in the sodality or the athletic teams. One priest may show greater interest in the Ushers' Society than in the Holy Name Society, or in the Rosary Society than in the choir. The active parishioners in these various groups come to consider the structure of their organizations so important that they have to have it recognized as such. A neglect of sacerdotal recognition of one group tends to make its members envious of the more-favored group.

The question of authority, the proper direction of lay societies within the parish, is much more complex than the discrimination between members and nonmembers or between one parish society and another. When a priest exercises close supervision over a group, the members sometimes feel that they are working for him and that the invaluable quality of lay initiative is being stifled. There are, of

6. Highly successful businessmen and professional men tend to maintain parochial prestige even though they are almost never active in the parish societies.

course, many parishionrs who are "chronic gripers" and who accept neither work nor responsibility in the parish societies. Still, even the most zealous and active parishioners sometimes complain about the priests' interference. This points up what Monsignor Hellriegel has said: "Innumerable efforts and much time are spent by priests on these societies, efforts often that *could be made just as well by non-consecrated hands*."[7] The effectiveness of a group in achieving its purpose is seriously hampered when clerical replaces laic action.

One of the clearest and most important conclusions we have made from our parochial research is that social efficiency, that is, the system of getting co-operative effort in the parish societies, is quite different from that in any other kind of social unit. This fact is particularly relevant to the authoritative lines of communication extending from the priests to the people through the voluntary organizations. An urban parish cannot be operated like a factory, a school, or even a family, and social efficiency cannot be achieved in the same way in all of them.

The priests frequently speak of their parishes as "one big happy family." They like to use this figure of speech in meetings of the lay societies, from the pulpit, and in private counseling. While the title "Father" may imply a paternal attitude, and while the priests may assume such a paternal attitude, the relationship is at best only remotely familial.[8] The urban parish is too large, the contacts are too few, and the parishioners do not exhibit a reciprocal filial attitude toward the priests. This is because the urban parish is typically a secondary associational grouping, while the family is a primary communal grouping.[9]

Unlike a school or factory, the parish contains a majority of persons who can refuse to co-operate. "Relatively few parishioners in the majority of the parishes studied are members of parish societies. By and large, parish societies are something of a hit-and-miss proposition which the parishioner can take or leave without any feeling of personal responsibility."[10] The size and the structure of parochial societies (as well as the problem of authority) are important ele-

7. At the National Liturgical Week in 1940 (see Mary Perkins [ed.], *The Sacramental Way* [New York: Sheed & Ward, 1948], p. 205).

8. See, however, the sense in which the "fatherly role" is a valid concept, above, chap. 10.

9. See below, chap. 14, for a discussion of the various concepts of social units.

10. Engel, *op. cit.*, p. 201.

ments in this lack of co-operation and this unwillingness to become members.

While a factory may contain five or six thousand persons—like a large parish—the nature of its operation and its structure makes similarity in size relatively unimportant. The factory is in continuous operation, and each person performs specific actions for specific ends, is motivated by sanctions and incentives, and is directed by delegated authority which leaves no choice except to obey or resign. The operation and the structure of parochial organizations have no advantages of this kind. The function is at best sporadic; it can be initiated, neglected, or altered in almost any way the volunteer workers desire. The priests can exercise their direct control only when the lay participants are positively willing to co-operate.

We have said above that in the urban parish only a small nucleus is so disposed.[11] This nucleus is in reality a clique of families and of close friends with whom the priests can best co-operate. The more outspoken parishioners who are not members of the inner circle sometimes talk about the "clique that's in control." The particularized relation between priests and parishioners refers again to one of the central problems of lay parochial structure. It is difficult to see how the personalized relation of the priest can or should be translated into a purely "professional" relationship.[12]

Is this nucleus, this handful of faithful parishioners who do all the work, elastic? The answer seems to lie in the multiplication of small nuclei instead of in the expansion of the nucleus into large formal groupings. Our detailed study of the meetings and activities of numerous lay organizations leads to the conclusion that effective co-operation cannot be achieved in groups of more than twelve to fifteen persons. Even in each of the smallest groups which do not strive for mass membership the actual work is done by less than ten persons. It is true that on single occasions large numbers of parishioners appear, as at Holy Name rallies, athletic contests, the May crowning, etc., but this is "attendance at" rather than "working with" a parish society.

The functioning of a lay parochial organization undoubtedly requires co-operative effort, but the renewed pleas of the priests for

11. This is not a peculiarity of parish groups only. For wider examples in American life see the study by Bernard Barber, "Participation and Mass Apathy in Associations," in *Studies in Leadership*, ed. Alois W. Gouldner (New York: Harper & Bros., 1950), pp. 477–504.

12. See above, chap. 10, for discussion of the "communal" role of the parish priest.

full co-operation of *all* the members of any society goes unheeded. The demonstrable fact is that there is an outer limit to the number of social relationships any person can maintain. The same is true of the relationships within a relatively small cohesive group. With each addition to the group the number of relationships increases geometrically. In a group of six persons there are fifteen pair relationships; in a group of twelve there are sixty-six. When a group passes beyond its limit of workable relationships, it must either proliferate (into subcommittees or separate groups) or resign itself to an increasing number of inactive members. This latter fact is attested by the long list of "inactive" members on the rolls of most large parish organizations.

If this conclusion is valid for any social unit, it is even more valid for a group made up of volunteer workers. Of its very nature, the voluntary contribution of effort to a parochial society inhibits large-scale, long-term co-operation. Many of the problems with which parish priests are plagued in large formal organizations may be converted into incentives for work in small informal groupings. Often a volunteer has pet projects and fads. He may have an exaggerated idea of his own importance or a desire for local prestige. These are "nonmaterial" incentives for parochial activity even though they cannot be called supernatural motives. As long as such a volunteer has a few fellow-parishioners who share his ideas and are willing to follow him, he may form a useful group in the parish. He demands a freedom of operation and association which could not be countenanced in a paid, full-time worker in any group.[13]

People of this kind are numerous in every urban parish. Personal interviews reveal that at various times they have "suggested good ideas" to the priests and officers, who "wouldn't listen." They tried to get the floor at meetings, but their ideas were either ignored or voted down. As a result they lost interest and complained that "nobody wants to co-operate around here." On the other hand, the priests tend to think of these people as "crackpots." They are the kind of persons who "always want to do things their own way, and, if they don't get their own way, they quit."

The history of any urban parish probably contains many examples of this failure of both effectiveness and efficiency, with its resultant

13. This distinction between the amateur volunteer and the paid professional is recognized as a social fact in the Red Cross, the YMCA, and other ameliorative organizations. Wherever possible the work is made to fit the volunteer rather than vice versa.

inactivity. They indicate the truth of the sociological generalization
that only a minority of the members of a large-scale unit like a parish
are willing to serve and co-operate in any specific organization.
Hence, if there are only certain restricted channels of social expression for them (the several, traditional, large, formal organizations),
the number of active participants in these formal groupings will be
few. This number of active people can be multiplied only if the
number of organizations (or their subcommittees) is multiplied and
only if these are small, natural (not artificial) groupings.

The concept of the natural group, or social clique, has been amply
demonstrated in modern sociological research.[14] Even in a factory
system people tend to do their best work when the realities of the
social system are recognized. The working nucleus is at its best
when its members have social bonds which go beyond the purely
economic. In the parish it does not seem sufficient to say, "They all
have the same religion. They're all Catholics and parishioners, and
they ought to work together." A social fact, clearly evident in the
urban American parish, is that the religious bond is only one in
many.[15] The informal groupings of lay persons actually existing in
the community tend to associate not only around a dominant personality but also around a combination of other elements: ethnic,
educational, sex, age, friendship, residence, kinship, etc.

These small informal groups have for the most part only relative
permanence. Some may endure for many years, but even in these
the membership changes. Some may have shorter duration, for it is
the very nature of informal dynamic social life that people regroup
themselves from time to time. This mercurial quality of informal
groupings is considered a defect by many Catholics, both lay and
clerical, who have accepted the system of large formal parochial
organizations as the only logical kind of social structure and who
put a high value on the continuance of traditional forms.[16]

14. Muzafer Sherif and Hadley Cantril, *The Psychology of Ego-Involve-
ments* (New York: John Wiley & Sons, 1947), survey the literature in this
regard in chap. x, "Ego-Involvements and Identifications in Group Situations."
See also F. J. Roethlisberger's *Management and Morale* (Cambridge: Harvard
University Press, 1941), W. Lloyd Warner's *The Social Life of a Modern
Community* (New Haven: Yale University Press, 1941), and William F.
Whyte's *Street Corner Society* (Chicago: University of Chicago Press, 1943).
15. See above, chap. 4, on the bases of solidarity in lay associations.
16. Montcheuil makes a penetrating remark on this point. "Real traditions
are not principles from which one can draw conclusions as to one's lines of
conduct in new circumstances. They are ways of existence incorporated into
a temperament, which determine a way of reacting more than they dictate
a solution. A true tradition is constitutive, not constituted. . . . One may wish

Some of the traditional organizations in the urban parishes exhibit a pride in their long-continuing history, but none of them has flourished continuously. Each has had periods of stagnancy and periods of activity. Fluctuations are part of the history of formal organizations; hence the relative transiency of informal groupings is not necessarily a major argument against their adoption. This is an aspect of the dynamism of parochial life which is emphasized in the prevailing conditions of modern urban areas. Lay parochial societies need not be perennial. There seems to be no compelling reason why they may not be allowed to die when their purpose is accomplished or when their members lose interest or regroup themselves.

It may be noted here that one of the greatest obstacles to the restructuring of lay organizations in urban parishes seems to lie in the traditional relationship between priests and people. In most instances initiative and authority lie firmly in the hands of the priests, and this is probably because ultimate responsibility is also the priests'. The principle of self-direction and of lay responsibility, basic to the modern concept of the organized lay apostolate, runs contrary to this tradition. While Catholic lay action is not separate from, and independent of, the regularly constituted lines of Church authority, the operation of informal groupings in the parochial structure is impossible without lay responsibility.

Abbé Michonneau complained that the French clergy reduced their parishioners to the status of mere listeners "even in organizations where they are supposed to do the talking. . . . They do not give anything; they are passive beings. The parish has become the business of the clergy; it is of no concern to the faithful."[17] This seems to be a valuable note of warning to both clergy and parishioners everywhere, even though this cleavage between clergy and laity is probably not so deep in American as in French parishes.

From this point of view the question resolves itself into that of the relationship between authority and responsibility. The freedom of the parishioners to form small natural groupings and the willingness and encouragement of priests for this type of association imply a working solution of the problem of authority and responsibility. Can

---

to be traditional, but he is not when he chooses a solution because he thinks it is traditional. In this event he is most often only routine and old-fashioned" (Yves de Montcheuil, *For Men of Action* [Chicago: Fides Publishers, 1952], pp. 152–53).

17. G. Michonneau and H. Ch. Chéry, *Revolution in a City Parish* (Oxford: Blackfriars Publications, 1949), p. 22.

one exist without the other? It is inconceivable that the priest can have all the authority and the lay people all the responsibility in the parish societies. The answer probably lies in the delegation of authority from the priest to the people and the concomitant assumption of responsibility by the laity.

In the last analysis there is no need to make exclusive alternatives of the large formal organizations, on the one hand, and the small informal groupings on the other. A blending of both is possible.[18] The negative features of both may be eliminated and their positive elements promoted. The mere fact of structure does not by itself guarantee either efficiency or effectiveness in the parish society. Structure is merely an auxiliary of function. The ultimate social test, and the most important social aspect, of any parochial group is its function—demonstrated when people act co-operatively toward worthy goals.

18. The practical technique for working out this "blend" of the two types of organization and the working solution of the blend of authority and responsibility, on the parish level, have been suggested as important projects for priests' workshops in human relations.

Chapter Thirteen

The School and the Parish

SINCE both religion and education are major institutions, they must have similar general institutional functions. Both church and school, therefore, function (*a*) as satisfiers of basic social needs of individuals; (*b*) as the operative bases of the social order; (*c*) as major instruments of social control; (*d*) as the patterns of social behavior of individuals; (*e*) as carriers of the society's culture; and (*f*) as social conservators.[1] These are the most generic functions of all institutions, and there can be little doubt that any system of human relations which fulfils the definition of an institution must also embrace its functions.

The essential distinction between institutions lies in the kinds of basic needs which are satisfied in a co-operative way, and the distinction between the church and the school lies in the fact that one satisfies the religious needs of people and the other the educational needs. The way in which each institution carries out the general functions further specifies it and distinguishes it from others. For example, it is empirically certain that both church and school function to conserve and transmit cultural values, to develop an appreciation of the social order, and to promote social progress and improvement.[2] Each, however, does these things in different ways, with different instruments, and on different levels of values.

These differences between the two basic institutions are fairly clear in that segment of the American institutional system where a cleavage is maintained between church and school, that is, with the Protestant denominations on the one side and the public schools on the other. The distinction is not so clear when a contrast is made between religious education and secular education, that is, between

1. J. O. Hertzler, *Social Institutions* (Lincoln: University of Nebraska Press, 1946), pp. 39–49.
2. See Marion B. Smith's contribution, "The School as a Social Institution," in *Sociological Foundations of Education*, ed. Joseph S. Roucek (New York: Thomas Y. Crowell Co., 1942), pp. 29–46.

the denominational schools and the public schools. It would seem, for example, that the Catholic parochial school is attempting to fulfil two distinguishable institutional functions, that of religion and that of education. The obverse may also be said, viz., that the Catholic parish, a religious institution, and the Catholic school, an educational institution, are both performing the same basic function: the religious development of the individual in society.

In the real operation of the parochial system there are two social facts which clarify this theoretical confusion of institutional functions. The first is that the parochial school is a subsidiary adjunct to the parish itself, just as the whole Catholic educational system is subsidiary to the whole Catholic Church. The second is that the content of the so-called secular subjects is secondary to the religious training of the pupils (just as the various functions and objectives of parish societies are secondary to the sanctifying and salvific function of the parish itself). Thus, the simultaneous collaboration of the religious and the educational institution within the classroom of the parochial school does not in practical operation engender confusion.

The point of discussion in this chapter is the sociological function rather than the religious function of the Catholic educational system. As institutions, both religion and education are expected to promote social solidarity, elevate social standards, and influence other institutions in the culture.[3] The extent to which the parish can and does fulfil these social functions has been discussed in various parts of this book. The question of whether or not the Catholic school system fulfils them requires analysis on various levels of both education and society. In other words, elementary, secondary, and college education contain certain distinguishing peculiarities, while the type of social solidarity differs in the total American society, the local urban community, and the smaller parish unit. The problem of this chapter is restricted to the relationship between the Catholic school and the Catholic parish and more specifically to the integrative sociological influence which the Catholic educational system has on the parish as a social aggregate.

There are several ways in which this problem can be stated. To what extent is it possible for the Catholic school to become an inte-

3. J. O. Hertzler, "Religious Institutions," *Annals of the American Academy of Political and Social Science*, CCLVI (March, 1948), 1–13, points out also three "personal" functions of the religious institution: it facilitates religious experience, it acts as an agent of social control, and it serves as a therapeutic agent for the individual.

grating agency for social relations on the parish level? In what ways has institutionalized Catholic education promoted or hindered the individual's actual participation in the parish unit of the Church? Does formal Catholic schooling make the student "parish-conscious" —help to give him a feeling of belonging to a socioreligious aggregate which has a definite function in the ecclesiastical structure? Does the Catholic educational system produce graduates who are loyal and devoted parishioners?

It may be argued, of course, that parochialism is an archaic, negative attitude which should not be developed. It may be argued whether the school, or the family, or any other agency of socialization should even attempt to concentrate on the development of local loyalties. Basic to this relationship between school and parish, and indeed to the whole analysis of Catholic parish life, is this problem of "parochialism" in the narrow sense of the term. Parochialism, like provincialism, has a connotation of warped narrowness and of ethnocentric localism which is apparently out of date in the modern city world of liberal, tolerant, and cosmopolitan attitudes. The fact that urban Catholics are participating more and more in supraparochial associations and interest groupings seems to indicate that they, like other Americans, are affected by the widening horizons of modern social life.

This factual current in social life cannot be ignored, but its existence does not mean that the trend is necessarily in the direction of social and cultural progress. The gradual loosening of the basic network of primary human relations characteristic of the simple, rural, communal society has been deplored by sociologists from Le Play to Zimmermann. The dynamic shift in social structures, in the patterns of group living as well as in the design of group values and goals, seems to have spelled the decline of local community loyalties. This upheaval is sometimes defined restrictively as a change of values and attitudes, a thing merely of the mind, but it has in reality become absorbed in the institutionalized processes.

The attempt on the part of Catholics to hold fast to their own religious system of education has been interpreted as one of the principal channels of un-American, antidemocratic parochialism.[4] The literature on this subject of the status and function of the

4. See Paul Blanshard, *American Freedom and Catholic Power* (Boston: Beacon Press, 1949), chap. iv, "Education and the Catholic Mind," and the rebuttal by James M. O'Neill, *Catholicism and American Freedom* (New York: Harper & Bros., 1952), chap. vii, "Catholic Education."

Catholic school in the American social structure abounds with charges and countercharges. Most of the writing by Catholics has been defensive in tone. They argue at great length to demonstrate that the Catholic school system is neither divisive nor undemocratic. Father John Walsh is more positive with his assertion that "the parochial school specializes in integration."[5] He was speaking of "the advantage of a unified, rounded-out, properly subordinated view of life" which is presented to the individual pupil in Catholic elementary schools.

Considered in both their structural and their functional aspects, the Catholic schools present the picture of an intricate and variegated social system. At some levels and in some aspects the Catholic schools are undoubtedly integrative, as Father Walsh suggests, but at other levels they seem to de divisive. A panel discussion at the convention of the National Catholic Educational Association in San Francisco in 1948 highlighted this latter point. It was designed to discuss ways of making the child less parochial, to teach him to participate in the "outside community," even the nation and the world at large. One of the participants, a pastor of an urban parish, complained that certain "pastors and principals live in a little world of their own, a world narrowed by parochial boundaries and inhabited only by the children of the parish."[6]

Such an admission of occasional lapses is not necessarily a sign of the total weakness or the failure of a whole system. Catholic educators have analyzed their own position and have insisted that the product of the Catholic school is prepared to take his place in the larger community, that differences do not always connote divisions and antagonisms, and that a democracy is composed of all kinds of people—some of whom are Catholic. They have countercharged that the opponents of the Catholic school system are themselves guilty of a narrow ethnocentrism, attempting to mold all American students according to their own peculiar, illiberal, and secularistic philosophy of values.

The preoccupation with both offensive and defensive tactics in this more general area where the attacks have been strongest has

5. John E. Walsh, "The Parochial School: Partner or Pariah," *School and Society*, LXXI, No. 1845 (April 29, 1950), 257–62; cf. William McManus, "The Catholic School and the Community," *Catholic Action* (N.C.W.C. Bulletin), November, 1951, p. 6.
6. See Gerald S. Walsh, S.J., "The Social Responsibility of Catholic Educators," *National Catholic Educational Association Bulletin*, XLV (August, 1948), 52–59.

emphasized the external justification that Catholic schools are, as Father Walsh says, "partners and not pariahs" in the American society. It is probable, however, that the internal vulnerability of the Catholic educational system has not been carefully analyzed. This is bluntly put in the question: Have the Catholic schools become so "American" that they have become less "Catholic"? This has nothing to do with either theology or patriotism; it is concerned with the social trend toward broad, associational types of human relations at the expense of primary, integrated, and communal relations.[7] While Catholic apologists have been showing that Catholic education makes students good citizens of the civic community, have they perhaps failed in awareness of the factors which help or hinder the student's participation in the parochial community?

This question cannot be adequately analyzed on merely the parochial school level. The Catholic educational system extends from elementary grades through high schools to colleges and universities. Each of these levels has its own peculiar problems and subdivisions, but each has also in some way an influence on the ultimate parochial attitudes of Catholic students.

The study of the parochial school may be clarified through an analogy with the sociological theory proposed by Perry in 1939. Perry maintained that the neighborhood is a focal point for restoring social order in the chaotic urban environment and that the neighborhood really centers around the elementary school.[8] Perhaps this concept could be paraphrased in the following hypothesis: Since people live and act out their Christianity in their parishes, they can spiritually revitalize society through the parish, and a focal point of parochial solidarity is the parish school.

This is an ingenious and fascinating hypothesis, since it suggests itself as the key to the large problem of parochial integration. But let us see whether the evidence supplied by the Catholic educational system substantiates it. Frank Kelly has pointed out that "the elementary school is the first breaking away from the fundamental unit of society—the family."[9] This suggests that the elementary school is socially divisive, that it weakens the primary and most important social bonds a child has. It does not, however, indicate a difference

7. See below, chap. 15, pp. 204–7, for the discussion of Professor Eister's suggestion concerning the basis of social integration.
8. Clarence Perry, *Housing for the Machine Age* (New York: Russell Sage Foundation, 1939).
9. National Catholic Education Association, *Proceedings of the San Francisco Convention, 1948*, p. 539.

between parochial and public schools in the social development of the child.

On the other hand, it is also true that the child at this point begins to make contacts with more fellow-parishioners and is developing his new social relations and bonds. Because of the association of elementary-school children with one another, their parents are also drawn into a new "interest circle" in the parish.[10] Some of these adults tend to get acquainted through an informal process of meeting the parents of their children's friends. Others go a step further and become associated in the formal groupings of a parents' club or a mothers' club.

The essential elements of social solidarity are present in this situation. The formal religious education of the children is the mutually appreciated social value among these parents. They are performing a function co-operatively in working toward better schooling. The medium for the associative process is present in the form of the organization and in the opportunities for social relations among parents. The co-ordinating link in this network of human relations is found in the faculty and, to some extent, in the principal and the pastor. This appears to be an excellent sociological matrix for the development of parochial solidarity.

The hypothesis that the parochial school serves as a fulcrum of parish solidarity is very plausible until we examine it a little more closely in the light of the actual social situation in the urban parochial environment. Let us start with the earliest step in the educational system. Few parishes can afford to operate a full-time day nursery school, but, where these do exist, they are patronized by parents from all over the city. In membership they are supraparochial schools, similar in this sense to the private elementary schools conducted by some religious orders. In so far as they have any solidaristic effect upon the children and their parents, they tend to dissipate parochial interest by overrunning parish boundaries. They may have a valuable function for the "higher integration" of Catholics, but they do not serve necessarily to bring members of the same parish closer to one another.

At the level of the elementary-school system the problem of parish solidarity becomes more complex. In every relatively large city

10. This appears to be a form of "communality," an association of people on a basis other than that of location. It is a phenomenon of modern urban life described by B. A. McClonohan, "The Communality: The Urban Substitute for the Traditional Community," *Sociology and Social Research*, XXX, No. 3 (March–April, 1946), 264–71.

there are private elementary schools, both religious and nonsectarian, which socially mobile parents find desirable for their children. These schools are more or less "exclusive" or "high class" by reputation if not always in reality. Sending the children to one of them is expected of families in a certain social status and is advantageous for the family which is aspiring to higher social status. If the school is Catholic, the effect will be to loosen parochial relations and to strengthen wider Catholic bonds; if the school is non-Catholic, the effect will be to weaken both.

The elementary parochial school does not suffer these sociological disabilities. It sems a valid generalization to maintain that the school operated by the parish itself is a medium or focal point for social integration within the parish. This concept has not been widely tested or studied in detail in a sufficient number of parishes to make it more than a tentative generalization. Our own research in this area has led us to three corroborating conclusions: first, that the "more faithful parishioners"[11] usually send their children to the parochial school; second, the children themselves are morally and socially closer to the heart of the parish at this time than at any later period of their lives; and, finally, the teachers in the school are a more important factor for this parish solidarity than either the children or the parents.

These three facts deserve elaboration. Scientific research on this question has indicated that loyalty to the parish is, or can be, strongest for the child who attends the parochial elementary school. While the educational function undoubtedly emphasizes the individual child and his development, it also helps to socialize the child for the home, the community, and the parish. Rautman goes so far as to suggest that children can be agents of social reform. He says that the child is "a most potent medium through which to influence the home" and points out that selected school projects may be employed for this purpose.[12]

The "dear Daddy" and the "dear Mommy" letters, composed and mimeographed by the teachers and signed by the child, are a blunt and specific use of the child as a medium of influencing the parents. In the parochial schools these letters have the child say that "it would make me feel so good if you went to Communion with the

11. That is, all of the nuclear and most of the modal parishioners. The marginal and dormant parishioners almost always send their children to other elementary schools, private or public.

12. Arthur Rautman, "Children as Agents of Social Reform," *Elementary School Journal*, L (1949–50), 277–82.

Holy Name Society (or if you would attend the Parent-Teachers' meeting, or helped with the annual bazaar, etc.)." This ingenuous approach does get measurable results in the participation of parents in parish organizations and activities. There are many more subtle instances in which pressure from the child, without the teacher's help, have brought parents back to the sacraments and improved their religious and parochial attitudes.

The sisters in the elementary parochial school are in a strategic position to exploit their social role in the parish. Because little children guilelessly "tell all," these teachers are probably better informed than anyone else about the primary social relations in the families of the parish. Their informal contact with parents before and after school hours, plus their intimate knowledge of home conditions, makes it possible for them to influence the parents toward closer parochial participation. The advantage of this situation for the development of parish loyalty rests upon the supposition that the teacher herself possesses an active parish-consciousness.

The concept of the parochial elementary school as a focus of influence in the urban parish is by no means a simple and sovereign generalization. There are several dysfunctional elements of parochial life to be considered. In those cities where Catholicism is still identified with an immigrant or lower-class culture, the socially unifying effect of the parochial school tends to be weakened. In some of the predominantly Protestant cities of the South, the children who attend the parochial schools are sometimes considered the "rougher element" of the juvenile population. This must also be taken with caution, subject to factual local studies. In writing about New Haven, Chapman says that the "impressionistic assigning of Catholic schools to the lower class does not precisely square with ecological analysis, which finds one Catholic church in one of the two best residential districts in the city."[13]

In so far as some Catholic parents recognize this low prestige element of the parochial pupils, they are tempted to send their children to the public school or to other private schools. The parochial schools are no longer "good enough" for them. This does not seem

13. Stanley Chapman, "Church Schools," *Journal of Educational Sociology*, XVIII, No. 6 (1944–45), 340–50. The assimilation of Catholics into the American culture, their gradual distribution over the whole class structure, and the continued construction of modern school buildings are changing this "impressionistic" evaluation.

to be true among Negro Catholics. Because of the deplorable condition of most of the Negro public schools throughout the South, Negroes in general hold Catholic elementary schools in high repute. Almost all the parochial schools are rated by them above the public elementary schools, and in some of the Catholic schools there are more non-Catholic than Catholic pupils.

It is nevertheless true that parishes, like individuals, families, and neighborhoods, have different social ratings, so that some are termed "high class," and others "low class." Parents may be very solicitous, and sometimes overcritical, about what they estimate to be the kind of children with whom their own offspring must associate in the parochial school. Many a pastor in a so-called lower-class parish has been chagrined to find that some of his parishioners prefer to send their children to school in a "better parish." This is the source of social disunity between pastor and parents as well as among parishioners and sometimes also between pastors of the parishes in question.

Another peculiar practice, which is not uncommon in the larger growing cities, is the continued fealty to a parochial school after the family has moved from the parish. The child may live at a considerable distance and may pass by two or three other parochial schools on the way to his old school. Whether the parents think that the change to a different school would disrupt the child's education, whether they believe that the old school is a much better one, or whether they simply have not become integrated in their new parish, the fact is that this practice is parochially divisive.[14] Some pastors in the "desirable" parishes try to discourage this pattern by charging a relatively high tuition for out-of-parish pupils. On the other hand, pastors with overcrowded schools sometimes request others to help take care of the overflow.

In the smaller communities, villages, and townships of the South these dysfunctional factors of the elementary school are apparently not so serious. If the community is predominantly Protestant, the Catholics frequently identify themselves more closely with the Church and insist as a matter of principle that their children should attend the parochial school. In some dioceses the bishop implements the canonical prescription of this serious obligation of conscience by

14. Fealty to the "old parish" is, of course, expressed in many other ways. Some of the downtown churches in rapidly changing urban areas still attract former residents to religious services. A person wants to be married or have his children baptized there; he may even stipulate that he wants to be buried from the "old parish" because it had been the "family parish" for generations. This is an interesting example of parish loyalty in reverse.

ordering that the sacraments be denied to those parents who fail to send their children to the Catholic school.

On the next educational level the Catholic high school loses many of the socially integrating advantages which are inherent in the parochial elementary school. While most Catholic elementary schools are parochial, most Catholic high schools are supraparochial. This is true of the composition of the school's population even when the high school is operated under the auspices of a particular parish.

In other words, whether we are talking about boarding academies, high schools operated privately by religious orders, central high-schools sponsored by four or five parishes, or the parish high school itself, all of them appear to be in some sense parochially divisive. They serve a segment of the Catholic population which necessarily goes beyond the parish boundaries. This population tends to be diffusive. The student body acts as a medium of contact and association, but it brings together people (not only students but families and friends) from various parishes.

The high-school freshmen who come from the same parish tend at first to associate with one another and to form a kind of temporary in-group. But before the year is over these parochial bonds dissolve and realign themselves into school ties. In the parochial high school the students from other parishes are sometimes expected to participate in the activities (e.g., choir-singing and religious devotions) of the parish where the school is located. In the diocesan and central Catholic high schools, and especially in the private academies and preparatory schools, such activities are not even generically parochial. The liturgy and the religious life of the student becomes more and more school-centered.

An even greater incongruity appears in the organizational and noncurricular activities of the high-school student. He can hardly be expected to belong to both the school sodality and the parish sodality, the school choir and the parish choir, the school athletic teams and the parish Catholic Youth Organization. It is sometimes said that these organized activities are basically a training ground for the future parishioner and that the student will be all the more competent when he takes his place in the parochial organizations. Whether and how the actual transition will be made from one to the other probably depends not only on the teachers and the graduate himself but also on the parents and the parish priests.

At the college level the problem is still further confounded. It is obvious that the Catholic college serves the largest area and, more strongly than the lower-level schools, pulls people away from their parishes. This is true not only of boarding colleges to which students are drawn from various dioceses but also of day colleges which are attended by students who live within commuting range. The bonds of friendship formed in college cut across parish and diocesan lines. The academic, cultural, economic, political, and even religious interests of the college student help to reduce his parochial orientation and affiliation. While his own personality is becoming more integrated and balanced, and his broader social relations are improving, his own parish is becoming more remote to him.

In both the high school and the college the various forms of group activity help to center the students' interest there. The sodalities provide for religious needs; the athletic teams, school dances, and parties provide recreational satisfactions; fraternities and sororities and numerous other campus groupings fashion new social bonds. The students form attachments to the teachers as well as to the school. This pull away from the parish continues after graduation when the school tries to keep alumni and alumnae interested in itself through its homecoming events, athletic contests, scholarship and endowment funds, building drives, etc.

In the secularized culture of the big city it would be naïve to suggest that a parish could arouse the same spirit of enthusiasm in its members that a winning football team can arouse in students and alumni. Some approach to this "group spirit" is found in the younger parishioners and sports-minded adults when their CYO team wins the city league title. But this is a specifically recreational phenomenon and does not touch the deeper loyalty and genuine social integration which the parish unit demands. Even the parents seem to be more interested in the school spirit than in the parochial spirit of their children.

The faculty and administration of the Catholic schools are, of course, key factors in this whole problem of the development of parochial solidarity. The teachers in the Catholic educational system, from kindergarten to university, are almost by profession nonparochial. This does not mean that they have a conscious antagonism or disregard for the parish as the basic social unit of the Catholic Church. The fact is that members of teaching Orders and congregations come originally from other parishes and even other regions of the country. They have been away from their native parishes for many years; they have worked in several other parish schools or in high schools and colleges conducted by their own Order; and their general attitudes and experiences in the religious life have been along the more universal lines of broader Catholicism.

At the elementary-school level, and to some extent in the high school, the teacher may be tempted to make invidious comparison between the present school and other schools with which he or she has been associated. On the other hand, there may be a tendency to think of the school and the class as just another school and class and not as an integral segment of this particular parochial structure. This is an aspect of the universalizing process which is present in every occupational function and which, in the nature of the case, seems to require some local limitation.

In the Catholic colleges and universities the teachers—lay, religious, and clerical—are so far removed from the parish that they are almost lost to it. Their status and role, and consequently their attitudes, are logically supraparochial, and this fact is reflected in the student. In our research it has often been noted that the student's participation in parish organizations, which was relatively low while he attended high school, decreases even further when he is in college. The fact that the college student has not been trained for and orientated toward parish activity is amply confirmed by the controversy which raged for a while in the pages of *America*.[15]

The absence of Catholic college graduates from the nuclear activities of the parish is a problem which requires more research and study. It is a fact so widely remarked by pastors that it must be accepted as a sociological generalization.[16] Part of the explanation may be found in the parish itself, but part is also found in the Catholic educational system. Continued affiliation as an alumnus tends to interfere with parish affiliation. It may be a sign of touching loyalty if the girl graduate wants to come back and be married in the college chapel, or if the boy graduate insists that his priest-teacher perform the ceremony for them. But this is also a sign that the logically nonparochial milieu of college life has extended beyond any usefulness which it may have had.

In counterstatement to the central question of this chapter, it may be argued that the Catholic educational system is not simply an auxiliary of the Catholic parish but an auxiliary of the whole

15. *America*, LXXXV, No. 17 (July 28, 1951), 418, and the discussions by correspondents in subsequent numbers; also *Commonweal*, LI (February 17, 1950), 511, where an attempted solution is discussed.
16. See above, chap. 4, on education as a factor of solidarity.

Catholic Church in America. The youth who come out of a Catholic school come into the world of social reality in which the traditional forms of parochial and territorial organization are being widely questioned. Tight, local community loyalties which might strengthen a single parish in Dallas or Mobile may not necessarily further the aims of the Church in the South or in the whole nation.

If formal schooling is supposed to prepare the student "for life," it appears sociologically valid to predict that the future life of the present Catholic student will be less and less parochial in the rigid narrow sense of the term. Preparing him for a social system and a cultural milieu which are gradually vanishing seems a frustrating process. The big-city parishioner seems to have become more and more a Catholic citizen at large. The broader group life of Catholics requires an appreciation of the importance of supraparochial activities like those of Grailville and the Men of Christ the King, of Friendship House and interracial groups, of *Integrity* and *Catholic Worker* and the American Catholic Trades-Union, of liturgical and social action groups of all kinds.

On the other hand, the Catholic student does not exist elsewhere than where he actually lives, and that in the last analysis is still the parish. From the point of view of personal and social salvation, the immediate, primary relationships are those which test the social virtues of the individual. The social processes are most frequent still in the family, the neighborhood, and the parish, and all the broader Catholic activities cannot take the parishioner completely away from the local scene.

Just as the democratic institutions do not function toward their proper goals unless they are used by alert and intelligent citizens, so also the rapidly changing parochial institution requires alert and intelligent parishioners. This was not so necessary when the "natural" social neighborhood and community surrounded the parish church and when religious patterns of behavior were almost automatically accepted by the larger portion of the parish. All this has changed, and the Catholic educational system seems an essential factor in the gradual adaptation of students to the exigencies of this change.

PART IV

Problems of Conceptualization and Research

Chapter Fourteen

Conceptualizations of the Urban Parish[1]

THE social structure of an urban Catholic parish is highly complex. At first glance this would not seem to be true, because the casual observer probably sees nothing but a large number of people who satisfy their religious needs at a particular parish church. On closer analysis, however, it will be noted that any social unit of a few thousand persons logically structures its social relations according to multiple patterns. It seems true also that the social scientist not only can but must conceptualize the parish in multiple ways in order to achieve meaningful analysis.

The analytical tool of multiple conceptualizations of the parish is obviously not an invention of the social scientists. Besides other approaches, a person could study the parish historically, theologically, canonically, and sociologically; and the sociological approach itself allows for numerous conceptual frameworks. The editors of a recent study of the Catholic parish in America remark that "there are, of course, several possible approaches to the living reality which is the parish," and they exemplify this patent observation by saying that the parish can be an institutionalized administrative unit, a social group in its own right, or a component of the larger ecclesiastical unit.[2] A quarter of a century ago Harbrecht spoke about the threefold aspect of the parish and discussed briefly the *legal* aspect from canon law, the *religious* aspect from pastoral theology, and the *socioethical* aspect from moral philosophy.[3]

1. An expansion of a paper read at the fifteenth annual meeting of the Southern Sociological Society, Atlanta, Georgia, March 28, 1952 (see *Social Forces*, XXXI, No. 1 [October, 1952], 43–46).
2. C. J. Nuesse and Thomas J. Harte (eds.), *The Sociology of the Parish* (Milwaukee: Bruce Publishing Co., 1951), p. 3.
3. John Harbrecht, *The Lay Apostolate* (St. Louis: B. Herder Book Co., 1929), p. 21. This book was designed to analyze only the last-named aspect and was subtitled, "A Social Ethical Study of Parish Charity Organizations for Large City Parishes."

This varied conceptualization of the urban American parish is not the same as the detailed subdivisions under which the parish is studied in the numerous textbooks and commentaries on the Code of Canon Law. These writings have in the past referred to different kinds of parishes in the Church, but they have now settled upon the three major types as territorial, personal, and mixed.[4] One of the first books written on the subject of pastors and parishes after the promulgation of the canon law of 1918 presented the following detailed subdivisions of the Catholic parish: (*a*) parishes and quasi-parishes; (*b*) territorial and personal; (*c*) secular and religious; (*d*) incorporated and independent; (*e*) removable and irremovable; and (*f*) exempt and nonexempt.[5] These various aspects of the parish, some of which are overlapping, must be known by the student of canon law, but they are not important to our present purpose.

The student of society may find it fruitful to analyze the normal large urban Catholic parish under any of the following aspects. Each varies in importance as a conceptual frame of reference for the research scientist. The parish may be considered (*a*) a legal corporation; (*b*) a superimposed association; (*c*) an institutionalized association; (*d*) a communal group; or (*e*) a cluster of subgroupings. It is also helpful for some purposes to conceive the parish as (*f*) a network of family relations and (*g*) a series of statistical categories. Even this list is not, of course, exhaustive or all-embracing.

a) The parish is a *legal corporation* according to two systems of law, the canonical code of the Church and the civil code of the state. Having its own canon law, the Catholic Church does not recognize or admit the right of the state to make laws governing the existence and operation of the parish, but in the *de facto* situation there are numerous instances in which the Catholic parish takes cognizance of the civil law.[6] This is not merely a reference to the acceptance of, and compliance with, codes which prescribe regulations concerning building, sanitation, fire prevention, etc. In-

4. See T. Lincoln Bouscaren and Adam C. Ellis, *Canon Law: A Text and Commentary* (2d rev. ed.; Milwaukee: Bruce Publishing Co., 1951).

5. Ludovicus Fanfani, *De iure parochorum* (Rome: Marietti, 1924), pp. 3–7. For a more recent work on this subject see Laurentius Agius, *Summarium iurium et officiorum parochorum* (Naples: D'Auria, 1953).

6. See Charles Augustine, *The Canonical and Civil Status of Catholic Parishes in the United States* (St. Louis: B. Herder Book Co., 1926), and for several interesting cases of pastors and parishioners before the civil courts see *ibid.*, pp. 305–25.

corporating as a legal entity under the laws of the state has been considered a helpful convenience by American parishes and dioceses.

The juridic notion of a pastor in Canon 451 implies that the parish is a moral person, a legal entity, a canonical corporation. A whole section of the Code (Canons 451–86) deals with the rights and obligations of pastors and necessarily discusses the parishioners.[7] The pastor is a priest or a moral person to whom a parish is intrusted with the care of souls to be exercised under the authority of the local ordinary. Scores of commentaries have been written concerning the canonical relationship between pastor and parishioners, and a further discussion of this aspect would be superfluous here.

The status of the parishioners in this canonical corporation, however, seems worthy of note, especially as it relates to the Catholic lay people in American cities. Abbo and Hannan remark that "the body of the faithful certainly constitutes a collectivity of which the law takes definite notice, since it is they for whom the pastor is appointed. In American civil law, this collectivity, if legally incorporated, is the repository of the rights and duties of the parish. It is not so under the law of the Church. If, then, it is said that the law of the Code does not deny juridic recognition to the body of the faithful as a collectivity, it is meant that it accords them this recognition in a very limited sphere, i.e., that of having all the resources of the parish, spiritual and temporal, administered in their behalf."[8]

As a legal corporation formed under the civil law of most states,[9] the urban Catholic parish has as its purposes and objectives "the holding and administering of property, real, personal and mixed, so that the same may be devoted to religious purposes, for the benefit of those who attend the Roman Catholic Church belonging to this corporation."

The members of this legal corporation under civil law also constitute the board of five directors who manage, administer, and control it. These are the "civilly" legal officers of the parish. The

7. See Bouscaren and Ellis, *op. cit.*, chap. v, pp. 188–227, and their definition from the point of view of the people, "a community of the faithful to which has been assigned its own rector with ordinary power in the internal forum for the care of souls."

8. John Abbo and Jerome Hannan, *The Sacred Canons* (St. Louis: B. Herder Book Co., 1952), I, 445–46. For a further contrast between the canonical and the civil legal corporation see Augustine, *op. cit.*, pp. 110–27.

9. The description of the parochial legal corporation given here is found in the official synodal publication of various American dioceses.

bishop is *ex officio* president; the vicar-general of the diocese is the vice-president; and the pastor holds the combined offices of secretary and treasurer. The two remaining members of the board are lay parishioners, formerly called "trustees," who are appointed by the bishop, usually for a term of two years. They are almost always successful professional and businessmen.

In practice, all legal and fiscal business of the parish is conducted by the secretary-treasurer, the pastor. The corporation charter forbids him to contract any debt over two hundred dollars and stipulates that "no real estate belonging to the corporation shall be sold, mortgaged or disposed of in any way without the vote and consent of all the five Directors."

The obvious intent of the parochial charter is that the effective legal control of the parish be in the hands of the clergy. The history of lay trusteeship in the parishes of the United States has demonstrated the wisdom and practicality of this arrangement.[10] The pastor, who is himself subject to higher authority in the administration of the parish, usually recognizes that the practical advice of the lay trustees can be very valuable. At the same time the laymen usually understand that their function is consultative rather than directive. The pastor is obliged to meet with them only on important financial decisions.

It is clear that the parishioners are not stockholders in this legal corporation, but they contribute the money and properties which the corporation administers. They are the "repository of the rights and duties" and the beneficiaries of the religious services and of the charitable, educational, and literary purposes for which the corporation was legally constituted. The two lay members of the board are not their elected representatives. Viewed in this light of civil law, the urban American parish is neither a spontaneously organized structure nor a mass-controlled organization. The lay people have no formal authority, direct or indirect, over the parochial corporation, but the corporation is an instrument of service to them.[11]

10. For a brief and reliable discussion of trusteeism see Theodore Maynard, *The Story of American Catholicism* (New York: Macmillan Co., 1941), pp. 187–96, 235–37.

11. This arrangement differs sharply from that of contemporary French-Canadian parishes. There the *fabrique*, or corporation, owns the real estate given by the parishioners for public worship; "it is the proprietor of the parish church, the rectory, and the sums of money assigned for the upkeep of those buildings and the celebration of the liturgical ceremonies." A lay warden is elected by the parishioners every year, and the three most recently

b) The urban Catholic parish may be called a *superimposed association* in the sense that the conditions for its existence are fixed by Rome through the local bishop. Canon 216 of the Code points out that every diocese must be divided into definite territorial areas, each with its own permanent pastor, people, and church.[12] Thus, the religious association of lay Catholics in any given parish is not a matter of choice by the people themselves as long as they reside within the designated boundaries. In practice, of course, some of the lay persons in any parish attend neighboring Catholic churches for religious services, and some participate in other parochial activities there, but a formally imposed and morally obligatory relationship still remains between them and the pastor of their own parish.

Of more importance than the territorial assignment of people to a definite parish is the fact that the general framework of their religious functions and objectives is also prescribed by church authorities outside the parish.[13] This means that, whenever the parishioners assemble for religious activities, they follow a pattern of worship and devotion which is *essentially* the same throughout the whole Catholic Church. The liturgical rituals of the Church, in so far as they are designed for public and corporate worship, can be termed ideal patterns of social relations. The moral and social behavior of parishioners, normatively posited in commandments, precepts, and rules of the Church, is also superimposed.

This accounts for the basic cultural universality of all Catholic parishes. At a certain minimum level there is permitted no variation, and this minimum is always centered around the essential values of the Roman rite. The regulatory patterns governing auricular confession, the form of Eucharistic consecration, and the administration of the other sacraments are rigidly fixed by the canon law of

---

elected wardens form the board of administrators. They "set limits to the authority of the parish priest; they also set limits to the authority of the bishop." This is written by the Most Reverend Maurice Roy, archbishop of Quebec, in *The Parish and Democracy in French Canada* (Toronto: University of Toronto Press, 1950), pp. 17 ff. Some American dioceses are "corporation soles," so that the parishes are merely part of the single local corporation, the diocese.

12. See also the discussion in *Dynamics of a City Church*, Vol. I of *Southern Parish* (Chicago: University of Chicago Press, 1951), chap. 2, "What Is the Parish?"

13. Hiller's concept of the "institutional group" is partly similar to our concept of the parish as a "superimposed association" in that the cultural system of the Church provides a common value-orientation for the members of the parish (Ernest T. Hiller, "Institutions and Institutional Groups," *Social Forces*, XX, No. 3 [March, 1942], 297–306).

the Church. At another level there are regulatory patterns fixed in each diocese by the bishop. For example, a bishop may dispense his diocese from abstinence on those Fridays which concur with national holidays or patronal feasts, while another bishop may refuse to do so. Each diocese has its own synodal decrees which are obligatory only on the parishes of that diocese.

From a sociological point of view this superimposition of basic cultural patterns from outside the parish is probably the greatest difference between the Catholic parish and the Protestant congregation. The latter has a wide range of selection which may be developed by its minister and participants. This is evidenced not only in the creedal divergences but also in the variety of worship services among the various denominations, as well as among the various congregations within the same denomination. These groupings tend much more to be institutionalized associations, in the sense discussed below, than superimposed associations.

c) The Catholic parish may also be conceptualized as an *institutionalized association*.[14] This is the fact which makes each parish a unique social phenomenon, different from every other parish. In other words, the patterned relationships in each urban parish have become institutionalized *locally*, by and for these particular people over a period of several generations in this designated territory of so many city blocks. In this sense, the parochial social system may be said to be a product of its own members.

As Wach remarks, "the sociologist of religion, interested in the study of the cultic group, cannot be satisfied with reviewing its theology as the foundation of the theory and practice of fellowship among its members."[15] Even the most sympathetic observer will note that the facts of social life in the urban parish frequently fail to conform to the expectations of social thought and behavior implied in the moral and dogmatic teachings of the Catholic Church.

This is simply another way of saying that, while there are many similarities among Catholic parishes all over the world, there are also distinctive features in each. The associative processes and pat-

14. The term "institutionalized group" used by Znaniecki seems to combine both concepts used above, "superimposed association" and "institutionalized association." His definition denotes "groups which are essentially cooperative products of their own members, but whose collective functions and statuses are partly institutionalized by other social groups" (Florian Znaniecki, "Social Organizations and Institutions," in *Twentieth Century Sociology*, eds. Georges Gurvitch and Wilbert E. Moore [New York: Philosophical Library, 1945], p. 212).

15. Joachim Wach, "Sociology of Religion," in *Twentieth Century Sociology*, p. 428.

terns are formed, maintained, and transmitted by these particular parishioners. They are affected by the age and sex composition, the occupational, marital, economic, and class status of the parishioners, as well as by the manner in which the parishioners perform the roles consonant with these statuses. They are affected by the various personalities which individuate each human interaction, by the goals toward which the roles actually function, and by the strong secular values of the American urban and industrial milieu.

d) The fourth way in which the Catholic parish may be conceptualized is that of a *communal group*[16] that is, of a number of people who are held together primarily by their high religious values. Clinchy, who is a close observer of religious behavior, says that "the central element in the structure of a group's existence is religion. . . . The heart and will of every culture lie in the beliefs of the group: that is, its religion. Without convictions about what is good, and without specific beliefs about its goals and the means to attain them, the group's *esprit* will decline, and the group will perish."[17]

This concept of the parish as a communal group rests upon the negative notion that the group will perish unless it holds values of a high order. This is one of Sorokin's most emphasized sociological principles: that people are truly integrated by their "systems of meanings and values."[18] Thomas and Znaniecki also use this principle when they call a parish "a kind of great family whose members are united by a community of moral interests."[19] Finally, Donovan remarks that "the members of the parish, both clerical and lay, share in a unity which stems from their common religious beliefs and which finds expression in their joint participation in group functions."[20]

These observations constitute the hypothesis that the *sharing*

16. MacIver's "communal type" of society, as distinguished from the "associational type," includes a number of factors other than high values (see R. M. MacIver and Charles H. Page, *Society: An Introductory Analysis* [New York: Rinehart & Co., 1937], pp. 8–12, 218–29).

17. Everett Clinchy, "The Efforts of Organized Religion," *Annals of the American Academy of Political and Social Sciences*, CCXLIV (March, 1946), 128.

18. Pitirim Sorokin, *Society, Culture and Personality* (New York: Harper & Bros., 1947), p. 127.

19. William I. Thomas and Florian Znaniecki, *The Polish Peasant in Europe and America* (New York: A. A. Knopf, 1927), I, 275.

20. John D. Donovan, "The Sociologist Looks at the Parish," *American Catholic Sociological Review*, XI, No. 2 (June, 1950), 68. Wach (*op. cit.*, p. 428) similarly says that "religious communities are constituted by loyalty to an ideal or set of values which is the basis of their communion."

of common values is the essential sociological and psychological factor of the Catholic parish as a group. Empirical research indicates that the *sharing of functions* is a much more practical factor of unity. In simple terms this means that, when people do things together which they think are worth doing, they tend to be drawn together. The interacting influence of co-operative functions seems to increase the group appreciation of values, which in turn leads to progressive interaction.

It is quite possible that smaller village parishes tend toward the ideal of the communal group. In the large urban parish, however, the great majority of lay persons seem to use the local church as a kind of "service station" for their religious needs: a place to go to Mass and confession, get married, and have their children baptized and their old folks buried. Their communal "social" bond with the priests and other parishioners is analogous to that which an automobile owner has with the gas-station manager and with the latter's other customers. It is somewhat like the professional relationship between dentist and patients.[21]

While the concept of a genuinely integrated communal group does not apply to the whole urban parish as a social aggregate, this does not mean that primary, communal relationships are completely absent from the parish. As a matter of fact, there is at the heart of every urban parish a group of parishioners who are united primarily through their high religious values. It appears that only these can fulfil Thomas and Znaniecki's definition of the parish as a "great family."

e) The fact that various functions are performed and various objectives attained in an organized way leads to the fifth concept of the urban parish as a cluster of *subgroupings.* Each of these has it own objectives, activities, and membership. The pastor is theoretically and ex officio the highest authority in all of them. Their ultimate objective must in some way conform to that of the parish as a whole: the sanctification and salvation of souls. But their immediate objectives help to specify the various groups.

It has been noted that the total parochial association is superimposed and maintained according to universal standards of the Catholic Church. Much more latitude is allowed in the origin and maintenance of the parochial subgroupings. The original impetus for the formation of a group comes sometimes from the people and

21. Brogan developed a similar analogy (D. W. Brogan, "The Catholic Church in America," *Harper's,* CC, No. 1200 [May, 1950], 40–50).

sometimes from the pastor. Occasionally its formation may be requested by the bishop.

These "parish societies" may be classified in many ways, according to age and sex composition, marital status, and religious conditions of membership, although these norms are not in every instance defined. They may be placed on a continuum indicating the degree of success or failure they have experienced in striving for their objectives. They may be divided as formally imposed or locally initiated, who orginated them and where.

Probably the most useful sociological approach is that which considers the main functions and goals of the parish subgroupings or "societies." (1) The *liturgical* groups are those which assist at the religious services performed in the church itself. The Acolyte Society, the choir, and the ushers take a more or less direct part in the services; the Ladies' Altar Society provides the appurtenances of the sanctuary. (2) The *sociospiritual* groups are sufficiently distinctive in their functions and objectives to be considered separately from those in the above category. They are organized into social groups for the primary objective of sanctification. They include, for example, the Children of Mary, the sodalities, the junior and senior Holy Name societies, and the Nocturnal Adoration societies. (3) In the category of *educational* groupings are included the parents' clubs, the Confraternity of Christian Doctrine, and study clubs of various kinds. (4) The *ameliorative* groups do the corporal works of mercy, St. Vincent de Paul conferences for men and the Daughters of Mercy for women. In a sense they act as the parochial "relief agencies" for the needy families and individuals of the parish. (5) Finally, the primarily *recreational* objectives are pursued in the Boy and Girl Scouts, Brownies and Cubs, boys' and girls' sport teams, and in the adult committees which promote these groupings.

It must be pointed out, however, that these formally organized subgroupings do not embrace all the parishioners in any parish. Although membership in these voluntary groupings is open to all (except the very youngest children), it is probably true to say that no American urban parish can claim that more than a third of its members are participants in the parochial organizations. Numerically therefore this concept suffers the same limitations as does the parish when considered as a communal group. It cannot be accorded a total application to the parish.

f) The concept of the urban American parish as a *network of family relations* is more subtle and more difficult to analyze. While it is probably false to assert that "religion runs in families," we have found that participation in parochial programs is frequently a "family affair." We noted this particularly in parish organizations: sons and daughters tend to be active in the youth groups when their parents are active in the adult societies of the parish.

In the actual functioning of the urban parish, however, there tends to be a discrete relationship of the individual qua individual to the parish center rather than a "group" relationship as a member of a family. In this the Catholic parish differs most markedly from the Jewish congregation, wherein a man is a member of the congregation as head of the family and others become members through him. In most urban parishes it is a notable fact that the members of a family do not usually attend Mass and other services together. If there are small children in the family, the parents attend Mass separately; the children of school age have their own Mass, at which attendance is obligatory; and the adolescents may go to still another Mass with their friends rather than with the members of their family. The majority of parishioners, however, come to the church without a partner or companion.[22]

It is interesting to note that pastors frequently estimate the size of the parish by the number of families rather than by the number of individuals who live in the parochial territory. Even in one of the largest downtown churches where over six thousand persons attend Mass every Sunday, most of them from hotels and rooming-houses, the pastor still says, "Our parish is made up of only about one hundred and fifty families."[23] This is probably a residual pattern of thinking derived from the era when community, family, and parish tended to be identified. It is also probably the result of the continued system of keeping the census files by families, according to which the data on all members of the family are kept on the same card.

From the point of view of the parishioners themselves, a con-

22. This is probably not true in suburban parishes or in places where most parishioners go to church in automobiles. Our statistical checks were made in city parishes where the church is within walking distance of most residences.

23. He refers, of course, to those who have a domicile, or quasi-domicile, in the parish. The transients, called *peregrini*, are not in a strictly canonical sense termed "parishioners" (see Canon 94, nn. 2, 3). Harbrecht (*op. cit.*, pp. 23–24) holds that the canonical axiom, "Quisquis est in paroecia, est de paroecia," applies even in this case. This fluid group constitutes a *de facto* category in the downtown parish, and the pastor quoted in the text remarked that "it would be impossible and illogical to leave them out of consideration in the actual operation of the parish."

sciousness of "family membership" in the parish appears to be present only in the nuclear parishioners and those of long residence. This occurs not only because these people are closer to the parish center but also because they are closer to one another. Continuous day-by-day association of the social researcher with these families brings out this fact more clearly than any over-all statistical analysis could achieve. These families know the main "Catholic families" of the parochial area; they identify themselves with them and are able to give a quite reliable account of their religious status.

The concept of the parish as a network of family relations is scientifically meaningful as a criterion of the transition from the relatively communal to the relatively associational structure of the urban parish. As an analytical tool for the understanding of the parish, this concept has greater scientific significance in the former type than in the latter. This is precisely because the importance of family membership in the parish tends to fade during a period of several decades, particularly in the urban parish of multiple dwellings. It would be fruitful to contrast this urban situation with the fast-growing suburban parishes, where the majority of families are relatively young and where there is frequently a deliberate attempt to foster community spirit and parish loyalty.

g) Besides the six general conceptualizations so far described, it seems useful also to think of the urban parish as a series of *statistical categories* into which the membership falls. The significance of a classification of parishioners lies in the comparison of one category with another and of each with the religious ideals and practices which the parish is promoting. In the first volume of *Southern Parish* these categories were employed in many ways according to age, sex, marital status, socioeconomic status, length of residence, amount of schooling, nationality background, etc.

One of the most frequently employed devices in this regard among American sociologists is the attempt to correlate denominational membership with social status. The influence of the Warner school and the preoccupation of some American sociologists with social stratification have resulted in a number of studies indicating the status of denominations.[24] This has not been pursued to its congregational or parochial refinement, even though it is obvious

24. W. R. Goldschmidt, "Class Denominationalism in Rural California Churches," *American Journal of Sociology*, XLIX, No. 4 (January, 1944), 348–55; Liston Pope, *Millhands and Preachers* (New Haven: Yale University Press, 1942).

to any observer that some parishes have "higher status" because they are in better neighborhods. Internally, however, most urban Catholic parishes include a fairly broad stratification. The correlation of religious fidelity with socioeconomic status is one of the most obvious applications of this concept in the sociology of the parish.

The use of these categories is a practical device for answering many questions concerning the religious observances of the large city parishes. Using age and sex categories, we have been able to show that parishioners of both sexes reach a religious ebb in their thirties and that at all ages females show better religious performance than males.[25] By rearranging the categories in various ways, we have found that single persons are more faithful to religious duties than married persons, those in Catholic marriages better than those in mixed marriages, certain ethnic groups better than others, etc. The value of this approach seems greatest to the parish priest who wishes to probe the weaknesses and recognize the strengths of his parish population in their formal religious observances.

Statistical categories based on religious practices have led to a convenient stratification of the urban parish. For example, the functional deficiencies of the parish may be measured by the size and composition of the "dormant" category, made up of those who are *in the parish but not of it*. The "marginal" parishioners constitute a number of people who are on the fringe of the parochial aggregate. "Modal" parishioners are the largest number of the ordinary "practicing" Catholics in the area. The relatively small class of "nuclear" parishioners is at the center of parish life, while an even smaller number may be called the "leadership group." Foregoing chapters of this book analyzed these major categories in some detail.

This brief account of seven ways in which the complex social structure of an urban Catholic parish can be abstractly analyzed is not meant to be exhaustive. A conceptual framework is valuable, after all, only in so far as it serves the specific purpose of the social scientist. There is probably no "best way" in which to conceptualize a social unit except the way which best helps the scientist to give meaning to his data. It is possible, therefore, that numerous other approaches may be devised and employed for fruitful empirical research.

25. See "The Profile of Catholic Religious Life," *American Journal of Sociology*, LVIII, No. 2 (September, 1952), 145–49.

We have found, for example, that the study of small informal cliques and of the various subneighborhoods of the parish provide a fascinating insight into the social relations of parishioners. The friendship cliques are not strictly parochial, like the organized subgroupings discussed above, but they tend to show the degree to which primary relationships are carried on with both Catholics and non-Catholics. The subneighborhoods are roughly defined areas surrounding a corner drugstore, grocery store, and/or bar. There are from thirty to forty such areas in the normal residential urban parish. They are valuable sources of knowledge concerning the type of both casual and frequent contacts which parishioners have with their immediate neighbors.

Running through almost all these approaches, however, are two concepts which are basic to the understanding of the urban parish; the first may be termed *functional,* and the other *structural.* The functional approach analyzes the social roles of the persons-in-action within the parochial system. For example, there can be no question but that the key persons in the operation of any Catholic parish are the priests. This is true not only of the direct "care of souls" but also of the whole problem of maintaining the social structure as a going concern. Thus the pastoral roles may be separately analyzed.[26]

Other full-time functionaries in the parish (schoolteachers, secretaries, janitors, etc.) play social roles which cannot be neglected, the study of which tends to give insight into the operation of the total parochial system. They are subsidiary roles which have been institutionalized over a period of time, and they are collectively important in achieving the general objectives of the parish. Also open to analysis are the roles of the lay persons who are acting either as individuals or as group members in the various voluntary activities which occur in every urban parish.

The structural approach ties together all these roles in the rank ordering and communicational system of the parish. The so-called "chain of command" or bureaucracy of any social unit is frequently unobtrusive and informal. This is an important factor, and sometimes a crucial one, in the urban culture where parishioners, like other Americans, have become imbued with the democratic ideology. Crisis situations bring to the fore the fact that in the ultimate analysis the parish is administered by the priests and not by the laity.

The evolving urban parish in America, where culturally attuned priests are the administrators, seems to be steering a psychologically

26. See above, chap. 10, discussion of the priest's roles.

difficult course between two extremes. The ecclesiastical constitution cannot allow the "congregational system" wherein the lay people run the church, while the active vocation of the parishioner would wither under an "authoritarian system" wherein the lay people are mere passive subjects of church administration. The priest-parishioner relationship is, of course, reciprocal. The laity cannot do without the clergy; the clergy cannot do without the laity. The relationship of these statuses has become structured in the parish and must be assumed to exist in all the various conceptualizations which have been suggested in this chapter.

Chapter Fifteen

Major Issues in the Sociology
of the Parish[1]

THE sociology of the parish is in some ways a clearly defined area of knowledge, but it is also a subarea of the more general field of the sociology of religion. Because of the insufficient and inadequate data so far collected in research, and because of an almost total lack of genuine hypotheses and theories, the sociology of the parish is still in an inchoative stage of development. In an effort to clarify this situation, Professor Francis has indicated certain tasks for American Catholic sociologists, and Professor Nuesse has pointed out the types of problems which require investigation in the American parish.[2] In the light of these serious suggestions it is interesting to note that the only American book which bears the title *Sociology of the Parish* is less sociological than it is canonical, theological, philosophical, and historical.[3]

1. The ideas developed in this chapter are based on "Major Issues of Parish Sociology," *American Ecclesiastical Review*, CXXVIII, No. 5 (May, 1953), 369–83.
2. Francis demands an increasingly rigid research technique and suggests three general areas of research: (*a*) American Catholicism as a cultural and social system, (*b*) various social problems in which Catholics are involved, and (*c*) the inner functioning of Catholic institutions (E. K. Francis, "Suggestions to American Catholic Sociologists for a Scheme of Research," *Lumen Vitae*, VI, Nos. 1–2 [1951], 160–65). In the same periodical Nuesse mentions six problem areas for research: (*a*) demographic trends, (*b*) religious observance, (*c*) associational participation, (*d*) ethnic and class systems, (*e*) integration of parish and community, and (*f*) ecology of the parish (C. J. Nuesse, "American Research Bearing upon the Sociology of the Parish," *Lumen Vitae*, VI, Nos. 1–2 [1951], 157 ff.).
3. In the present writer's opinion the best technically sociological contribution to *The Sociology of the Parish*, ed. C. J. Nuesse and Thomas J. Harte (Milwaukee: Bruce Publishing Co., 1951) is John D. Donovan's chap. iii, "The Social Structure of the Parish," pp. 75–99. His unpublished doctoral dissertation at Harvard University, "The Catholic Priest: A Study in the Sociology of the Professions," is also an excellent sociological contribution to the literature in this field.

It has become a textbook axiom that good theory comes out of good research in the sense that hypotheses can be tested and validated by factual knowledge. "Experts are not made by standing on the sidelines and theorizing. They have to come in contact with the real problem to know its nature and make effective use of their academic knowledge."[4] It is true also that good research provides new theoretical insight and raises new problems of research. The stimulation of insight and discussion among scientists is one of the most important results emerging from research. It is almost trite to say that this process of analysis and comment by fellow-scientists is of immense value in the scientific search for truth, because challenging questions are raised, new problems are recognized, paradigms for further research are devised, and knowledge is expanded.

There are at least three levels on which theory and research can be combined for the further development of the sociology of the parish. On the highest and most abstract level there is "the all-inclusive speculation comprising a master conceptual scheme," a kind of system-building which is more philosophical than scientific and for which there is not nearly sufficient research data in the sociology of the parish. At the lowest level there are "the minor working hypotheses evolved in abundance during the day-by-day routines of research." For the most part, the basic research and theory involved in the *Southern Parish* project, and in the chapters of the present book, belong on this lowest level. It is to be hoped that, when sufficient research of this kind has been done in various parishes, a series of dependable generalizations can be made concerning parochial life.

In between these two levels are found what Merton has called "theories of the middle range,"[5] and it appears that the research required for this type of theory can be done only after comparisons and analyses have been made of a relatively large number of "lower-range" research projects. In a limited way, some of these items have developed from the comments and criticisms made by the reviewers

4. M. E. Tracy, quoted by Pauline V. Young, *Scientific Social Surveys and Research* (New York: Prentice-Hall, Inc., 1939), p. 1. But it must be noted that one may be an expert in the theory and art of painting without ever having painted a picture. Similarly, a social scientist need not be the administrator of a college, a hospital, a city, or a parish before he can study and understand the social relations and functions of these organizations. On the other hand, it is also true that the administrator himself frequently has little competence for objective sociological analysis. See Appendix.

5. Robert Merton, *Social Theory and Social Structure* (Glencoe, Ill.: Free Press), 1949, p. 5. See his valuable chaps. ii and iii on the relation between sociological theory and empirical research.

of the *Southern Parish* report, *Dynamics of a City Church*. Commentators for the most part discussed the work from the vantage point of their own specific interests, with the result that a large variety of interpretations was presented. From the point of view of theory and research, however, several major issues were raised which are basically important, around which there has developed serious and intelligent discussion and from which certain modest theoretical generalizations may eventually emerge.

These "middle-range" items constitute some of the problem areas which require deeper analysis and further research in the field of parochial sociology. I have selected seven of these controversial issues for further discussion, but not with the intention of "settling" any of them. On the contrary, they are presented here because of their significance and their provocativeness and especially because they seem to admit of no easy answers. They represent the partial comment of five social scientists, Professors La Violette, Lynd, Wach, Eister, and Francis; of two priests, Fathers Reinhold and Schuyler; and of a Catholic social-actionist, Miss Bartelme.

The order in which these questions are here discussed does not mean to indicate an order of importance. As a matter of fact, their degree of importance may vary from time to time and from place to place. These major problem areas are as follows: (1) the impact of urban change on the religious behavior of Catholic parishioners; (2) the Church as a power structure in relation to the larger society; (3) social integration as a consequent of free religious choice; (4) the social implications of the sacraments and the liturgy; (5) the motivation of religious behavior; (6) the need for structural reform of the urban parish; and (7) the use of evaluative methodology in the sociology of the parish.

1. *Impact of urban change on the religious behavior of Catholic parishioners.*—This problem area is a social phenomenon which requires much more study and analysis.[6] Professor La Violette has dis-

6. The pioneer research done by Douglass and Sanderson on the urban Protestant churches placed emphasis on the influence of the city upon the Church as a total structure rather than upon the moral and religious practices of Church adherents (see H. Paul Douglass, *1000 City Churches* [New York: Harper & Bros., 1926]; *The Church in the Changing City* [New York: Harper & Bros., 1927]; *Church Comity* [New York: Harper & Bros., 1929]; *The City's Church* [New York: Friendship Press, 1929]; Ross W. Sanderson, *The Strategy of City Church Planning* [New York: Harper & Bros., 1932]; see also Samuel C. Kincheloe, *The American City and Its Church* [New York: Friendship Press, 1938], and Murray H. Leiffer, *The Effective City Church* [New York: Abingdon-Cokesbury Press, 1949]).

cussed the "assumption that in earlier days a closer conformance to the ideals of the Church existed."[7] In a traditional social system like the Catholic parish the older parishioners frequently allude to their younger days when "everybody was more religious." They imply that, together with all the other changes they have experienced in city life, there has been a change for the worse in religious observance and moral behavior. They give the impression that the modern generation is widely flaunting the precepts and practices of the elders.

The problem here is twofold: In what ways do the patterns of religious behavior now differ from those of our forefathers? What urban factors have been at work to bring about these differences? Satisfactory answers to both of these questions require not only carefully planned research but also a certain amount of difficult judgment and immediately involve the use of "evaluative methodology" discussed below. Central to this research problem is also the question: What scientific criteria can be used to distinguish what is better and what is worse in the generalized religious customs of a city church?

Certain social facts are so well known among urban parishioners that they require little elaboration. There has unquestionably been a decline in church attendance at (and in some parishes an abandonment of) traditional evening services, sermons, Vespers, Rosary, Benediction, etc. The proportion of mixed marriages is increasing. Relations between priests and parishioners are becoming less primary and more formalized. There has also been a decrease of interest and activity in the formal parochial subgroupings as well as in those gatherings like church suppers, parish festivals, and dances, which used to bring together large numbers of parishioners of every age in social intercourse.

On the other hand, there has been an increase in the frequency of the reception of Holy Communion and of the sacrament of penance by both sexes and at all age levels. Adult male attendance at Mass has increased both numerically and proportionately, and the recently instituted evening Mass in some cities has drawn overflow crowds.[8]

7. Forrest E. La Violette (Tulane University), *American Sociological Review*, XVII, No. 2 (1952), 254–55.
8. Since the completion of the data collection for the present volume, three new factors have been introduced: the evening Mass, the relaxed rules on the Eucharistic fast, and the air-conditioning of some city churches. It will be important to study the effects on religious practices of these "modern urban adaptations."

Nocturnal Adoration of the Blessed Sacrament has attracted large numbers of men. The First Friday in honor of the Sacred Heart and the First Saturday in honor of Our Lady of Fatima have brought increasing numbers to the city churches. The week-end retreat movement for both men and women is growing everywhere in our cities. The Block Rosary and Family Rosary have shown remarkable vitality. Other revitalized and popular expressions of religion are the Cana conferences, Christian Family circles, the liturgical movement, the Third Orders, Catholic Action, interracial councils, and similar socioreligious programs and activities.[9]

The factors of urban change are numerous and serious, and everyone recognizes them as having an effect upon the lives of more and more segments of the population. Housing is overcrowded, recreation is largely passive and commercialized, education and the professions are becoming more specialized, leisure time is increasing, the material standard of living continues to rise, and the means of communication and transportation are more available. Some of these aspects of urbanization affect also the people in smaller towns, and even in rural farm areas, in the sense that an "urban philosophy of life" is spreading throughout the country.

Much is said and written about secularism today and about the fact that cities are the centers of secularism. Have all these changes had a "secularizing effect" upon the Catholic urban parishioner? Have they made it more difficult for a person to be a forthright, integrated Christian? It is to be expected that in our dynamic society the modern executive is not like the industrialist of fifty years ago; and it is to be expected also that the modern Catholic parishioner does not fit the mold of a half-century ago. While it would be presumptuous to say that the Catholic Church has successfully met the challenge of American urbanization, it seems reasonable to make the tentative hypothesis that urban Catholic spirituality, while different, is not of a lower grade than its predecessor. At least, this hypothesis is worthy of serious consideration and scientific testing.

The factors of urban change and the process of change itself and its results must be studied *specifically* in relation to their significance to Catholics in parish life. A comparative research model would not be too difficult to construct. A simultaneous study could be carried

9. Most of these are nonparochial religious activities which seem to be adaptations to meet the demands of urban life, and their further expansion will unquestionably affect the strictly parochial functions and structures. See above, chap. 11.

on in two contemporary parishes, the one in a city which is presumed to be relatively dynamic, and the other in a village which is presumed to be relatively static. Perhaps in a city parish where dependable records have been maintained, the most recent ten-year period could be compared with the last decade of the last century.[10]

Testing the hypothesis that urban Catholicism is different, but not worse, than it used to be is complicated by the need to evaluate the many different modes of religious expression. The greatest difficulty probably lies in the selection of scientific criteria by which to judge what is "better" and what is "worse." Running through the comparison, of course, are certain central and expected religious observances like attendance at Sunday Mass, making the Easter duties, infant baptism, and validity of marriages. These are the perennial Catholic patterns of behavior which can be aptly used as norms of comparison and which lend themselves to measurement by rates and percentages.[11]

2. *The Church as a power structure in relation to the larger society.*—In this regard Professor Lynd has touched upon an explosively controversial concept. He is interested in the sociology of the Catholic parish because he regards the Catholic Church "as the best-organized international power structure operating across the world today." He thinks of the Church in technical terms as a "social apparatus," advancing rapidly, using planned programs, and having a stout but flexible policy which aims at enhancing welfare programs consonant with its doctrines in the general society.[12]

This raises the general but significant issue of the impact of Catholicism on the modern world. If this subject is put in terms of the struggle between the value systems of communism and Catholicism, or of the constant competitive effort between Protestantism and Catholicism to win converts to their respective religious beliefs and practices, it is not likely to cause controversy or protest. The American generally, and above all the objective social scientist who is American-trained, prides himself on a kind of cool aloofness from

10. Robert Redfield's *The Folk Culture of Yucatan* (Chicago: University of Chicago Press, 1941), a study of four communities on a continuum, is an example of the first; Everett C. Hughes's *French Canada in Transition* (Chicago: University of Chicago Press, 1943) is an example of the latter.
11. Comparisons made in previous chapters of this book and in *Dynamics of a City Church*, Vol. I of *Southern Parish* (Chicago: University of Chicago Press, 1951), have been within the parish aggregate. They do not measure change in religious practices between urban and nonurban environments.
12. Robert S. Lynd (Columbia University), *Annals of the American Academy of Political and Social Science*, CCLXXIX (1952), 228–29.

ideological struggles which are based on religion.[13] It is true that the values of the Catholic Church are in competition with, and sometimes in conflict with, other systems of values. But this is not the precise point at issue here.

A man like Lynd tends to ask the question: Values for what? or *Knowledge for What?* (the title of one of his best-known books). He recognizes that the values of Catholicism must involve the institutionalized structure of the Church as well as the people who make up the membership of the Church, but he does not descend to the level of men like Blanshard who seem to think that a "lust for power" is inherent in both the institutions and the functionaries of the Church. Professor Lynd's position (if I understand him correctly) seems to be this: If the Catholic Church has a negative outlook on human nature, holding that man is "fallen" and prone to "sin," and if the Church defines its role as the permanent agency to control men in less sinful directions (standing as an organization at the right hand of secular power), then we may fear the power strategy of the Church will be more likely to maintain and to strengthen its own power in the secular world by compromise with going institutions than it will be to trust man in his condemnation of the going institutions and in his fight to erect other institutions more conducive to supporting good social personalities and good social behavior.

Briefly, Lynd's central concern is the Church's attitude toward man as fundamentally sinful and the resulting authoritarian structure which attempts to offset this sinfulness. The point here is not that Lynd misinterprets Catholic theological dogma, attributing to Catholicism a teaching on fallen human nature which is essentially Lutheran and Calvinistic. The point is that he, like others, sees in it a threat to the democratic procedures of change. In other words, in what manner will this well-organized social apparatus, called the Roman Catholic Church, affect social functions, relations, and structures? The Church is committed to the apparently monumental task of restoring society with all its forms and institutions to Christ. This means that the Church aims at exerting a tremendous moral,

13. Kolb argues that the positivistic sociologist acts this way because he does not hold the ontic status of religious values and is thereby involved in this dilemma: as a scientist he must teach a "truth" which will destroy the socially integrating values of religion; as a citizen he must allow people to adhere to the "religious illusions" which help to integrate social life and institutions (William L. Kolb, "Values, Positivism, and the Functional Theory of Religion: The Growth of a Moral Dilemma," *Social Forces*, XXXI, No. 4 [May, 1953], 305–11).

cultural, and social influence over all aspects of human society. In this sense, the Church is an internal power structure with procedures which will necessarily eventuate in a changed society.[14]

There can be no doubt that, to a fearful and misinformed outsider, the sacred authority of the hierarchy and the loyal devotion of the laity look like the makings of a different sort of "power structure." The misapprehension of some non-Catholics in this regard seems to stem from two general misconceptions. The first is the belief that the monarchical and hierarchical administrative structure of the Church is almost totally inconsistent with the American democratic way of life.[15] The second is a failure to realize that (except for the religious institution) American Catholics have been culturally trained in the same traditions as other Americans and participate side by side with non-Catholics in the same social structures and forms and institutions.

These two misconceptions, as well as the political misapprehensions of some non-Catholics, can be allayed to some extent through the systematic study and reporting of the Church as a social system in American cities. It is a truism to say that people fear what they do not know. Catholicism as a social and cultural system is an unexplored area to millions of American Protestants. It is a jungle of myths even to the sociologists of religion who, as Lynd says, have found it a "hard-to-penetrate area." Fears, suspicions, and antagonisms are almost always associated with lack of knowledge. It must not be a matter of surprise when non-Catholics think that the Church's power structure has a Fascist flavor (which is as abhorrent to American Catholics as it is to them).

On the modest plane of social research of the parish—the grass-roots level of Catholicism—this question of the internal structure of the Church and of its influence on the local community cannot escape the attention of the social scientist. The universal missionary function is at work there: the intention to convert and embrace all within reach. We have indicated that the social role of the parish

14. J. Milton Yinger's *Religion in the Struggle for Power* (Durham, N.C.: Duke University Press, 1946) is a sympathetic study of moral suasion and not, as the title may suggest, a study of the authoritarian struggle between religion and the state, the economic system, etc. "In the last analysis this is a study of power. It raises the question: How much influence does religion exercise over the behavior of men? How much, in the competition with other powers, is it able to control behavior *in accordance with its own standards?*" (*ibid.*, p. 15).

15. This is also part of the problem which bothers Professor Eister, whose comments are discussed below in the third major issue.

priest extends into the civic community.[16] Much more must be learned about the specific ways in which priests and laymen "interfere" with local nonsacred institutions and the ways in which Catholics organize as pressure groups to obtain their objectives. Little systematic knowledge has been assembled on the parish level of the extent to which priests and laymen co-operate in social reforms, encourage the union or the management side in labor disputes,[17] get involved in political parties, influence commercial and business morality. We have also indicated above that the voluntary association of Catholic lay people in parish societies is a basically democratic process.[18] Further detailed studies of these subgroupings in action are required to understand the relation between the democratic attitudes of lay persons and the effective attainment of the objectives of the various groups.

In so far as it affects the local community, the genuine ideological influence of the Church is a moral and spiritual ascendancy which must ultimately affect the cultural patterns of thought and behavior of the whole society. It is said to be like the yeast which liberates and elevates and expands the "dough" of society. In spite of the traditional mores and the resistance to change found in even the most dynamic society, the Church is always dealing with human beings who have the power of choice. In general terms, that choice is still between God and mammon. The Church places its highest values before the individual human conscience, through which its influence must penetrate to all social institutions, promote the highest social and moral behavior, and clarify and strengthen the beliefs of men.

If it is true that human beings tend toward consistency in both their internal patterns and their external behavior, the influence of the Church over their hearts and minds must be an influence also over their conduct. The social scientist distinguishes between sacred and nonsacred behavior, and he is able to study cultural trends to

16. See above, chap. 10. The so-called social encyclicals call upon both priests and laity to accept moral responsibility in the general community. Davis remarks that the *Five Great Encyclicals* (New York: Paulist Press, 1939) "reveal in striking fashion the mental process by which supernatural absolutism is applied to social issues" (Kingsley Davis, *Human Society* [New York: Macmillan Co., 1949], p. 546).

17. Liston Pope's *Millhands and Preachers* (New Haven: Yale University Press, 1942), is an outstanding study of the way in which local Protestant churches reacted to industrial and commercial activities. No comparable study has been made of Catholic parishes in similar situations.

18. See chap. 12 on the internal structure of parish societies.

determine which is predominant. In so far as the Church succeeds in replacing secularism with supernaturalism in society, it functions unquestionably as a moral power structure and works toward ends which are logically within its legitimate values.

3. *Social integration as a consequent of free religious choice.*— The question involved in these two terms is what Allan Eister has called a "head-on collision." He challenges the assumption that the Roman Catholic Church or any other formal religious organization can be the likeliest agency for the social reintegration of Western society.[19] This statement is said to be in disagreement with the "liberal democratic view" that the best guaranty of social unity is the principle of individual freedom to choose one's way to God and salvation.

Perhaps no one knows better than a social scientist that there is a fundamental divergence between these two theoretical approaches to social integration. The liberal Protestant view does not necessarily and always hold that everyone's religion is objectively true (or that one religion is as good as another), but it does hold the principle that everyone should be free to choose his own way to God. As a matter of fact, the Catholic Church officially indorses the principle that people must be allowed freely to choose the truth and follow it.[20] But the Church always and necessarily teaches that objective religious truth is one, that the Church is the divinely appointed guardian of that truth on earth, and that all other denominations and sects are to some degree in error.[21]

But the thesis here under consideration deals with the matter of social integration. Is social unity better achieved on a basis of consensus on doctrinal values and practices (such as the Catholic Church strives for) or on a basis of "agreeing to disagree" (such as Eister seems to encourage)? Anthropological studies of various societies and communities throughout the world tend to conclude that integrated social relations usually occur when there is major

19. Allan W. Eister (Southern Methodist University), *Southwestern Social Science Quarterly*, XXXII, No. 4 (1952), 281–83. See my *Dynamics of a City Church*, p. 4, and above, chap. 4, on solidarity.

20. Canon 1351: "No one is to be forced to embrace the Catholic faith against his will" (see the important contribution to this question by George W. Shea, "Spain and Religious Freedom," *American Ecclesiastical Review*, CXXVII, No. 3 [1952], 161–72).

21. This sort of statement is undoubtedly a central irritant to Protestants, but not all have been irritated by it (see Murray Leiffer, *Garrett Tower*, XXVII, No. 1 [December, 1951], 17, and G. S. Dobbins, *Review and Exposition*, July, 1952).

consensus on the highest beliefs and valuations.[22] Within the ethos, or the "ideal core" of the culture, religious and moral beliefs are objectively scaled toward the top of the value heirarchy.

The approach to this problem involves the whole question of scientific objectivity. It is not merely a question of whether social consensus comes out of the free choice of individuals or out of the authoritarian sanctions which a Church sets up. It is also a matter of the social scientist's suspicion that a man who is committed to the whole Catholic value system will be unconsciously biased toward interpreting his data on social integration. It is conceded that the researcher in social science will undoubtedly have his own "sectarian bias," which is indicated by his selection of a particular area of research in the sociology of religion.[23] He goes scientifically astray, however, not by stating his "bias" but by trying to conceal it, or by forcing his discovered social facts to coincide with his bias. This is, of course, the scientifically unforgivable sin.

A social scientist, however, may still tentatively hold the hypothesis of social solidarity based on consensus of values, even though limited research in urban Catholic parishes indicates that Catholics are for the most part united more on secular ideologies than on common religious beliefs. For example, we have found that white Catholics are often closely integrated in overt social relations with white Protestants, co-operating actively in various groups and organizations but refusing to have any association with Negroes who are their fellow-parishioners and members with them in the Mystical Body of Christ.[24]

22. Although there is still much dispute about the origins, cultural diversity, and historical development of the religious institution, there is no longer any doubt among social scientists about its universality and its function as a socially integrative factor (see, e.g., Robert H. Lowie, *Social Organization* [New York: Rinehart & Co., 1948], chap. viii; Franz Boas [ed.], *General Anthropology* [New York: D. C. Heath & Co., 1938], chap. xiv by Ruth Benedict).

23. Eister agrees on this point. In an unpublished manuscript, "Note on Objectivity, Value Commitment, and Social Science," he writes that "there is really no *scientific* excuse for the scientist to refuse to commit himself to any values involving some choice or decision which he openly expresses when the matter is controversial and even when it lies within his own field of investigation and study" (p. 6).

24. See above, chap. 4. This constantly recurring example of racial relations may indicate that for some people the institutionalized caste system has almost the force of religious dogma. Indeed, the use of biblical arguments in favor of segregation occurs among persons who have otherwise deeply religious and fundamentalist convictions.

This is a serious sociological problem because the research data on urban Catholicism seem to challenge a hypothesis which appears to be historically demonstrable and to which most social theorists cling. There are many avenues open to research in this field. Have the nonsacred values in the local community developed an integrative force equal to, or surpassing that of, the traditional religious values? Has secularization in American cities reached a kind of limit, so that we are now going through an interim phase of anomic thought patterns which will soon give way to a restructuring of the religious and moral beliefs of the people? If we are in a transitional stage of this kind, it may be scientifically fruitful to investigate the following questions: Is the size (territorial and numerical) of the typical urban parish a factor in the apparent diminution of religious solidarity? Does the small rural parish demonstrate the social integration which is lacking in the city congregation, and, if so, what sociological factors are significant? Is there any influence from the ethnic composition of the parish population, the occupational roles of the parishioners, their social status, their local and regional mobility?

The issue raised by Professor Eister, and particularly his assumption that freedom of religious choice is a principle of social integration, requires scientific analysis and research. If I understand him correctly, he appears to have assumed this position through a fear of the institutionalization and formalization built up around the profound religious insights of Catholicism. He believes that every institutional organization, even the Church, must rigidly eschew any claims to divine sanction or sacrosanct status. From this point of view, this issue is similar to that of Professor Lynd, who fears the influence of an authoritarian ecclesiastical power structure upon the freedom of thought and action of people in a democracy.

In spite of these fears and biases which may surround the issue, the assumption that social integration can be a consequent of free religious choice does not appear to be logically tenable. While freedom of conscience is a sacred right of individuals which may not be morally impugned, there is no inherent reason why it should be expected to result in social unity. Nor can it be logically accepted merely because large numbers of Americans seem to believe it. The principles of democracy and universal brotherhood in the United States may help to achieve a social unity and an integrated culture *which allows for fundamental differences of religious beliefs.*

But it has been a quasi-nationalism which has embraced antagonistic religious loyalties and which has perhaps substituted for a system of unifying religious values.[25]

Two observations may, therefore, be made concerning the relatively peaceful coexistence of fundamentally differing religious bodies in America: first, this phenomenon has arisen *in spite of* (not because of) our different religious beliefs; and, second, we Americans have perhaps subordinated, through a spirit of religious indifferentism, our religious values to patriotic and nationalistic values. American Catholics, at least on a theoretical and doctrinal basis (if not on the basis of day-by-day social relations), offer a principle of unity quite different from that of Professor Eister. Catholics maintain that wide religious consensus tends to diminish group antagonisms and thus increase national unity and social integration.

4. *Social implications of the sacraments and the liturgy.*—Father Joseph Schuyler says that the "tremendous potentiality" of the sacraments and the liturgy "for achieving social harmony in Catholic and civic life" must be studied by the sociologist of the parish.[26] From one point of view, his hypothesis is a deeper and more abstract support of my own stand against Eister on religious consensus as a principle of social integration. It is an important concept, and it is given some consideration in a paper on "Parochial Solidarity" read by the author at the 1949 Convention of the American Catholic Sociological Society in Chicago. It is doubtful, however, that the subject is treated in the manner which the reviewer seems to suggest.

In a sense this problem also overlaps the question of motivation of religious behavior mentioned below. The operation of divine grace[27] through the sacraments provides a real social unity (in the higher ontological order), since baptism introduces persons into a social Body of Christ, and the Eucharist—the Sacrament of Love—unites them more closely to God and to their fellow-men. The liturgy, through the actual social participation of the laity in reli-

25. Arnold Rose, however, suggests that there is a mounting tension between Catholics and Protestants in American cities. His thesis, though supported by a few factual errors, that this is due to conflicting value systems, tends to bear out the hypothesis on value consensus and social solidarity (Arnold and Caroline Rose, *America Divided: Minority Group Relations in the United States* [New York: A. A. Knopf, 1948], pp. 54–60).

26. Joseph B. Schuyler (Woodstock College), *Woodstock Letters*, LXXXI, No. 1 (1952), 100–101.

27. See above, chap. 4, for the discussion of "solidarity by divine grace."

gious services, provides a social situation for group prayer, thought, and action.

These "social implications" of the sacraments and the liturgy have been discussed time and again in popular as well as in learned Catholic periodicals. God's grace *does* unite Catholics on a spiritual plane, and it *should* motivate them to live more harmoniously in the day-to-day social relations in which they participate. This doctrine has been widely taught and preached as a compelling *motive* for the improvement of the actual social relations among Catholics.

But the social scientist works on a lower plane. He must grub among the profane and the measurable. He readily admits that the external social behavior which he observes, the words that he hears, may well be activated by sacramental grace and liturgical ideals; but he also regrets to admit that he cannot measure the functioning of divine grace in itself. He is, however, brought up against some hard facts. When he studies a Catholic parish in which the rich and the poor have no social contact, and less sympathy, with each other, where whites and Negroes are separated by rigid caste lines, where the successful materialist enjoys higher social prestige than the tubercular saint who is dying of starvation—he asks himself where is the social and externally observable fulfilment of the sacramental and liturgical ideals?

The social scientist expects to see no miracles, and he must always be careful to distinguish *what ought to be* from *what is*. But he also respectfully agrees that there is great wisdom in the biblical dictum: "By their fruits you shall know them." Although there are deep social implications in religious doctrines, there appears to be no guaranty that the implications will become explicit in the social conduct of parishioners. Even in those areas of social behavior where the sociologist recognizes behavioral integration he is reluctant to attribute it to elusive spiritual influences.

The preacher, the theologian, the social philosopher, perform a socially valuable service when they explain and urge the necessity for implementation of socioreligious ideals. They demonstrate logically the intrinsic connection between the order of grace and the order of nature. They explain carefully that, in the life of the integrated Christian, human co-operation with divine grace must result in the striving for both personal and social perfection. But the social scientist reports what he sees and hears. He analyzes these reports and tries to generalize on that which is relevant and significant *within the selected area of study*.

The question of immediate interest to the social scientist, therefore, is not the social implication of the sacraments and the liturgy but their social results. An area of fruitful research could be staked out here. Two categories of people could be studied and compared within the same community. The variable element would be the presence or absence of sacraments and liturgy. The constant element would be the actual social integration and social awareness exhibited by each group. In other words, the Catholics, who have the advantage of the sacraments and the Mass, could be compared with the non-Catholics who do not have these advantages.

Out of a controlled study of this kind there could be discovered in some rough way the extent to which the social implications of sacraments and liturgy are realized. It is one thing to assert that these sacred rites should have social implications; it is quite another thing to demonstrate the social effects which they have actually produced in a given parish. A realistic awareness of the facts of social life is ultimately more valuable for the progress of both religion and social science than the most masterful effort to demonstrate a priori that social solidarity ought to flow from certain doctrines and rituals.

5. *Motivation of religious behavior.*—The analysis of motivation is one of the most difficult areas into which the social psychologist or sociologist can venture. At the same time it is one of the most important, since the social results of the false imputation of motives are frequently serious. Motivation is complex and multiple, and its relation to specific human actions is frequently obscure. In a discussion of religious practices Wach suggests the importance of a systematic analysis and study of the fact that "identical behavior might be motivated quite differently." He remarks that the subjective approach—by interview and questionnaire—would provide an opportunity to achieve "a greater understanding of what considerations (feelings, values) actually motivate people's attitudes and actions."[28]

In the hierarchy of motives for social behavior it is undoubtedly true that the "highest" is the love of God. When the social scientist observes the external patterns of religious behavior in a parish,

28. Joachim Wach (University of Chicago), *Journal of Religion*, XXXII, No. 2 (April, 1952), 139–41. He points out also that Protestant theologians, educators, psychologists, and sociologists have frequently of late stressed the necessity of analyses of motivation. A popular Protestant application of this interest is John Sutherland Bonnell, *Psychology for Pastor and People* (New York: Harper & Bros., 1948).

he must assume that the agents are motivated, at least to some degree, by divine love. But this assumption is not scientifically verifiable with any degree of accuracy simply because the main factor involved is immeasurable and imponderable. This does not mean that saintly people go completely unrecognized. The procedure of canonization shows that the Church employs extraordinary criteria for discerning (after death) the sanctity of a person who has been steadily motivated by divine love.

The social scientist is constrained to study the social relations of living persons in contemporary groups. He knows in a general way that the motivational roots of human behavior are multiple and intertwined. His specific problem lies in trying to get at other than surface or assumed motives. People attend Mass, receive the sacraments, and participate in parochial activities for many and mixed reasons. They may have built up a habit pattern more out of imitation than out of conviction. The desire for social prestige may help or hinder their religious behavior, depending upon the cultural pressures of the community. Furthermore, their motives may vary from one time to another, from one situation to another, and run the gamut from divine love to conventional habit and even to personal gain.

The present tools of social psychology are admittedly inadequate for the measurement of motives, but the scientific attempt must be continued. Some of the techniques devised are ingenious: depth psychology or psychoanalysis, Rohrshach tests, apperception tests, thematic approaches, etc. Most of these are financially prohibitive in the study of a large social unit like the urban Catholic parish.

There remains the technique of the straight interview in which the individual parishioner explains his own behavior. Here the snare of rationalization, innocent though it may be, tends to trap the researcher. Every experienced social scientist realizes that some "downward revision" is usually necessary when a large group of people is questioned about attitudes, beliefs, what they "would do," and why they have acted in a certain way.[29] It is probably the recognition and expression of this fact by social scientists which has helped to gain them a reputation for cynicism among religious-minded people.

29. That is why my chapter on the "Catholic Mind of the Parish" was hedged around with numerous cautions and why the statistical results as published make the interviewees appear even "more Catholic" than they actually are (see *Dynamics of a City Church*, pp. 259–61).

Despite these difficulties, the findings of motivational analysis, in so far as they are reliable, would be extremely helpful to the Church and to the parish. If in any given situation there were even a general knowledge of the motivational factors of religious behavior, the clergy and laity could co-operate to manipulate those factors for favorable and desired results. Induced changes in institutional patterns and in social structures could promote the positive factors and discourage the negative.

The insistent instruction and preaching of the Church constantly emphasizes the highest motives for human conduct. This cannot be otherwise, for the Church by its nature must function in an inspirational way, and—it may be added—the Church is no amateur in the techniques of propaganda. While this particular spiritual impact on the individual conscience must not be diminished, it may find a helpful ally in a study of the more prosaic motives for the maintenance of a social conscience.

In other words, there is a need to understand the extent and manner in which nonspiritual motives affect religious behavior.[30] This is a study not simply of the actual social conditions existing in any parish but of the means-end relationship in which the social conditions become motives (or are rationalized as motives) for religious behavior. This knowledge could contribute much to the Church's attempt to improve the behavioral ideals of its members on the parish level. The problem in the realm of practical application is not only to raise the standards of motivation and to purify them; it is also to know the natural motives for social behavior in order to manipulate them.

6. *Need for structural reform of the urban parish.*—This is mentioned in some way or another by several persons who are interested in the sociology of religion. Father Reinhold suggests the need for a "complete rebirth from the source" and takes a dim view of twentieth-century urban Catholicism. Miss Bartelme talks about reforming the parish in a shape that would promote maximum spiritual participation by its members. These suggestions dig deeply into the whole problem of the present social structure of American urban parishes. The reviewers, in this regard, seem to have been

---

30. The analysis of motivation for both personal and social behavior is almost always associated with philosophical Freudianism. For a dispassionate modern work on the subject see James Vander Veldt and Robert Osenwald, *Psychiatry and Catholicism* (New York: McGraw-Hill Book Co., 1952), esp. chap. ix, "Evolution of Psychoanalysis."

influenced by the so-called "radical" innovations occurring in some European parishes.[31]

This is another major issue which confronts the Church in our dynamic urban culture. Although it deals with a matter that rests on the decisions of the hierarchy, and is more in the realm of social action than in that of theory or research, the sociologist must find it a fascinating question. For both clergy and laity it may well be the most important question that has come out of the controversy on parish sociology. Everett Hughes remarks that sociological studies of parishes and congregations have an "administrative bearing" because in America these religious units are something of an enterprise. "How to make such an enterprise succeed without contradicting its mission, that is the question."[32]

The scientific spirit is one of inquiry, and the social scientist cannot but ask to what purpose and to what extent the parochial aggregate functions. Is the territorial and social structure of the urban parish the best possible arrangement through which the day-by-day work can be carried on for the "care of souls"? How is it succeeding and how is it failing in its exalted objective—the sanctification and salvation of American urban people? Out of further research and analysis there may come suggestions for structural changes and possibly for certain substitutes and supplements.[33]

The parish structure is a man-made system evolving out of the experience of the Church, decreed by the Council of Trent, and ordered by the canon law of 1918.[34] This is solemn and official ap-

31. H. A. Reinhold, *Books on Trial*, X, No. 2 (1951), 105–6; Betty Bartelme, *Catholic Worker*, XVIII, No. 3 (1952), 5. The general statement by Cardinal Suhard is that "society, especially Western society, is going through a structural reform which is breaking the continuity of its traditions, upsetting the working of established rules and questioning accepted values. The resulting disorder and the consciousness of inadaptation, in every sphere, justify the feeling so often and ambiguously expressed by the words: 'The world is in revolution'" (Emmanuel Cardinal Suhard, *The Church Today* [Chicago: Fides Publishers, 1953], p. 95).

32. Everett C. Hughes (University of Chicago), *Faith and Thought*, February, 1952, p. 6.

33. See below, Appendix, for the fifth point of discussion. Although most studies have been made of urban Protestant congregations, Hallenback remarks that "the Roman Catholic Church not only has had a greater genius for adaptation, but with centralized resources and some measure of administrative control has met the changing needs of cities with greater success" (Wilbur C. Hallenback, "The Organization of Religion," in *American Urban Communities* [New York: Harper & Bros., 1951], pp. 476–95).

34. See John Harbrecht, *The Lay Apostolate* (St. Louis: B. Herder Book Co., 1929), chap. i; also C. J. Nuesse and Thomas J. Harte (eds.), *The Sociology of the Parish* (Milwaukee: Bruce Publishing Co., 1951), chaps. i and ii.

proval of the parochial system which cannot be lightly disregarded by clergy or laity. At the same time it must be realized that the Church over the centuries has shown itself an excellent anthropologist in understanding the institutions of a people and a competent social engineer in adapting new forms when they are needed. It is conceivable that our urbanized, industrialized society, which is unique in the history of the world, requires a unique restructuring of religious forms and institutions.

This is the question for which the serious student of society must try to provide an answer if his research is to be of service to the Church. There is at present a growing storehouse of sociological knowledge upon which the Church can draw in order to introduce some changes. The decision for some reformation within the present parochial structure need not wait until "all the facts are in." Society keeps moving, and continuous change is one of the central facts of our American social life.

The study of change and of social experimentation is in itself an area for social research. While it would be temerarious to maintain that the territorial parish has outlived its usefulness in American cities, it is necessary to realize that the vitality and flexibility of the Church (as a social system) allows and invites constant efforts at improvement. These experiments must not be shrugged off as the fringe activities of the discontented minority within the Church. In some instances they may be that, but underlying all of them is the psychological and sociological need for meeting the challenges to the spiritual life from a changing culture.

The "reshaping" of social relations and social structures within the Church now appears to be a trend toward extraparochial activities or "interest communalities" on the part of the laity. Urban parishioners seem to be satisfying their spiritual and social needs in groupings of their own choice rather than in the parish aggregate to which they "belong" by virtue of residence. There seems to be a trend also to large, loosely structured mass movements like the informal Christopher clubs. On the more technical side there has been a multiplication of modest urban chapels around which small groups cluster and in which the relation between priest and people is closer and more informal. In short, all these examples seem to show that in our urban society ascribed status in predetermined groupings has become culturally and psychologically less acceptable than achieved status in voluntary structures.[35]

35. See above, chap. 11, on the various forms of association among urban lay Catholics.

Until professional social scientists are employed for the purpose, the actual social engineering which maneuvers these changes will be done by the clergy and people who constitute the groups to be changed. Meanwhile the social scientist may continue to build up the body of knowledge on social and religious change with an awareness of this major issue of "social restructuring." While the culture lag theory has certain limitations, it has emphasized the type and rate of change in the nonsacred institutions. Social engineering for a better society has frequently depended upon the knowledge of extrareligious institutional and structural changes. It appears that the comparative knowledge gained from them could be helpful in understanding the possibilities for reshaping the urban parishes.

7. *Use of evaluative methodology in the sociology of the parish.* —Among the various approaches that could be made to the sociological study of the parish, Professor Francis seems to think that the evaluative approach is the least sociological.[36] This belief is in some ways a disturbing one, first, because evaluation is most important in the very area in which the social scientist works and, second, because no scientific work, whether in the sphere of social or physical phenomenon can escape evaluation. In the sociology of the parish there is great scientific significance in a comparison between the observable, measurable, religious behavior of Catholics and the ideals of behavior which the Church proposes. This is true precisely because it requires the application of value standards which are inherent and explicit in the statement of the problem. This is not merely a philosophical function. Rendering a judgment of fact about values which are present in a social system is not the same as making a moral appraisal or value judgment.[37]

This question resurrects the perennial discussion concerning the essential role of the social scientist. Nettler has claimed that the "distinctive function of the sociologist is to ascertain the probability with which certain types of social events will occur under certain conditions" and that the "evaluative methodologists" corrupt the

36. E. K. Francis (Notre Dame University), *Review of Politics,* XIV, No. 2 (1952), 273–76.

37. Whether or not the social scientist will become an advocate of certain values either within his profession or outside of it is another question (see the statement of Professor Eister above, p. 205, and the discussion on this point by Richard C. Fuller, "The Problem of Teaching Social Problems," *American Journal of Sociology,* LXIV, No. 3 [November, 1939], 415–35).

role of scientists by becoming moralists.[38] This position reduces the scope of sociology to an almost exclusively predictive science and tries unsuccessfully to ignore the inescapable scientific instruments of both value premises and value norms.

The central function of a Catholic parish as a socioreligious system is demonstrated externally in the formal religious observances of the parishioners. But even this elementary statement could have no meaning unless one knew that the religious functions of a Catholic parish are *intended to be carried out differently* from those of a Jewish synagogue or a Protestant congregation. This is a social fact. It is not a value judgment in a moralistic sense. This difference, this ideal function, can be learned only through a knowledge of the normative patterns of the Catholic Church. In other words, function does not exist for its own sake, nor is it studied scientifically for its own sake. Thus an intelligent understanding of religious behavior demands a comparison between *what is* and *what is intended*.

It is unrealistic to suggest that this is a "theological" rather than a sociological approach. This is like saying that the sociological study of the recreational institution or the political institution must be labeled a recreational approach or a political approach. The total community approach which we have employed in the study of *Southern Parish* includes an analysis of all the functions which are carried on within the parochial structure: educational, familial, ameliorative, athletic, and many others. It is obvious that all these could not be contained in a single volume which designedly treated only the parochial religious functions. But that is not the question at issue. The fact is that the study of each of these would have been merely an inconclusive list of social items of no sociological significance if they had not been related to, and evaluated by, their respective norms.

Perhaps the scientific question involved here is not the use of norms but the selection of the kind of norms to be used. This is indicated by Professor Lynd's puzzlement over my use of the term "complete supernatural ideology," and by Professor Francis' reference to Linton's ideal culture and real culture and to Max Weber's

38. Gwynne Nettler, "Toward a Definition of the Sociologist," *American Sociological Review*, XII, No. 5 (October, 1947), 553–60. See, however, Arnold M. Rose, "The Selection of Problems for Research," *American Journal of Sociology*, LIV, No. 3 (November, 1948), 219–27, and Gunnar Myrdal, *An American Dilemma* (New York: Harper & Bros., 1944), Appendix 2.

ideal types used as culture constructs. What we face here appears to be a semantic problem in relation to the methodology employed.

Unfortunately, sociologists tend to differ in the terms they use for the same social phenomenon. For example, I have distinguished three levels of abstraction. First, there is the *complete ideology* of the Catholic Church, as officially expressed in its written and stated traditional doctrines of faith and morals. This is precisely what Linton means by the "ideal pattern" of a culture, and it seems to fit what Parsons calls the "utopian level." Second, the *practical ideology* of Catholics is the actual set of norms according to which Catholics guide their religious life. It includes an admixture of secular thinking and nonreligious values. This is what Weber means by the "ideal type" and what Linton calls a "culture construct." It is only that part of Linton's "real culture" which has to do with attitudes, thinking, and beliefs. The third is the *actual level of behavior*, those phenomena which can be seen and heard and measured and which become patterned in the sense that many people do the same things in relatively the same way. They constitute the other part of Linton's "real culture" which has to do with the actions learned and shared by a group.[39]

The methodological procedure is then something like this: The sociologist does not learn the *complete ideology* by studying the actual behavior of Catholics. He must study that separately and from official ecclesiastical sources and use it as a valuable heuristic device. The actual data gathered in sociological research are the precise, detailed, day-by-day collection of facts obtained from participant observation among the parishioners themselves. This is the *behavioral level* which alone can be studied directly. From these facts one may then scientifically construct the *practical ideology*, which is certainly a real existing cultural phenomenon.

The presentation of the research report may explicitly spell out the differences among these three levels of social phenomena. This clarifies both the method and the content of the study. On the other hand, the research report may omit any mention of the complete ideology and allow the reader to guess what it might be or to study the official sources for himself. But the evaluative methodology must be present in both cases, explicitly in the first, and implicitly—with the danger of being garbled and misused—in the second.

This does not mean to say that evaluation is the most significant

39. See *Dynamics of a City Church*, pp. 259–60.

aspect of sociology or that the analysis of the statistical difference between actual behavior and ideal norms is the ultimate function of sociological research in the parish.[40] But it does mean that, without an evaluative methodology, the other functions of sociology, including prediction, are largely reduced to scientific incoherence and sociological insignificance.

In summary, it may be said that these seven major issues in the sociology of the parish tend to overlap. Two of them view the reciprocal influence of Church and society: (1) the manner in which urban society affects religious practices and (2) the way in which the Church influences the society and community. Two of them revolve around the problem of social integration: (3) whether individual choice can be accepted as a principle of social unity and (4) the fact that the sacraments and the liturgy intrinsically imply social integration. The three remaining issues involve more or less technical problems of social analysis: (5) the possibility of studying the motivation of religious behavior, (6) the question of reshaping the parochial structure, and (7) the evaluative approach in the sociology of the parish.

Although these questions of theory and research overlap, they are neither complete nor exclusive in themselves. Each of them requires more discussion. Other problematic issues of parochial sociology will undoubtedly appear as the constant work of research and study goes forward. Because we are still far removed from the master conceptual scheme which will be theoretically satisfying in this area of social science, it seems important that we approach the theories of the middle range with great humility and that we continue the factual research on the lower level. The concrete and specific exemplification of obtainable social data in the religious institutions is the raw material without which the sociology of the parish cannot be defined.

40. This is what Professor Francis calls the main question: "What sociological significance should be ascribed to the fact that actual conduct in one parish digresses from a postulated norm?"

Chapter Sixteen

Ethical Limitations on Sociological Reporting[1]

I<small>N</small> HIS primary task as the discoverer of new knowledge, the modern scientist is governed by the obligation to search for truth, to be objective, to discern the relevant, and to check meticulously the data. There is also at present a tendency to incorporate in this code an awareness of the scientist's responsibility for the use that is made of scientific knowledge. For example, the concern of some physical scientists over the disposition and extension of their atomic discoveries has been great.

The literature of science and of scientific methodology, however, reveals little systematic concern with the ethical problems arising from the relations between the scientist and the objects of his observation and experimentation. This may be due in part to the conceptualization of phenomena as "objects." Only "subjects" have rights which must be respected. Thus the generalized framework of science has at present no place for the development of a relational ethic governing the duties of the scientist to his "objects." Within this scientific perspective any experiment is possible so long as it conforms to the canons of method; any scientific report is permissible so long as it is rigorously stated and true to the observation of the scientist.

The scientist whose objects of research are human beings must necessarily be uneasy over these limited methodological rules. The experiments on living human bodies made by Nazi doctors gained them infamy rather than fame. The theoretical literature of American psychiatry hides the identity of most of its "cases." Sociologists and anthropologists frequently attempt to disguise the communities they study. These instances indicate a recognition of the fact that

1. This chapter was done in collaboration with William L. Kolb, Newcomb College, Tulane University. For a condensed version see *American Sociological Review*, XVIII, No. 5 (October, 1953), 544–50.

men are subjects as well as objects and that, even when studied as objects, they retain their rights to privacy and respect. The social scientist, more than any other, incurs responsibilities which extend beyond the procedural ethics of science itself.

The norms defining such responsibilities are most pertinent to the sociologist, but they never have been systematically formulated. The practitioner in psychiatry, social work, and medicine may generalize about his data, but he also protects the client or the patient. This expected anonymity seems to be guaranteed more by professional and medical ethics than by the ethics of science. Similarly, the priest who handles numerous cases of conscience, marriage problems, and other human problems may make scientific deductions about his data. But he protects the persons involved on the basis of the high standards of his sacred role rather than on any prescriptions of the science of human relations.

The sociological researcher is not primarily or essentially a priest or a doctor, a social worker, or a reformer. In his relations with the human objects of his study he is not a practitioner but a seeker of truth. Thus his ethical norms must evolve from a code of science rather than from a code of art. His problem, therefore, may be briefly stated as follows: Are there ethical limitations on the "complete" objectivity of a research report in social science? In other words, is it morally permissible for the sociologist to report *all the truth* he has discovered in his investigation, or are there certain boundaries of human decency which he may not cross?

It is assumed, of course, that the research reporter is not a pure and simple muckraker or a deliberate debunker. Although some of his conclusions may be considered scandalous by the general public, let us assume that he is not primarily or professionally interested in the sensational. As an ethically responsible person, he is unwilling to be scandalous or vulgar or to make exposés simply for their own sake. He may be assumed to have a feeling for the sensitivities of people and a respect for their rights so that he will not deliberately violate the norms of fraternal charity.

It is precisely at this point that the need seems greatest for a set of objective norms of responsibility in sociological reporting. The above assumptions demand personal value judgments on the part of the reporting scientist which tend to be relativistic. That these assumptions have not always been fulfilled is demonstrated by several widely published research reports which have been termed sensational, and even salacious, by the nonscientific reading public. The personal decision on how far to go in scientific objectivity seems to depend on the scientist's own sense of decency, which in turn is undoubtedly influenced by the prevailing values in the culture and in the practices of fellow-scientists. Sociologists, like other scientists, are fallible; and an element of subjectivity, perhaps of personal bias, is present even in the most conscientious research report.

Because of this internal variability of judgmental norms and because of the external impossibility of a simplicist adherence to the view of human beings as either pure objects or pure subjects of research, it seems neccessary that we attempt an outline of an ethical code to govern the relation of the sociologist to the persons who are subjects of his study. Such a code will not relieve the social scientist of moral choice, but it may serve as a guide for the making of responsible decisions. As a tentative formulation of this code we discuss here only the area of small-group or community studies and only the question of the selection of research data for publication. This is in itself a complex question, the answer to which differs widely according to the *kind of data* which are in hand and according to the *manner of presentation* of the data.

Under the former heading it seems obvious that historical material allows more latitude for reporting than contemporary material. Every study of a small group or community seems to require a brief sketch of historical background, and through this research the scientist may discover certain skeletons in the closet. Their revelation may be pertinent to the understanding of the functioning group and will probably not intrude upon the living group's reputation. On the other hand, contemporary data may include knowledge about certain personages and situations which requires prudent handling and perhaps even omission.

Within the area of contemporary material it seems necessary also to distinguish between studies of primitive and civilized communities and persons. It is to be supposed that the details of social life among the Samoans were not reported to these people, and, if any reputations suffered from the study, it was only among non-Samoans. There have been instances, however, of anthropologists' reports getting back to the American Indians, causing some dissension and suspicion among the members of the tribe. In either case the social scientist must consider these peoples as the subjects of human rights, even though the prospect of moral damage may not be great.

The more pertinent kinds of research projects have been among the contemporary civilized groups and communities, and the present discussion is focused upon these studies. What ethical rights has the researcher to reveal facts which these persons resent or which may in some way harm their reputation? Are there any general norms which can be employed for the selection or rejection of data in the research report?

The kind of data obtained in social research implies also that some social facts in our society are considered *sacred*, while others are more or less *profane*. The analysis and reporting of behavior patterns which involve high traditional values (like religion, family and sex, ethnic and group loyalties) seem to demand special discernment before they are revealed. While there are great variations of value concepts concerning matters which are not sacred (such as efficient social processes, economic and political activities, housing and recreational problems, etc.), these areas generally seem to allow a maximum of freedom in reporting.

The knottiest problem concerning the kind of data seems to revolve around the distinction between *public* and *private* facts. This is something more than the difference between hidden and open knowledge. By definition, the sociologist deals with social and group relations which involve a plurality of persons. In a sense, therefore, his data are already known to some persons, and they can rarely be completely private and secret. It is obvious that widely known information may have a wide margin of expression in the research report.

The whole research report of a small group or community does not fall easily and simply into the four dichotomies mentioned above. There is a fairly well-established distinction between the primitive group and other groups, but the complete report will undoubtedly include both public and private data. The moral decisions of the research reporter are, therefore, multiple and continuous, judging each separate datum according to the latitude of expression allowed to it. The ethical restrictions on the social scientist seem strongest when his research raises the problem of reporting on behavior regarded as private or which may threaten reputations.

As the second element in the ethical problem of selection of data for publication, there is the *manner of presentation*. What we say of this involves also all the preliminary remarks made above. In other words, whether the material is public or private, sacred or nonsacred, whether it treats about civilized or primitive groups, historical or contemporary situations, it can be prepared for publication in a variety of ways. It is at this point in the preparation of his final report that the scientist is faced with decisions which have broad ethical implications. Here it is a problem not only of what to tell but also of how to tell it.

American sociologists have usually followed the custom of providing anonymity for the subjects of community study. It is common practice in so-called total community studies to shroud the identity of the group in pseudonyms like "Yankee City," "Cottonville," "Middletown," "Jonesville," "Riverside," etc. Anyone, however, who is intent upon discovering the location of any particular community study can usually do so. Thus there is a further ethical duty for internal disguises requiring that the researcher alter, or recombine, or even omit, certain identifying characteristics. While it is true that no living group can be completely obscured by these various devices of anonymity, this type of presentation undoubtedly allows a relatively wide margin of expression.

The happiest situation for the social scientist is one in which statistical analysis of, and reporting on, large numbers of people are possible. Usually in such cases there is not a problem of direct identification or of serious violation of privacy. It is obvious of course that statistics derived from a large population will be more meaningful and scientifically useful, and they also are less likely to give offense, than statistics derived from a small identifiable group or community. In the latter case an analysis of the statistical material may reveal situations which are distasteful to the subjects of the study.

Frequently, however, the highest value of a research report lies precisely in its expert interpretation by the skilled social analyst; and this interpretative presentation of sociological data has become almost essential in the modern research report. But it also creates an ethically problematic area for the scientist. If the scientist limits himself to the social meaning of the data, he may escape the pitfalls of interpretation. But there is a tendency today to carry psychological interpretation over into the area of social relations, so that attempts are made to state and explain the motivations of social behavior. It appears that this psychological interpretation of motives is an area which allows minimum freedom in sociological reports and requires the greatest honesty and objectivity of the reporter.

The ethical problem of the social scientist seems most serious when he presents a descriptive analysis of a relatively small group or community.[2] Even when the project is reported pseudonymously

2. It is difficult to discuss rules without citing cases in which they apply. By omitting in the following discussion a number of instances in which the social scientist suffered the repercussion of the community, we are subjecting

and the interpretation of motives is held to a minimum, indirect identification is almost always possible, and there is likely to be a subtle and unintended violation of real or supposed human rights. These descriptive studies are dynamic, and they are being multiplied. They show the actions of persons and the functions of groups. It is with this descriptive type of small community study in mind that the following moral generalizations are offered.

In preparing a research report on a small community or group, the sociologist has a moral duty toward several different individuals and groups. Because his obligations to each of these differ in kind and degree, it seems necessary to set forth briefly the various categories into which they fall.

1. For practical as well as moral reasons, the social scientist must consider the wishes and needs of those persons who have allowed, invited, sponsored, or co-operated with the study. City officials, management of a factory group, officers of a labor union, the pastor of a church—all are examples of persons who have some concern with the results of sponsored research. The scientist's obligations to them include truthfulness about the nature and scope of the study, the honoring of confidences, scientific objectivity, and honest reporting. Because of the crucial position of such individuals in all group studies, respect for these obligations has become deeply ingrained among social scientists.

2. The social scientist has obligations to the source from which research funds were obtained. Like anyone who enters a contractual agreement, he has a duty to employ these funds honestly and usefully and to abide by the agreement concerning publication and ownership of data and by any other explicit provisions contained in the contract. In basic research it is to be expected that the scientist will not permit an agreement to be made that will interfere with his integrity as a scientist, so that obligations to the source of funds will not interfere with the responsibilities of the scientist to his own discipline. Nor will these obligations be allowed to interfere with the rights of the persons being studied.

3. The publisher too undoubtedly has a call upon the moral consideration of the research reporter. He has the right to expect an honest and thorough report. In his contract with the author he is usually protected by a libel clause which places responsibility upon

---

ourselves to our own norms of ethical limitations. At least a half-dozen cases, however, are known to every American social scientist, and he can easily judge whether the research-reporter in these cases violated these various norms.

the writer, but it may be expected that beyond this legal technicality the scientist will not include material which will embarrass the publisher.

4. Social scientists in general may be said to have a claim on the findings of the social researcher. While this right must probably be balanced against the rights of the individuals and the group under study, the scientist's colleagues have a moral expectation that the findings will be made available to them in a serious, honest, and competent report. The progress of science is built on such an ethic of free exchange of knowledge, and it is hindered by secrecy and suppression. Social scientists increase their store of knowledge and improve their understanding and their teaching and research skills by having access to basic research reports.

5. Another kind of group has a similar claim, perhaps not on the individual scientist but certainly on the discipline, to receive the findings of social research. At a minimum, this includes the key persons in a community or group who are in a position to implement the data through action programs of social improvement. It may be morally expected that, even if the scientist does not give general publication to his material, he will feel obliged to reveal pertinent data to those "who can do something about it." In the long run, all worth-while knowledge should become generally available, and it is particularly important that social science knowledge ultimately become the possession of all the people.

6. Finally—and of central concern—the research reporter must respect the rights of the community studied, its subgroups, and its individual members. They are the source about whom and from whom the essential data are obtained. In a descriptive study, the higher the functionary within a group, the more likelihood that he will be identified and that his social behavior and personal reputation will be placed under scrutiny. A person's rights to his secrets, his privacy, and his reputation may vary according to circumstances, but they are intrinsically present in a society like our own which in its central tradition accords dignity and worth to the individual. The sociologist has not discharged his obligations when he has made an effort at disguise, ambiguity, or anonymity. He is always faced with a moral problem of how much to tell about the lives and habits of the members of the community.

The above categories are merely an attempt to indicate the different persons and groups toward whom the research reporter may have some moral obligation. They do not and cannot specify the relative seriousness of the various obligations in each instance of reporting. The extent to which full objective reporting is to be engaged in must be determined in large measure by prevailing circumstances. Recognition of this fact is of crucial importance in any effort to develop a code of ethics for sociological reporting.

This circumstantial nature of the problem of truth-telling means that, while telling the truth cannot be per se wrong or harmful, the ethical question of whether or not to include a certain objective fact in a publication arises always in relation to persons and circumstances. Thus complete objectivity, or telling all the truth in all circumstances, is not necessarily a morally good act.

Even if it were humanly possible for the scientist to discover all of the detailed facts of social behavior in a group, he is morally bound to be selective in his reporting. This is true for several reasons. There are various kinds of secrets which may not be ethically revealed without permission of the persons involved. An important secret which is given in confidence, or which the interviewer promises to protect, undoubtedly places the strongest obligation on the scientist not to reveal it. But in the course of his investigation and observation the researcher will also discover natural secrets which, by their seriousness, demand the confidence of the reporter.

There is also the problem of detraction—the injury of another's reputation by revealing what is detrimental but true about him. This implies, of course, that the true but harmful fact concerning the person or group is not already widely disseminated. There can be no detraction or further moral injury done by repeating the information of facts through which a person has already lost his reputation. Here it seems necessary to make a disinction between objective and imaginary derogation of reputation. The social scientist can hardly be held morally responsible if the subjects of his study find insults in the report which are not really there.

It seems obvious also that the revelation of true research data is circumstantial or relative to the commonweal. Sometimes truth is social dynamite, and its revelation may be either inopportune or actually damaging to the public good. At other times the needs of society may demand that a truth be revealed even though it may bring some incidental harm to an individual or group.

The balancing of the obligations to various individuals, groups, the community, and society under varying circumstances calls for judicious evaluation in each instance by the research reporter. If we assume that the scientist accepts the values of human dignity and worth, so that he will not needlessly injure any of these persons and groups, we may proceed to indicate several general guides which may be ethically useful in the preparation of the research report. There are, in essence, the following four variables which must be related to one another in attempting to arrive at moral decisions in sociological reporting.

a) The sociologist's definition of the nature of science.—Some positivists seem to regard science as a fascinating game played according to a set of rules.[3] It is doubtful that the sociologist using this conception of science may ever legitimately overrule the rightful claims of the people studied. The simple wish of the people to conceal certain aspects of their behavior must then be considered sufficient to bar the report of that behavior.

If one regards science as a search for truth as an end in itself, the demands of the objectivity of science will carry much weight in the decision to publish all pertinent data. Within the Western tradition the search for truth is generally considered one of the highest functions of the human mind, and it might seem at first glance that such a function must transcend the rights of the individual. Yet there are reasons why this may not be so. Except in history, the truth for which the social scientist searches is nomothetic, not idiographic, truth. It may be necessary to base generalizations on certain idiographic items, but man has the entire span of his career on earth to discover and disclose such items. Certainly a particular item of current behavior turned up in a community study need not be used to support a generalization if such use inflicts injury on the people being investigated. Searchers for knowledge and truth for their own sake can afford to await the historian's revelation. There is plenty of time.

There is a third conception of pure science. Social scientists may believe that science is both a rigidly ruled game and a search for truth which is valuable in itself, but they usually also believe that science, well developed and used by experts or disseminated among the people, can make for a better life. Such conceptions range from an adherence to a purely evolutionary doctrine of the adaptive value of science to an acceptance of one in which science, together with

3. "Science after all is only one of the games played by the children of this world, and it may very well be that those who prefer other games are in their generation wiser" (Carroll C. Pratt, *The Logic of Modern Psychology* [New York: Macmillan Co., 1939], p. 57).

religion and philosophy, will help man discover his true place in the universe. There is also in the modern world a sense of urgency about accomplishing this mission of pure science. Considerable pressure arises within this perspective to ignore the rights of people who are scientifically studied. Despite this pressure it remains true that a wilful disregard for the rights of persons and groups to their privacy, reputations, and secrets will tend to destroy the very values which the scientist hopes his basic research can render more achievable.

Frequently the scientist makes a community or small-group study not as a pure scientist but in one sense or another as an applied scientist. He may carry on the research for what he himself considers desirable practical ends; he may be employed by officials of the community or group or by those of the larger society; or he may be employed by some private group with a specific, selfish, or altruistic interest. In all three of these instances there is pressure to report all the significant findings even though injury may be done to the objects of the study. Nevertheless, the sociologist must abide by the rule that he exercise every effort to determine whether or not the values to be implemented by the study and the probability of being able to achieve them through the use of its findings justify the harm done to the members of the community or group.

Preoccupation with applied science is frequently accompanied by the temptation to look for and publish data which will further the realization of what the researcher himself regards as the good society or community. He is most likely to believe that all his data must be revealed in all circumstances. It appears to us that a scientist of this persuasion is most in need of the virtues of tolerance, compassion, and love, because he is in danger of placing considerations of the "good" society above all consideration of individual rights and injuries.

The hired scientist, moreover, cannot avoid responsibility for revealing data injurious to individuals and groups by pleading loyalty to community or nation or by indicating his contractual responsibilities to a private group. It will be seen below that any scientist may have moral problems concerning duty to nation and community, and duty to the objects of his study, but in any event responsibility for injuring others remains. Loyalty to community or nation may require injury to individuals, but in such cases the scientist shares with all other responsible agencies whatever guilt is incurred. In instances of purely contractual research the scientist must accept full responsibility, because loyalty to nation or community is not involved. He is free to refuse the job, and, if the values of the employing group are wrong or do not justify the amount of injury done, the scientist himself must accept the moral responsibility.

b) Determination of the extent to which persons or groups will be injured by the publication of data concerning their behavior.—We have already discussed the importance of the extent of injury in several contexts. Frivolous science and even the search for scientific truth for its own sake cannot justify any degree of injury; but, as one moves into the realm of pure science as important to society or into the various types of applied research, the degree of injury becomes important. In the latter instances the determination of the extent of injury to persons or groups by the publication of social data is a continuous moral problem in the preparation of a research report. It is also the hub of the whole problem which we are discussing. Those instances in which the scientist can foretell with certitude that serious damage will accrue to the subjects of his study seem to be very few in number. It may also be assumed that, unless the scientist is studying a relatively disorganized, criminally inclined group of people, the largest proportion of his data will be free of derogatory implications.

It is the in-between area of probable moral injury that is difficult to determine. To know what the effect of exposing a group's secrets will be, to realize how seriously a person's reputation may be damaged, and to visualize the effects of violation of privacy presuppose knowledge on the part of the scientist which he may not have. This knowledge can be approached to the extent to which the scientist "saturates" himself in the social relations of the group which he studies. It probably cannot be achieved by the aloof scientist who simply culls the reports of those who have done the actual and basic data-collecting. It may be said that, the more intimately the research reporter himself has associated with the group, the more likely is he able to discern the probable future damage to reputations.

Since there is a great difference between imaginary and objective derogation of reputation, the sociologist may tend to brush off the former as irrelevant and uncontrollable. Human decency, however, seems to require that the scientist make an effort to inquire even into this possibility of psychological and subjective injury. The scientist cannot guard against all such contingencies and against the unexpected and unwarranted complaints of people, but he should do his human best to avoid them ahead of time and to be sympathetic to them if they come.

If the sociologist attempts to interpret the social behavior of the people he studies, he must assess the responsibility of the people for their own actions. While it is true that no individual is either fully responsible or completely controlled in all his behavior, the scientist must also determine to the best of his ability the degree of actual responsibility of the persons concerned. Otherwise, false sentimentality may result in the denial of the fact that a person must accept the consequences of the acts for which he is responsible. In other words, while the scientist protects the rights of persons and groups to the fullest possible extent, he cannot erase the responsibilities, duties, and obligations of the subjects of his study.

c) The degree to which people or groups are actually members of a moral community in which the scientist is also a member.—At the core of the Western value system is a belief in the basic dignity and worth of the human being. This belief is founded on different assumptions according to the particular stream of tradition in which one locates it: the Fatherhood of God, natural law, universal human needs and aspirations, or human reason. Within these traditions men are bound to one another in a moral community which is something more than the "psychic unity" of the human race. Membership in this community requires that the individual's rights to privacy, secrecy, and reputation be respected, even though the human beings studied may not be members of the sociologist's own social community or society.

This belief also implies that a man or group can renounce membership in the moral community by choosing modes of action which violate these basic values of human dignity and worth. It seems probable that men like Stalin and Hitler, organized groups like "Murder Incorporated," the Ku Klux Klan, dedicated anarchists, and some others, have placed themselves outside the moral community and have surrendered the protection of its norms. This must be alien doctrine to the sociologist who is positivistic in his approach to values and ethics. Yet in actual practice this has been one of the standards which he has used in his own research or in accepting the research of others.

The decision of the sociologist to place particular persons or groups outside the moral community involves great responsibility, and he must be careful that his criteria of judgment permit tolerance, compassion, and wisdom. This is especially the case when he finds among the subjects of his research "unpopular" racial, religious, and political groups, prostitutes, homosexuals, drug addicts, the psychologically ill, the poor and powerless. It is hardly questionable that these people remain members of the moral community and hence retain their claims of privacy, respect, and secrecy against the reporting scientist. The moral seriousness of their behavior or the urgency of social needs may require a limitation of their rights, but the scientist is burdened with the responsibility for protecting them to the fullest possible extent.

In the face of the great moral and social evils of the twentieth century the recognition of the universal moral community should also have some impact on the reform-minded sociologists. Some of these have implicitly believed in the existence of a moral community, but one so restricted in its membership that large segments of American society have been regarded by them as falling outside of it.[4] A scientist interested in social reform must recognize the rights even of those groups which he considers obstacles to reform, whether they are businessmen, labor unions, farm blocs, religious fundamentalists, or others. This is not to say that the utilitarian sociologist must give up his hopes for reform, but rather that he must recognize these groupings as members of the same moral community to which he belongs.

It seems to us that the recognition of basic human rights which accompany membership in the moral community is an important instrument for the avoidance of mere subjective criteria by social scientists. It is objectively true that there are moral evils and modes of action which place the perpetrator outside this community. We have recognized of course that we must know as much as possible about such people and that the scientist need have little inhibition in the report he provides about them. All other persons and groups, no matter how distasteful to the personal norms of the scientist, seem to require the respect of fellow-members in the moral community.

d) The degree to which the larger society, the local community, or the group needs the data of the research.—Balancing the judgments of the extent of probable injury to the subjects of a study and the degree to which such subjects are members of a common moral community is the determination of the extent of urgent social need for the revelation of data. Real urgency must be defined in terms of

4. E.g., if a Marxian social scientist wants to exclude capitalists, or a gentile sociologist places Jews outside the moral community, he appears to be vitiating not only the need for moral responsibility but even the definition of social science.

the pressing needs of group, community, or society; or in terms of some impending disaster of which the scientist, but not the community or group studied, is aware. Rights and duties are never unqualified in society, and one of the conditions seems to be that the society sometimes has a prior right to information which is necessary and useful for itself even though it may be harmful to an individual person or subgroup.

The social scientist may find himself in one of several moral situations when he is trying to determine whether or not the social need is greater than the individual or group right. If the duly appointed authorities of a community or of the larger society believe certain information to be vitally needed, there is a prima facie case for the scientist to reveal such information. However, these authorities must really prove to the scientist that this need exists. If he does not know and cannot find out from the authorities whether there is an urgent need or a true utility for certain data from his studies which will be harmful to individuals and subgroups, he appears to be free of moral obligation to reveal it. If he is certain that the information is neither necessary nor useful, he may in good conscience refuse to reveal it even though the authorities demand to know it. It must be recognized that his freedom in such instances is moral, but not always legal, and he may have to pay a price for his refusal.

In a similar manner the ethical relation which the scientist has to the group studied may require the revelation of information damaging to individuals or subgroups. Here in the local community which he has studied he is likely to be the best judge of the need and utility of his data. If he understands and accepts the basic values of the group and takes his obligations to the group seriously, he may find it imperative to disclose data which may violate the privacy or injure the reputation of some members of the community. In this case, since he cannot plead ignorance, and since there was no demand from competent higher authority, the responsibility for the assessment of urgency rests squarely upon him.

Finally, even though neither the higher authority nor the community places any demands upon him, he may become aware of facts which are vital to the maintenance of the social group studied. In these cases he must not only accept the responsibility for violating the claims of individuals but also arrive at his decision with very little outside aid. In clear-cut instances where the comparison and balancing of the rights of the various claimants can be easily accomplished, the decision may be easily reached. But it is certainly in this area that the researcher will be forced to consider most thoroughly the importance which he himself has placed upon the value of his data and its relation to the needs of the group.

In all these last-mentioned types of moral situations, it may be possible to give the information to those who need it without revealing it in the published report. There is an assumption here, of course, that the scientific objectivity of the study will not be distorted by the omission of certain facts. At the same time, in our American social structure, there is frequently a claim on the part of the members that, if knowledge is urgently needed by the authorities of the group or community, it is perhaps also needed by the members themselves. The scientist must again balance this claim against the rights of the individual in question as well as against the urgency of social need for this particular datum.

Enough has been said in discussing the four sets of variables (as well as the kind of data, the manner of its presentation, and the different types of persons involved in ethical relations) to indicate the main outline of the path along which the scientist must seek to arrive at any concrete decision concerning the selection of research data to be included in a published report. There are no easy answers in that precise area of the conflict of rights where answers are sought.

The complexities exhibited in this discussion indicate that the problem of ethical limitations on sociological reporting cannot be reduced to the simple either-or proposition of a conflict between the scientific objectivity of a research report and the ethical inhibitions of the person who writes the report. It is apparent that the sociologist must act simultaneously according to a highly developed procedural code for scientific reporting and a code of ethics based on the belief that the objects of his study are also subjects. These codes are not irreconcilable, but the resolution of specific conflicts between them may be a very complex task, involving the claims of many groups and the interrelationships of the four variables. Yet the sociologist must resolve them. If there is a tendency for the sociologist to become more scientific, he must also become increasingly sensitized to the rights, feelings, and needs of the people he studies. Treating them as subjects means that to the best of his ability he will treat them with justice, understanding, compassion, and, in the last analysis, love.

APPENDIX

Appendix

Utility of Social Science for Religion

I T APPEARS that the sociologist of religion must concern himself
with two questions: (*a*) Is it possible to study religious groups with
the tools and methods of social science? (*b*) Is a study of this kind
useful, not only to social science, but to religion?

The first question need hardly detain us. The work of Pinard de
la Boullaye, Max Weber, Émile Durkheim, and others in Europe has
demonstrated the answer.[1] Books like Joachim Wach's classic *Sociology of Religion*, Liston Pope's *Millhands and Preachers*, and J. Milton Yinger's *Religion in the Struggle for Power*, as well as numerous
monographs which have appeared in American scientific journals,
have shown that the sociological approach to religion is respectable,
reliable, and valid.

This does not mean that the sociologist turns theologian or that
religious mysteries can be reduced to scientific formulas. It does
mean that the trained social scientist is competently at home wherever people associate and function co-operatively in the pursuit of
known goals. While religious functions are sacred, and religious
aims are higher than those of any other social institutions, the fact
remains that they are *social* functions and aims. The economic man
is also the religious man, and, if social behavior can be successfully
studied in the former role, it can also be successfully studied in the
latter.

The second question—concerning social science's utility to religion—seems of much more importance to all who are worried about

1. Weber and Durkheim have been severely criticized by philosophers and
ethicians for their positivistic tendencies. Despite these strictures, their pioneer
work in the sociology of religion provided insights to the whole problem discussed here (see Simon Deploige, *The Conflict between Ethics and Sociology*
[St. Louis: B. Herder Book Co., 1938]; Henri Pinard de la Boullaye, S.J.,
L'Étude comparée de religions [2 vols.; Paris: Beauchesne, 1922, 1929]; Max
Weber, *Gesammelte Aufsätze zur Religionssoziologie* [Tübingen: Mohr, 1920–
21]; Talcott Parsons, "Theoretical Development of the Sociology of Religion,"
Journal of the History of Ideas, V [1944], 176 ff.).

the balance of the sacred and the secular, the conflict between faith and reason, the assumed incompatibility between religious functions and social science research. This question of *Cui bono?* ("What good is it?") is raised by religious-minded people and must be answered by the social scientist, whether the latter regards himself as a pure scientist merely in the search of knowledge for its own sake or whether he considers himself a kind of applied scientist whose conclusions should be of benefit to society.

In order to focus the question more clearly, and because our own research has been largely in the area of parochial systems, the test of utility will be made here on the sociological study of the Catholic urban parish as a social unit. The arguments to prove this utility of social science for organized religion, and the various empirical evidences provided in this book, imply much wider generalizations and applications. If we substitute Protestant congregations for Catholic parishes and Protestant religious practices for those of the Catholic Church, the same general thesis concerning the utility of scientific research can be demonstrated.

In other words, every religious group, whether Catholic, Protestant, or Jewish, must have a local history and must be composed of people who follow institutionalized patterns of religious behavior. The human experiences which constitute its history, and the human relations which characterize its present existence, are the essential material of sociological research. No religious group, especially in its administrators, is completely unaware that it has both problems and potentialities within its system of social relations. The trained social scientist can help to sharpen and focus this awareness even though the religious and theological differences among the various groups are deep-seated and weighty.

The specific question here is: Why make a scientific social study of the Catholic urban parish? What "good" can come from the sociological approach to an institutionalized system which the Catholic Church has employed for centuries? Elsewhere I have made a tentative answer to this question in the assumption that "a vigorous parochial system not only bespeaks an internally strong Catholic social structure but also promises solidarity for the larger community and nation in which it exists. . . . The sociological roots of Catholicism are in the parish."[2]

2. See *Dynamics of a City Church,* Vol. I of *Southern Parish* (Chicago: University of Chicago Press, 1951), p. 8. See also T. S. Eliot, *The Idea of a Christian Society* (New York: Harcourt, Brace & Co., 1940), where he re-

This tentative assumption is open to question because the parochial system is a man-made institution and because the Church employs many other institutional mechanisms in carrying out its primary spiritual function. At some time in the distant future the Church may emphasize some other form of social structure as the basic social unit of the Church, but at the present time (and probably for many decades to come) the sociological basis of Catholicism is the parish. Hence it seems important to study things as they are and to analyze and appraise objectively the social unit in which and through which most Catholics strive for eternal salvation.

The remainder of this appendix is a brief exploration of some of the reasons why the sociological study of the urban American parish is a vital enterprise, which has the utmost utility for the Church itself and for the society in which it exists. In general, these reasons evolve from the premise that knowledge of objective facts is a preliminary essential to the proper and intelligent functioning of any social group or community. If this knowledge can be achieved and analyzed through sociological techniques, the Church has at its disposal a potent instrument of internal and external progress.

1. The Catholic Church in America has grown with the nation. At the middle of the twentieth century it has reached a point where it may profitably "take stock of itself." It has successfully passed through the youthful stage of establishing itself in what had been an alien Protestant culture. It has been preoccupied with proving itself an institution which could resist attacks from organized Knownothingism, Klanism, and other antagonistic ideologies; which could overcome the internal problems of trusteeism and of ethnic disputes among immigrant clergy and laity; and which could build a tremendous physical plant of churches, seminaries, schools, convents, and hospitals, in spite of the relative poverty of most of its membership.

Catholicism in America is an urban religion in the sense that more than 80 per cent of its adherents are city dwellers. It has become a

marks that "the traditional unit of the Christian Community in England is the parish. . . . How far the parish must be superseded will depend largely upon our view of the necessity of accepting the causes which tend to destroy it. In any case, the parish will serve my purpose as an example of community unit. For this unit must not be solely religious, and not solely social; nor should the individual be a member of two separate, or even overlapping units, one religious and the other social. The unitary community should be religious-social, and it must be one in which all classes, if you have classes, have their centre of interest" (p. 28).

"success" there in the cities, which tend to be the models and fore-runners of American cultural change. The brick-and-mortar phase is almost passed; the "build-up" has been phenomenal. If the process of urbanization continues in this country, it is almost inevitable that the largest urban religion must have an influence in its development.

Impatient criticism has been made of the Church's failure to evolve with other social institutions and to develop with contemporary civil society. "She has remained frozen in feudal forms which worked in times past. In our time, instead of being fused with society as she was in the middle ages when the parish and the commune had the same extension and the same life, the Church is 'absent' from the City. She hovers over humanity instead of being incarnate in its flesh and blood. In her message to men she has everything she needs, even more than she needs, to animate the contemporary structures and to draw up plans for the future, but she does not use her resources. She lets strangers, or adversaries, take the decisive initiative on questions of doctrine, culture or action. When she acts or speaks it is often too late. In scientific research, social legislation, or humanism she has few innovators. It is not in this way that she will win the world to Christ."[3]

The Church in America, particularly the urban Catholic parish, is ready for a thorough analysis of the present objective facts of its existence. Its values are eternal, and its doctrines are incorrupt; but these are concretized by human agents in a social system. This concrete day-by-day operation of Catholics in an institutionalized structure is the present foundation upon which the future is to be built. The planning of new directions, of new forms, of greater vitality, must be projected from a thorough knowledge of the present.

2. The Catholic Church is existing in urban America, which is the most fluid and dynamic society the world has ever seen. The members of the Church are members of this society, and there is a tremendous mutual influence between their religious and their secular roles. Even the holiest, most intelligent, industrious, and able priest needs help in understanding and interpreting this society. In their own social organizations high-powered and high-salaried business executives recognize this need and are turning more and more to the social scientists for help. The clergyman is performing a much more valuable function than the business executive, but he is doing it with the same people in the same society. The priest's aloofness from, or disregard of, the scientist indicates a neglect of these nat-

3. Emmanuel Cardinal Suhard, *The Church Today* (Chicago: Fides Publishers, 1953), p. 99.

ural instruments which can be made to subserve supernatural work.

The man who is most involved in the activities of a social group, whether the manager of a factory or the pastor of a parish, is frequently unable to grasp the significance of the social change occurring all around him. Usually he has neither the training nor the objectivity nor the time to make the social analysis which would be most fruitful for the objectives of his group. That is why the trained and careful social researcher is in such great demand today. His services can be of paramount importance to the Church, not merely by gathering facts, but by helping to interpret these facts in relation to the changing society.

This point was made by an experienced parish priest in reviewing a study on parochial sociology: "When a priest offers the holy sacrifice he is tempted at times to assume all is well back of him in the church and throughout the parish. Complacency is his enemy. The priest needs a rear-view mirror. This book picks up some of the reflections that would fall on such a mirror in one parish. The priestly reader will ask what images would fall on such a mirror if a study were made in his parish."[4] Using the same figure of speech, another priest remarked that this research publication "mirrors the three parishes I pastored in my forty-one years as a priest. I dare say that every priest exercising the care of souls in a parish will find the book a revelation of what needs to be done to improve his field for a better harvest."[5]

3. The puzzling inconsistencies of our urban social behavior, oversimplified in the dichotomy of religion and secularism, seem to have resulted from the dynamic shift in our social structures and institutions. This means that the volatile character of our group values and goals, which disturbs the minds of religious people, cannot be interpreted separately from the changing patterns of our group living. Sometimes an elderly pastor is naturally bewildered because the large city parish which he administers is so different from the little village parish in which he grew up during the first decades of this century. He may find psychological security in the role of *laudator temporis acti*, or he may be frustrated by present social conditions while he bemoans the "good old days," but neither attitude is profitable in God's service.

4. Book review by Francis J. Gilligan in *Worship*, XXVI, No. 5 (April, 1952), 271.
5. Book review by Anthony Rothlauf, in *Integrity*, Vol. VI, No. 3 (December, 1951).

The Catholic parish in America, even among the urban immigrants, was once a simple, primary, social community. But it seems now that the sense of community, which once existed even in the "old neighborhoods" of the city, has largely vanished. The large parish in the big city is now a complex, secondary, associational structure. This is not necessarily the fault of the Church or the fault of the people or the priests; it may not necessarily be a "fault" at all. The social relations and structure of a parish cannot exist completely apart, and different, from the social relations and structure of the society within which it exists. The changing customs, patterns of behavior, even the mores, of the one affect those of the other.

How can the Church understand, interpret, and meet these structural and relational changes in modern urban society? None of the great theologians and moralists of the past ever experienced this particular kind of society. Urban America is unique in the history of the world. There is not available, even in the vast storehouse of Catholicism's social experience, a systematic body of knowledge to which the Catholic can go for help. Just as in times past the Church has turned to philosophers and physical scientists for help in philosophical and physical problems, so it must now turn to social scientists for help in social problems.

The oft-repeated mission of the Church to bring all Americans within its fold does not necessarily presage a perfect "City of God" on earth, but it does require at least an elementary recognition of the new and unique in American society. What Father Murray says in a different context seems to apply here. "In the providence of God and by the intelligent zeal of the Catholic citizen there may be a Christendom again; but it too will be imperfect and not ideal. And no one can foresee in detail its form. What was true and valid in the old will find place in the new, but the new will be new in all its texture."[6]

4. The social scientist's contribution to the work of organized religion was sought by the late Cardinal Suhard, who recognized the "crisis of growth and change" in modern society. He praised the "extensive research of scholars, sociologists, and technicians," and he advised them to "draw up an objective evaluation of our urban civilization of today with its gigantic concentrations and its

6. John Courtney Murray, "Governmental Repression of Heresy," from the Catholic Theological Society of America, *Proceedings of the Third Annual Meeting* (Chicago, 1948), p. 38.

continual growth: with the strains of its inhuman production, its unjust distribution, and its exhausting forms of entertainment."[7]

His authoritative voice spoke from France, where the religious faith of the man on the street has come upon unhappy days. It is said that in France and other parts of Europe the masses of the people (who in the last analysis are the constituents of the Church on the parish and neighborhood level) have become alienated from the Church. In an almost desperate attempt to reach the people, the Cardinal sponsored the programs of priest-workmen and city missionaries. These measures could have been adopted more successfully a generation ago had there been objective sociological studies of the religious and social conditions of French Catholics.[8]

As far as we can learn from the few research projects so far conducted in American parochial life, the loyalty of the Catholic masses is much stronger here than in France. This is largely a guess and an assumption. There are many differences between the two countries, and it is only through patient and tedious research that we can honestly judge the present condition of American Catholicism. However, if we wait another generation, the Church in America may be suddenly confronted with the need to apply hasty measures of dubious value. The groundwork for planned and sound adaptions to social needs may best be laid at the present time.

5. Whether or not the Church is flourishing in its urban American parishes, no Catholic priest or layman will argue that the Church's social institutions are beyond improvement. The central religious function of the Church is predicated on the perfectibility of the human individual and of human society. The fact that the Holy Spirit will always be with the Church and the fact that the sacramental system provides a tremendous flow of supernatural grace are no guaranties of a steady linear social and spiritual progress.[9] Religious institutions are human institutions,[10] and they too are subject to the fluctuations of human actions and social pressures.

7. Emmanuel Cardinal Suhard, *Growth or Decline?* (South Bend: Fides Publishers, 1948), p. 83.

8. The experimental character of the priest-worker movement, as well as its lack of a basic scientific preparation, is perhaps indicated in the crisis which it encountered in the winter of 1953–54. It appears that the movement must now proceed in a modified form and at a more cautious pace. For a balanced account of the problem see Friedrich Heer, "Die Arbeiterpriester in Frankreich: Ursprung und Hintergründe," *Hochland*, XLVI (April, 1954), 326–41.

9. See above, chap. 15, pp. 207–9, for the discussion on the social implications of liturgy and sacraments.

10. This term is used here in its technical sense and does not deny the "divine origin" of religion. As Hertzler says: "Religion is a universal attribute

Some priests contend that the whole parochial system (especially in its rigid territorial aspects) is outmoded, that it has outlived its usefulness, and that new social structures are required to meet the exigencies of our urban, industrial society. Others maintain that the territorial parish is the best social mechanism ever devised by man for the practical day-to-day operation of Catholicism in the lives of the laity. There are numerous intermediary opinions between these two extremes; but all are centered on an issue of vital importance to American Catholicism: Is the parochial system, as it now operates in our urban American society, an adequate instrument for the salvation and sanctification of souls?

This question cannot be answered, and these opinions cannot be tested, by an appeal to the Bible, to Thomas Aquinas, or to canon law. The mere fact that there is this diversity of opinion among clergymen and that zealous laymen are also concerned about the problem should make religious people eager for any scientific studies which may help to provide answers. Improvements and changes can best be instituted if we have at our disposal a studied analysis of the objective facts of parish life.

It is the function of the social researcher to discover the facts, to analyze them, and to make tentative generalizations. These in turn must be tested in similar situations with the use of similar methods. Without this conscientious preliminary labor we cannot have valid judgments to offer in the controversy over the parochial system; we can have only questionable opinions limited to some specific area and to some particular experiences.

6. Personal opinion and subjective evaluations are not scientific expressions of actual social conditions any more than they are scientific guides to the practical improvement of social structures and institutions. The overworked and harassed priest, like the enthusiastic and energetic layman, tends to judge only from the surface of the parish. He sees the immediately visible and the easily measurable behavior of the parishioners. His natural optimism and loyalty to the Church may provide a state of mind in which it will never occur to him to question the obvious.

The high birth and marriage rates (which are not exclusively Catholic phenomena) and the urbanward migration of the postwar era have not only increased the numbers who receive the sacraments

---

of man at every stage of his culture and in every period of history. In all races and in all times there is a *human experience* and a congeries of problems which is specifically religious" (J. O. Hertzler, *Social Institutions* [Lincoln: University of Nebraska Press, 1946], pp. 124–25).

of marriage, baptism, and confirmation. They have also helped to account for the fact that the parish school is crowded, confessions are more numerous, and the Sunday-noon Mass congregation overflows onto the sidewalk. This obvious and bustling activity may obscure the fact that this is a numerical but not necessarily a *proportional* growth. The priest may not even suspect the number of dormant Catholics who are living in his parish. These signs of a flourishing parish may make it seem unnecessary to make a thorough periodical census of the parish, with the result that urban Catholicism continues to "prosper" in blissful ignorance.

Even the most casual survey of the parish by a trained social scientist will bring to light objective facts which will dim this nimbus of optimism. It will open up areas of spiritual activity and suggest procedures through which large numbers of people may receive the benefits of religious ministrations. In other words, scientific social research uncovers not only the negative elements of the parochial system but also gives new insights into positive programs of improvement. Above all, it lifts the veil of illusion and permits the observer to judge critically and objectively.

7. In one sense, the dedicated religious adherent is often guilty of an attitude of presumption. He realizes that religion is above science and feels that the higher level requires no help from the lower. This is shown in the outright dependence on a few memorized philosophical maxims or theological tenets as an explanation of, or excuse for, certain realistic social situations. An incontinent scoffing at social science and social engineering usually accompanies this attitude. After all, the Catholic Church has been in business for two thousand years, while social science is a newcomer with overextended ambitions.

Father Joseph Fitzpatrick exposes this presumption when he says that "Catholics have a tendency to allow their faith and their philosophy to substitute for knowledge that can be gained only through competent empirical research."[11] In other words, there is a legitimate and necessary area of truth which is not readily discerned by the trained philosopher or understood by the competent theologian. The presumption that social science has nothing to offer for the improvement of religious groups seems to be a misunderstanding of Divine Providence in human relations. God expects us to employ our minds, our talents, and our training in the pursuit of knowledge, in the formulation of plans, in the application of solutions. Any technical

11. Joseph P. Fitzpatrick, "Catholic Responsibilities in Sociology," *Thought,* XXVI (autumn, 1951), 389.

sociological study of the parish is an instrument in the hands of alert priests and of zealous laymen for the better understanding and operation of the parish.

8. The emergence of a vocal and educated laity is a relatively recent phenomenon of urban American Catholicism. The change from immigrant status to native status over the last two generations means that American Catholicism is culturally unique. "The intensely sentimental Catholicism of Spain; the fiercely Puritanical Catholicism of Ireland; the relaxed and affectionate Catholicism of Italy; the reasonable and sophisticated Catholicism of France; the deeply devotional Catholicism of Hungary and Poland—all were displayed in American parishes."[12] Most of the ethnic differences are now disappearing, and what remains has gradually blended with the distinctively American pattern of social behavior.

Just as the Church, without changing its substantive features, adapts itself in accidental features to the social institutions of China, France, the Philippines, Mexico, and other countries, so also must the Church here adapt itself to American culture. This adaptation seems to have occurred more rapidly in the laity than in the clergy, and some of the spiritually disastrous results appear to have been due to lack of understanding and direction by the clergy. Souls are not saved nor is society Christianized, by ignoring the culture of the people among whom this work is done, or by merely wishing that the culture were different, or by constantly condemning it.

It would be a serious failing in the lay apostle and in the sociologist of religion to forget that *civis idem et Christianus*, that the individual person is both a citizen and a Christian, and specifically that *civis Americanus idem et Christianus*. The "vital law of continual adaption" must be applied to the fact that the Church is of the people in a more pertinent sense now than it ever was. "This is the situation to which Cardinal Manning referred in his famous utterance that, as reinforced by Cardinal Gibbons' repetition of it, made such an impression on Leo XIII: 'A new task is before us. The Church has no longer to deal with Parliaments and princes, but with the masses and with the people. Whether we will or no, this is our work; we need a new spirit and a new law of life.' "[13]

12. Thomas Sugrue, *A Catholic Speaks His Mind* (New York: Harper & Bros., 1952), p. 42. This small controversial work was discussed with indignation by some religious reviewers.
13. John Courtney Murray, "Contemporary Orientations of Catholic Thought on Church and State in the Light of History," *Theological Studies*, X (1949), 219.

The Catholic laity, in this time and in this place, constitute the overwhelming majority of the members of the Church. The Catholic clergy is, in a true sense, the servant of the laity.[14] It is also the servant of all those non-Catholic Americans whom the Church would like to enfold in its universal embrace. Most of these are in some way "Americanized," and they are not likely to be attracted in large numbers to a transplanted species of German or Irish Catholicism or to parishes which retain the cultural patterns of Spain, Poland, France, or Italy. The student of social relations and structures, the expert in cultural patterns and institutions, can provide interpretations of American society for the practical use of religious administrators.

9. American Catholic social scientists are only beginning to apply their energies and talents to a study of the Church as a social system. These men and women—most of whom are relatively young—have a thorough understanding of the relation between religion and social science. As educated Catholics they have an adult knowledge of religious functions, of the ideals and aspirations of religious society. As parishioners they have had intimate experience of the parochial social system. As trained scientists they are able to make an effective contribution to the urban American Church.

In some ways the European social scientists have done much more work in the sociology of religion than have the Americans. Their findings have sometimes met with clerical suspicion and opposition, but they continue their studies with the frankness and humility which characterize the true scientist. They have even formed an international congress for the study of the sociology of religion. It may be said, however, that American sociologists have enjoyed a type of scientific training which enables them to pursue a more empirical kind of research—and to that extent probably more valuable.

If the young social scientist is not permitted to employ his training in the study of religious groups, he will apply his competency to research in other fields—housing, race relations, delinquency, marriage problems, etc. This is socially valuable research, but one need not be a Catholic to do it, nor does the progress of the Catholic Church benefit from it, except indirectly. In a sense, these

14. The popes have termed themselves "servant of the servants of God," and this title is widely understood and accepted by the laity. At the same time Pius XII cautions that "those who exercise sacred power in this Body are its first and chief members" (*Mystici Corporis* [New York: America Press], p. 10).

Catholic sociologists are at the core of the whole problem discussed in this appendix. The esteem or disesteem in which they are held is a matter of vital importance to the Church. Without them the sociological analysis of the urban parish cannot be done.

10. Seminarians who are themselves in preparation for the priesthood are sometimes employed for parish work during the summer vacations. This gives them some small acquaintance with parish routines; they may act as rectory doormen, sacristans, bookkeepers, secretaries, perhaps as catechists in a children's vacation school. Such experience is excellent, but it cannot substitute for the work of trained social scientists, nor can it supply the type of knowledge available through a scientific study. Seminarians are future priests, prospective guides in social relations and social groups, and their training needs scientific implementation.

At some time in their academic career seminarians take a course called "Pastoral Theology," which is intended to teach them the practical aspects of the pastoral function in the parish. This academic procedure suffers the difficulties present in all "vocational training" processes but has an added hindrance in the lack of a scientific literature of socioreligious relations. While the textbooks which supply "ready answers for the busy pastor" are valuable instruments for the parish priest in action, they do not provide a deep analysis of social structures and institutions for the seminarian.

The result is that there is a definite lacuna in the seminary training program, and in the seminary library, which can be filled by up-to-date sociological studies of the parish and the church. At the present time, if he has the interest, energy, and time, the seminarian must scratch his own way through the parochial labyrinth without much practical help either from the older generation or from the books. He sorely needs some dependable studies which can demonstrate the social trends in parish life, give him an insight into organizational problems, and prepare him for the leadership role which he must later assume.

11. Every year hundreds of newly ordained American priests enter eagerly upon their first contact with parochial realities from the vantage point of the parish rectory. They are fledglings, apprentices whose faltering steps are guided by their experienced superior, the pastor. This is a time-consuming and often erratic process. One may speak in high praise of the leisurely apprentice system of yore in which a young man learned his trade under the careful tutelage of a master-craftsman. The modern urban parish

is not a leisurely place, and there is no essential logic in allowing the newly ordained priest to "start from scratch" even when the priest in charge of his practical training is a master-pastor. There are also many pastors who have a shrewd insight into the social conditions of their parish but find it extremely difficult to transfer this insight to their assistants.

The young priest in the parish frequently has to learn through the hit-or-miss technique or by circumventing the categorical negatives which are thrown in the path of his zealous efforts. This may be a by-product of the hierarchical structure or of fairly rigidly institutionalized pastoral roles, but it is also undoubtedly the result of his own unpreparedness in social science. In spite of these difficulties it is true that he may in time become an expert parochial assistant and a successfully functioning pastor. But even the assistant who begins his priestly career in an ideally administered parish will be all the more eager to improve himself through the study of reliable parochial research findings.

12. In all human institutions and social structures the roles and statuses have a relative permanency, but the agents, or official incumbents, are relatively short lived. This may appear to be an absurdly superficial observation, but it has implications of deep importance. It is true that the generic pastoral role is not created by the newly appointed functionary, but it is also true that this role is not left unchanged during the years in which he holds office. The specific pastoral role in a particular parish is forged out of the accumulated wisdom, information, and experience of decades of hard work. For practical social purposes almost all this evaporates when the pastor grows old and dies.

This is more than a "dead loss" to the Church. It is the squandering of a social heritage. The Church does not allow theological knowledge to die; it carefully nurtures the development of dogma and preserves over the centuries the institutionalized varieties of liturgical practices. This preservation is due not only to the essential importance of dogma and liturgy but also to the fact that there have been trained and alert thinkers and writers in these fields. Enough has been said to show that social relations are extremely important in our times and that trained social scientists are available to analyze and report on them.

The fact that pastors and other ecclesiastical functionaries have often failed to hand on to their successors the benefit of their experiences is no reflection on their clerical competence. On the contrary, it is probably a proof of their complete dedication to the immediate work on hand, as well as of their professional absorption in their specific pastoral roles, that they were unable to sift and analyze their experience in a scientific way. They have had some brilliant ideas, and have suffered some heartbreaking disappointments, in the direction of personal and group relations of lay Catholics. These events have not been analyzed and systematized into a body of reliable scientific knowledge for the use of successive incumbents of the ecclesiastical roles.

In the last analysis all the arguments demonstrating the utility of social science research for the improved functioning of organized religion must be focused from a scientific rather than from a religious orientation. Science properly seeks truth; religion properly uses truth. Since truth is one and cannot contradict itself, neither the scientific researcher nor the religious adherent need have any fear of truth. The extent to which the social scientist will be encouraged to study religious groups and to publish his findings will largely influence the extent to which objective social truth will be effectively employed for the benefit of the Church.

This is another way of saying that one of the major functions of professional social scientists is to impart their findings not only to colleagues but also to nonspecialists through publication and teaching. The clerical religious functionary and the active lay Catholic are nonspecialists in social science, and they are immediate beneficiaries of this major function of the social scientist. As Parsons says: "This function derives above all from the fact that science contributes to human life in two directions, first in giving men knowledge about the world in which they live so that they may orient themselves more intelligently to it, and second in making it possible, through technological applications of the findings of science, to satisfy human needs and wants more effectively."[15]

15. *Op. cit.*, p. 5.

Indexes

Index of Names

Index of Subjects

Index

functions of, 165
graduates and parishioners, 167
and modal parishioners, 171
and nuclear parishioners, 171
and parish, 165–77
and social mobility, 171
and solidarity, 166–67, 169
and supraparochialism, 177
see also Education
Science, and religion, 1–6, 248
Secrets, and research, 228
Sect type of religion, 139
Secular groups, in parish, 52–53
Secular Institutes
approbation of, 148
definition of, 141
Secular values
and marginal parishioners, 62, 66
and parish, 199, 205
and religious values, 206
Selection of data, and research, 225
Seminarians, and sociology, 246
Sermons, and parishioners, 134
"Service station," parish as a, 188
Sex categories, and religious observances, 91 ff.
Single-role theory, and religion, 3–4
Sisters, social roles of, 172
Social barriers, breakdown of, 48
Social categories, 12, 70, 83, 156, 189, 191–92
Social engineering, 138, 214
Social facts, sacred and profane, 221
Social functions, and structures, 155, 163, 167, 181
Social group
definition of, 9
and nuclear parishioners, 25, 49
parish as a, 18
Social implication, of sacraments, 241
Social mobility
and families, 171
and schools, 171
Social participation
as criterion of parishioner, 18 ff.
and mobility, 95
of nonmobile families, 99
and religious observances, 106
Social reform, and children, 171
Social relations
of laity, 138–53
limits of, 161
Social roles
concept of, 3–4, 109
co-ordination of priests', 125
of laymen, 151

of parish priest, 121–37
reciprocal, 136
of sisters, 172
Social science
and Catholics, 245–46
definition of, 226 ff.
and religion, 1–6, 235–48
task of, 218
see also Sociologist; Sociology
Social solidarity
and age levels, 53–54
concept of, 42, 49, 55
and consensus, 43–44, 204–5
democracy and, 206–7
by divine grace, 48–45, 207 ff.
and education, 50, 170 ff., 166, 174
and ethnic background, 50–51
factors of, 47, 52
functions of, 42, 46
and liturgy, 207 ff.
and love, 45
and marriage choice, 50
mobility and, 95, 98
and modal parishioners, 40–55
and parish societies, 51–55
through religious choice, 204–7
and size of parish, 206
of social classes, 49
by social virtue, 45–46
on supraparochial level, 47 ff.
of vocational groups, 150
Social status
of nuclear parishioners, 26–29
and parents of school children, 173
of parish schools, 172–73
of parishes, 173, 192
of parishioners, 49, 127–28
and religious behavior, 107–20
and social role, 109–10
and social values, 110
and social virtue of women, 116–19
Social structure, and function, 155, 163, 167, 181
Social virtue
in community, 46–47
in parish, 49
and race relations, 47 ff.
and social status of women, 116–19
and solidarity, 45–46
Society
and the Church, 200–201, 204
and parish, 142
perfectible, 241
Sociologist
and behavior, 1, 203–4
and community, 220, 229–30

263